When you're asked to

DO THE IMPOSSIBLE

Anthony J. Le Storti

When you're asked to

DO THE IMPOSSIBLE

Principles of Business

Teamwork and Leadership

from the U.S. Army's Elite Rangers

The Lyons Press
Guilford, Connecticut
An imprint of The Globe Pequot Press

The Lyons Press is an imprint of The Globe Pequot Press.

10   9   8   7   6   5   4   3   2   1

Printed in the United States of America.
Book design and composition by Diane Gleba Hall.

ISBN 1-59228-171-0

Library of Congress Cataloging-in-Publication Data is available on file.

To Anthony F. Le Storti
My father
A source of quiet strength and great courage

To Gerry Kelly and Mike Parr
Classmate and roommate, brother Rangers
Killed in action

To Rangers, Past, Present, and Future
For courage and dedication in leading the way

Acknowledgments

This book has become a reality because of the vision, enthusiasm, and support of several people. I am very glad for the opportunity to name them and express to them my sincere gratitude.

When You're Asked to Do the Impossible will readily be viewed as the product of my efforts, yet I know that it is born at least as much from the deep conviction and abundant support that I received from Lorraine, my wife. She helped to initiate the project, contributed to the research effort, and designed the cover graphics. More important, she believed all along in its success, and her energy sustained me in bringing this book to life. In Lorraine I have been blessed with the font of love and support that made this work possible.

I am also especially grateful to my cousin Joseph Le Storti, the other Ranger in our family. More a brother than a cousin and someone I respect greatly, Joey provided early and unwavering support of this book. He contributed substantially to the direction and underlying structure of this work, he facilitated connections to invaluable resources, and he even provided the basis for the title.

This book benefits tremendously from the contributions of knowledge and experience provided by the individuals whom I interviewed. Their generous gifts of time and information were beyond my expectations. World War II hero Sid Salomon provided a deep and vivid connection to the

Ranger tradition. Contemporary Rangers Colonel Kurt Fuller, Lieutenant Colonel Mark Meadows, and Lieutenant Colonel Dave Anders, quiet professionals who were quick to point out that they were simply sharing what they had learned from others, contributed the state of the art of Ranger thinking. Fred Walker, Nick Panagakos, and Alex Gorsky, Rangers now in civilian roles, demonstrated the potential of and modeled Ranger leadership in business and government service. Betsy Scarcelli and Joyce Juntune, "can do" leaders in business and education, provided examples of leadership outside of the Ranger tradition yet consistent with its principles.

It is important to note that much of what is offered here is a result of what I have learned from others. I am greatly appreciative of the authors and editors of resources that provided the background for this work and which are respectfully cited in the endnotes. I am also grateful to the leaders and teams, both military and civilian, from whom I have learned so much through the years.

Scott Christie, Larry Martin, Mark Meadows, Betsy Scarcelli, and Fred Walker previewed sections of this book and offered constructive editorial suggestions. I am very grateful to them for their investment of energy and for their comments, which added both substance and polish to this work. Special thanks to Rose Marye Boudreaux for a fine job of copyediting and also to Tom Gass for his contribution of a great cover concept.

I also wish to express my gratitude to Mr. Bruce Zielsdorf and Major Kenneth McDorman of the U.S. Army Office of the Chief of Public Affairs for their aid in gaining approval for the use of Army interviews and photographs. I am also grateful for the help offered by the public affairs offices of the Ranger Regiment and the Special Operations Command.

Besides those who contributed directly to this work, there are those whose support during my military service fostered my development and, in effect, prompted this writing. The first of these are Rangers. There is a sense in which becoming a Ranger represents success as an individual in one of the severest tests that a person can undergo. There is another sense, however, in which it results from the support and encouragement of brother Rangers. For the latter, I am deeply indebted to my Ranger Buddy Bill Jones and the other members of Ranger Class 5-67 and to Captain Fishman, Sergeant Biondo and the Ranger Instructors of that class who challenged us beyond our imaginations and brought us to an accomplishment that imprinted us forever.

Likewise, this is an opportunity for me to express gratitude to those whose leadership and mentoring fostered and guided my growth as an officer. Colonel John Bennett oversaw my development as an ROTC cadet and helped launch my career. Captain Robert Jakes, my first company commander, provided me with early validation in my role as a troop leader. Major William Gooch, a quiet combat commander, enabled my efforts in Vietnam through his steady demonstration of trust.

Finally, *When You're Asked to Do the Impossible* would probably still be a dream except for the vision and personal support of two other individuals. I am indebted to Andrew Stuart, my literary agent, who believed in this work from the beginning and worked diligently to achieve its publication. I am likewise grateful to George Donahue, senior acquisitions editor at The Lyons Press, whose clear sense of this book's value and whose support throughout the publishing process brought this work to fruition.

Contents

Part I

THE TRADITION

Introduction   3
1. Rangers Lead the Way!   9
2. Move Farther, Faster, and Fight Harder   32

Part II

THE INDIVIDUAL

3. Don't Forget Nothin'   41
4. Be the Best   54

Part III

THE TEAM

5. Select the Best   67
6. Forge the Team   75
7. Be Agile, Versatile, and Responsive   99
8. Create Positive Synergy   128

Part IV

THE LEADER

9. Be, Know, Do   147

10. Visualize, Describe, Direct   179

11. Be Prepared for Anything   211

12. Accomplish the Mission   231

13. Learn Like Crazy   249

14. Drive On!   273

APPENDIX A

The Ranger Creed   275

APPENDIX B

Standing Orders Rogers' Rangers   277

Notes   279

Index   291

Part I

THE TRADITION

Introduction

Had my nightmare come true?

Here I was back at Ranger School. I had commanded combat troops in Vietnam, and, as with most warriors, there had been challenging moments of reflection. But they had come during the day and the evening. The nightmares seemed reserved for Ranger School—a place where men are challenged beyond their imaginations. Ranger School is where the U.S. Army's elite warriors are forged. Here comfort is replaced by deprivation, safety is replaced by danger, and psychological security is replaced by constant challenge. Here one's physical courage, intelligence, and leadership ability are challenged every moment. Not everyone who comes here stays. Not everyone who stays succeeds.

In my nightmares, I am reassigned to Ranger School for training. I protest. I keep pointing at the coveted Ranger Tab that I wear proudly on my left shoulder. But my superiors insist that I must return. But today isn't quite like in my nightmares.

Today I am here as a guest at graduation ceremonies. This afternoon, my cousin, Joey Le Storti, the other Ranger in our family, will be graduating from the Long-Range Surveillance Unit (LRSU) leaders course that is also conducted at the Ranger School. He has arranged for me to attend this morning's graduation ceremonies for a newly minted Ranger class. Proud wives and parents are in the stands. They have come to see their husbands and sons receive the Ranger Tab, that badge of immense prestige within the military.

The Tab identifies you as one of the Army's elite. You have been tested in mind and body more than most human beings ever will be, and you passed.

The ceremonies begin with impressive demonstrations of Ranger prowess. People are dropping from helicopters and sneaking onto land from small boats in a river. Explosions are going off, and Rangers are fighting hand to hand. For the family members and other guests, these demonstrations are exciting, even thrilling. For the graduating class watching from the side, the demonstrations are mostly something to laugh about and enjoy. These Rangers have just survived eight weeks of constant challenge and considerable danger. They have had their skills and leadership tested mercilessly. Their body fat has been burned away. They are still largely dazed from the sleep and food deprivation. This afternoon, as they join their families to munch on the "Ranger Burgers" that they have been dreaming about for weeks, their families will ask about how the demonstrations relate to the training they just endured. They will try to provide a description, and they will fail. They will learn for the first time what we Rangers sitting in the stands know: they are part of a brotherhood, but it is a brotherhood forged by a very special experience. They will find out as early as this afternoon that, except with another Ranger, they will never be able to talk about the experience of Ranger School in any meaningful way.

They are about to get their Tabs. I know they feel great. But there are several of us at this ceremony who already have the Tab, and we know something that they do not yet know. This will be one of the proudest moments in their entire lives.

So this is not my nightmare. On this return, I am safely in the viewing stands. A few years ago, it was my turn out there. But the ceremonies were not here at Fort Benning, and there were no family members invited. There was no demonstration and no two-star general on hand. We were at Eglin Air Force Base in the Florida Panhandle. It was late November. We had just come in from several days of intense field operations and had been given a belated Thanksgiving dinner. This was nice of the Ranger Instructors, since we had been living on one C-ration a day for some time—except on those days when they had "forgotten" to give us even that meager amount of sustenance.

But we were just as proud, and dazed, as these new graduates. Our nation, however, was at war, and our training had an extra edge to it. We knew where our skills were going to be tested. It had been ingrained in us throughout this torturous experience that this training wasn't for our benefit; it was an "insurance policy" for the men we would lead in combat. We had been told that Gen. William Westmoreland, the commander of U.S. forces in Vietnam, had asked for Rangers. His feeling was that, if he had a couple of thousand Rangers, he could win the war. At the time, independent Ranger units did not exist (although they would be formed as Long Range Patrol Companies were converted to Ranger Companies in 1969). The current plan was to spread these elite soldiers throughout the Army. When the really demanding challenges came up, Rangers either would be in command or would be available to advise how to handle them. It was fall 1967. In a couple of months the Viet Cong would celebrate the New Year in devastating fashion. In fact, the name for that celebration, *Tet*, would change meaning forever.

Since almost half of those who enter Ranger training do not make it to the end, Ranger graduating classes are relatively small. So I am not sure if "Westy" got all the Rangers he wanted. But we were all to find out that battle victories in jungles, highlands, or rice paddies would not be enough. The Vietnam War would divide our country in a way not seen before or since, and even battles won in combat would be lost again at the peace talks.

But this graduation was in the fall of 1997. I had been out of the service for some time and thoughts of Vietnam were far from my mind. The Persian Gulf War had helped to cleanse the American psyche. Rangers had served with distinction during that conflict, as well as in the interventions in Panama and Grenada. And they had done so as quiet professionals generally away from the limelight. I looked with deep pride at the Rangers in uniform around me. I thought, "We cannot go to war again. These elite young men are too strong, brave, and talented to be wasted."

But on a dark night four years later, in the fall of 2001, U.S. Army Rangers would parachute into Afghanistan. They would be the first ground troop unit to reply to September 11, and they would come from the sky in an in-your-face jump that told the terrorists and their supporters that America had been bloodied, but was strong and ready to restore justice. U.S. Army Rangers, as has always been their tradition, were leading the way.

: : :

Although a brief historical sketch and some anecdotes are included, this book is not intended to provide a detailed history of the Rangers, nor is it a book about military operations per se. It is, instead, an effort to learn from these elite warriors who are often asked to do what others would consider impossible. They have things to teach us. For example, how do you select people who can take on the greatest challenges? How do you prepare and support them? How do you motivate and lead them? How do you make decisions and plan in the face of great uncertainty? How do you accomplish so much with so few? These are some of the questions addressed in this book. We will not look to borrow or duplicate Ranger approaches for civilian pursuits. That would be a silly and mistaken effort. Rather, we will attempt to abstract lessons from Ranger training and operations that offer answers that can be applied in civilian domains.

It needs to be emphasized also that this is not a book that equates business or other civilian pursuits with warfare. Anyone who thinks that business is like war has never fought a war. At the end of a business day, the market may be down, you may have lost a customer, or you may be worth less on paper than you were this morning. At the end of the day in combat, the bottom line is in terms of lives lost, people mutilated, and families that will never be the same. In transferring the lessons from Ranger training and military operations, some analogies are offered, but they are not intended to be tight analogies that equate business, health care, government, or even law enforcement with war.

There are, however, good reasons to study Ranger methods and Ranger leadership. These elite warriors operate in complex, fluid, and chaotic situations. They stand ready to respond to new and unexpected challenges. They think strategically and tactically; they plan very well and improvise just as well. They are asked to lead important initiatives, often being called upon to deal decisively with key tasks and to leverage fleeting opportunities. Their knowledge, skills, and courage are challenged on an ongoing basis. They deal with the concrete and the intangible, and they must continually prepare for the future while alertly operating in the present. They must learn constantly, adapt quickly, and respond expertly. Yet at the heart of it all, they are about individual ability and courage, morale and esprit, smart thinking and aggressive doing, teamwork and leadership.

This book, therefore, focuses on the lessons to be learned from Rangers regarding high-stakes teams, those teams that take on the most important or most difficult challenges. This is a book for business teams and task forces that must save the company by developing important new strategies, by inventing new products or services, or by responding to new crises. It is for hospital trauma units and government emergency response teams that must perform at peak performance levels on demand. It is for educators who must take on decades-old problems in order to reinvent education or resuscitate schools. It for law enforcement officers whose jobs were always difficult and have gotten even more challenging recently.

Here we will look to a new source for guidance. For, although they are not usually spotlighted, we have among us smart, daring warriors who regularly prepare for and deliver the impossible. They have lessons to teach, and, while their challenges are greater and often more fateful than most people will face, this book is an effort to learn from them.

1

Rangers Lead the Way!

U.S. Army Rangers are among the most elite, if not the most
elite, combat soldiers in the world. Being a Ranger is a function
of attitude and state of mind, as well as a matter of skill and
training. It is the fraternity of a highly select group within
the profession of arms that few will attempt to join and into
which even fewer will be initiated. To be a Ranger is a mark of
excellence indicating a degree of success that few will achieve.
The challenge of being a Ranger is to prove your ability to lead
and command while undergoing significant mental, emotional,
and physical stress. For those who have mastered this challenge,
the coveted title of "Army Ranger" is their reward.

— Maj. John D. Lock, U.S. Army Ranger,
To Fight with Intrepidity[1]

The Tradition

The Ranger tradition precedes the birth of the American nation. Ranger is
an English term found in writing as early as the fifteenth century, although
it was apparently used as a spoken reference much earlier. Rangers were
armed men who traversed the frontiers as scouts or who provided defensive
support to outlying areas. Because they were a mobile group that roamed or
"ranged" between outposts along the frontier, such fighters became known
as Rangers.

CHURCH'S RANGERS

In the North American colonies, early references to Ranger operations appear during the occasional conflicts between Indians and the British colonists in Virginia (1622), Maryland (1648), and the New England settlements (from 1675). Capt. Benjamin Church of Massachusetts is often named as the first American Ranger. Church and his company of Rangers defended colonial settlements during the King Philip's War. This unit included friendly Indian scouts, and its tactics were largely learned from Indians. Stealthy and daring, Church's Rangers are credited with winning the decisive engagement that ended that war. Church stressed military order and discipline. His memoirs are considered the first American military manual, thus beginning a Ranger tradition of learning and developing standard operating procedures.

ROGERS' RANGERS

Other early Ranger units operated successfully in defense of British colonists in Georgia, Florida, Virginia, and along the Canadian border. Like Church's Rangers, they employed unorthodox fighting methods that blended Indian tactics and frontiersmen skills. But the most famous of the early Ranger units would come to be when Great Britain found itself embroiled in the French and Indian War (1754–1760), the North American version of the Seven Years' War it was fighting in Europe. Impressed by earlier successes, the British sought to again organize Ranger units to combat French forces and their Indian allies in the northern colonies. Accordingly, the Ranger Company of New Hampshire Provincial Regiment was formed and placed under the command of Capt. Robert Rogers. Thereafter known as Rogers' Rangers, and immortalized in the novel *Northwest Passage*,[2] this unit became famous for its daring, stealthy reconnaissance patrols and raids in the Lake George and Lake Champlain regions of New York. These Rangers covered distances of as much as fourteen miles a day and stayed in the field for days and weeks at a time. Depending on the weather, they traversed frozen landscapes on snowshoes or they traveled by boat and crossed overland to new waterways while carrying those boats. Because they patrolled so far and for so long, they often found themselves running out of provisions and using their frontier skills to survive as best they could.

Over time, the Rangers grew in number and conducted many of what would now be known as long-range patrols. Their silent reconnaissance missions became legendary, as did their courage and daring in the many skirmishes and battles that they fought. As the leader of the elusive and deadly force, Rogers was referred to by his Indian enemies as *Wobi Madaondo* (White Devil).

In late 1757, Rogers was tasked with developing a program to train new Rangers. This first "Ranging School" taught tactics and developed Ranger discipline. In order to offer cadets the benefit of his experience and also to provide operational guidelines, Rogers composed twenty-eight Rules of Discipline to govern Ranger operations. Probably by way of transformation in *Northwest Passage*, nineteen rules emerged. These became known as Rogers' Rangers Standing Orders, and to this day they are among the very first things given to candidates at the U.S. Army Ranger School. Rogers had established a Ranger tradition of tough discipline, immediate readiness, and daring long-distance operations.

The Rangers went on to fight for the British in the French West Indies and against the Cherokee Indians in the middle Atlantic colonies. When hostilities broke out between the British and their North American colonists, some veterans of the original Rogers' Rangers would commit their leadership and expertise to the cause of the American rebels, and new Ranger leaders would emerge as well.

MORGAN'S RANGERS AND THE SWAMP FOX

In 1775, the Continental Congress formed six companies of riflemen, to whom General Washington referred as the Corps of Rangers. Known for their remarkable marksmanship, these Rangers under the command of Capt. Daniel Morgan soon gained the highest respect of their British adversaries. Morgan's Rangers helped to defeat a large British force under Gen. Burgoyne at the Battle of Bemis Heights, and they inscribed their name in military history with their cunning victory in the Battle of Cowpens. Utilizing their crack shooting ability and executing a surprise double envelopment at Cowpens, the Rangers killed 110 and captured 830 British soldiers while suffering 12 dead and 61 wounded.

While Morgan and his Rangers were very successful, the exploits of another group of Rangers caused the British great consternation and gained great fame for their leader. Partly as a response to the brutality of British Gen. Cornwallis, a group of Rangers was formed under the command of Brig. Gen. Francis Marion. Although the British had largely taken South

Carolina after the Battle of Camden, Marion and his men ran the British ragged with raids that harassed the enemy, disrupted supplies and communications, and kept the rebels in a spirit to fight. The much-feared Lt. Col. Tarleton and his Green Dragoon took up the task of neutralizing Marion. After one long and futile pursuit, Tarleton stopped his troops at the Ox Swamp, telling his men that the devil himself could not catch that "old fox" (Marion). Marion thus became known as the Swamp Fox, and his Rangers continually entangled the British forces.

Ranger tactics soon spread to other militia units. Forsaking the tradition of European warfare, some colonial militia bedeviled the British with their surprise attacks and quick-moving small unit operations. Preferring marksmanship from defilade rather than lining up in an open field, these "irregulars" became thorns in the British side.

One British officer in referring to Marion's Rangers complained that they did not "sleep and fight like gentlemen," they were rather "like savages . . . eternally firing and whooping around us by night, and by day waylaying and popping at us from behind every tree!" Due largely to Marion's disruptive tactics, South Carolina was recovered and secured by the Continental forces. Gen. Nathanael Greene praised the Swamp Fox, saying,

> Certain it is no man has a better claim to the public thanks, or
> is more generally admired than you. History affords no instance
> wherein an officer has kept possession of a country under so
> many disadvantages as you have; surrounded on every side with
> a superior force; hunted from every quarter with veteran troops,
> you have found the means to elude all their attempts, and to
> keep alive the expiring hope of an oppressed Militia, when all
> succor seemed to be cut off.[3]

MOSBY'S RANGERS

Unorthodox thinking characterized the approach of John Singleton Mosby. At the beginning of the Civil War, Mosby enlisted in the cavalry unit commanded by Confederate Gen. Jeb Stuart. Influenced by Morgan and Marion, Mosby approached the general with an idea: instead of going into traditional bivouac over the winter months, he would like to lead a group of guerrilla fighters to continually harass Union forces. In 1863, Stuart granted his request, and ten cavalrymen became the first of Mosby's Rangers. His force would grow to several hundred, and he trained his troopers well.

Mosby's philosophy was, "If you are going to fight, be the attacker."[4] He sought to spread Union forces thin and then attack their weakest point. His night raids deep behind Union lines created great fear among Union soldiers and their supporters. One exploit in particular exemplified his cunning and daring. One night, he and some of his Rangers, pretending to be messengers, approached the house where a Union general was staying. Surprising the occupants, they captured the general. They also captured two captains, thirty enlisted soldiers, and fifty-eight horses without firing a shot! Mosby, then a lieutenant, was promoted to captain and would eventually be promoted to colonel. His ongoing tactical operations were as daring as this event. In skirmish after skirmish, he harassed the Union army to such a degree that the region between Washington, D.C., and Richmond, Virginia, became known as Mosby's Confederacy. He continued to fight for a short time after Lee's surrender to Grant until it became obvious that the Confederate effort was lost. He then disbanded his Rangers.

: : :

We see some patterns in this first generation of Rangers. The soldiers generally volunteered. They were hardy individuals with strong skills such as woodcraft or marksmanship. They could march or row for hours and/or they were capable horsemen. They could operate in all climates and could live off the land if necessary. They were disciplined in their operations and stalwart fighters. They mastered unorthodox tactics and techniques. They were elusive and deadly, and they took on unusually demanding challenges—often fighting when and where others dared not. Together they founded the tradition of the American Ranger.

World War II

DARBY'S RANGERS

You Yanks bloody well surprised us. We expected to grind you to bits. Instead, some of my best Commando instructors have been hard put to keep up with you. A cracking good bunch, you Rangers.

—Colonel Vaughn, British Commando
Training Instructor[5]

Following the Civil War, the Ranger tradition largely lay dormant until the onset of World War II. Army Chief of Staff Gen. George C. Marshall decided that the Army could benefit from having soldiers from throughout the Army trained in the manner of the much-admired British Commandos. Having completed their training, these soldiers could then be reassigned to their original units where their special expertise could be valuable. This "yeast" concept would be revived during the Vietnam era, but it went through an almost immediate change in early 1942. On the recommendation of Brig. Gen. Lucian Truscott Jr., Marshall approved the formation of an American combat unit similar to the Commandos. General Eisenhower liked the idea of a special unit but did not prefer the designation of "Commando," since it was so associated with the British. Truscott, remembering his history, suggested "First American Ranger Battalion" in reference to the courage and accomplishments of Rogers' Rangers.

The new command was given to Maj. William Orlando Darby, a dynamic West Point graduate. Darby and his officers handpicked the Rangers from the volunteers that answered the call. At least part of Marshall's original concept was retained in the formation of the 1st Ranger Battalion; the volunteers did come from several units and branches of the Army, so the new unit benefited from a diverse base of knowledge and experience.

Darby moved the new battalion to Scotland for what would be exceedingly grueling and dangerous training conducted by the British Commandos. It was there that Darby instituted what remains an important Ranger tradition to this day, the concept of the Ranger Buddy. Darby allowed each Ranger to choose a fellow Ranger and to form two-person teams that would stay together through training and eventually combat. Rangers would learn quickly to back each other up, aiding, supporting and encouraging one another whether in training or in combat. "Never send one Ranger to do something," became a Ranger operating principle.

> We're the toughest and we're the best,
> You'll find us leading all the rest.
> Darby's Rangers, toughest Rangers.
>
> —Marching Cadence, 1st Ranger Battalion[6]

As their marching cadence proclaimed, Darby's Rangers would lead all the rest. After the perilous and exacting training at the hands of the experienced

Commandos, a small band from the Ranger battalion would be the first American troops to fight against the Germans. Taking part in a British-led raid on the port at Dieppe, France, the Rangers acquitted themselves very well in what would be a failed mission. But many Ranger successes lay ahead—beginning in North Africa.

As part of Operation Torch, the invasion of North Africa, the Rangers were given the kind of mission for which they would become famous. Tasked to destroy or capture the coastal defenses of the port of Arzew, Algeria, the Rangers made an amphibious landing in two places. They knocked out the artillery positions that defended the port and captured a major fort, all with the loss of only one Ranger. Being a special unit, the concept of Rangers was not always understood, nor were they always properly employed. But they did conduct a very successful raid in Tunisia, and they provided reconnaissance and a daring behind-the-lines attack that significantly contributed to the victory at El Guettar.

Darby, whom Gen. George Patton viewed as "very gallant," personally led these actions.[7] From the training in Scotland to the raids in North Africa, Darby took the lead. Enduring the same tribulations and hardships that his men endured and subjecting himself to the same dangers, Darby exemplified the title "Ranger" and provided his unit with a hard-to-surpass model. For its actions in Africa, the battalion received its first Distinguished Unit Citation, and the reputation of the Rangers was building on both sides of the conflict. Axis Sally, the German propagandist, labeled the Rangers the "Black Death" and promised that none of them would be taken alive.[8] Meanwhile, Darby convinced General Eisenhower to activate two additional Ranger battalions, and all three units were ready for the next stop, Sicily.

Officially designated "Ranger Force," the "Spearheaders" of the 1st, 3rd, and 4th Ranger Battalions landed with the lead elements of Operation Husky. While one group of Rangers seized the high ground and neutralized the coastal defenses at Gela, another unit destroyed fortified installations at Green Beach. For his personal heroism during the invasion, Darby was awarded the Distinguished Service Cross. General Patton soon began using the Rangers as armed reconnaissance sending them behind enemy lines. Ambushed on one of these missions, the Rangers countered so effectively that they killed many of the enemy and captured 165 prisoners without sustaining a casualty.

Then followed Operation Avalanche, the invasion of Italy, with Rangers in the lead. Attacking with total surprise, they seized the town of Mairori and the critical Chiunzi Pass and helped capture Salerno. They received another Distinguished Unit Citation, and began moving north to Naples. They fought in several battles, including Cassino, but were often misused as conventional infantry and thus suffered more casualties than usual. But as fighting drew to a stalemate, the Rangers reverted to their special role, leading the invasion of Anzio and helping to seize the port and establish a beachhead that allowed Allied forces to come ashore.

Shortly thereafter, the Rangers, again being used as conventional infantry, were assigned to attack the town of Cisterna. Although Darby had doubts, intelligence reports indicated that only light German resistance was to be expected. The 1st and 3rd Battalions walked into a German trap. Unlike the predictions of the intelligence report, the lightly armed Rangers encountered units massing for a major German counteroffensive. Panzer tanks, antiaircraft guns, and artillery, reinforced by a fresh paratrooper regiment, fired directly at the Rangers. Although fighting bravely, the 1st and 3rd Rangers were soon encircled and destroyed. Darby and the 4th Rangers made an aggressive effort to rescue their brothers, but were blocked by heavy tanks, artillery, and automatic weapons. Of the 767 Rangers from the 1st and 3rd Battalions, only 6 managed to escape death or capture. But the Rangers had inflicted 5,500 casualties on the enemy, and they forced the Germans to commit forces that were to be used in the planned counteroffensive. The Rangers bought two days for the Allies, enough to save the troops at the beachhead from being pushed back into the sea. Decimated, the Ranger Battalions would be deactivated rather than reconstituted. But four months later, two more Ranger Battalions would spring to life, and they would be given "the toughest, most desperate, and dangerous mission" in the greatest military invasion in world history.[9]

RUDDER'S RANGERS

Formed at Camp Forrest, Tennessee, the 2nd and 5th Ranger Battalions trained hard in the United States and even harder with the Commandos in England. They were preparing themselves for an impossible mission. Operation Overlord, the invasion of Europe at Normandy, was a daunting enterprise in itself. The German forces had had years to fortify the "western wall" of Europe, and they had done so diligently. The obstacles and forces that defended the beaches were immensely intimidating. But overlooking the beaches were two even more terrifying elements that provided special concern. At Pointe-du-Hoc, the Germans had placed six 155-mm artillery guns. With a range of about fifteen miles, these guns could control both Omaha and Utah Beaches and could rain fire on the vulnerable invasion forces. The problem: the guns were positioned atop a sheer, twelve-story-high cliff. Also overlooking Omaha Beach, near the town of Vierville, was Pointe de la Percée. Here was located a stone farmhouse, believed to be fortified, with a commanding view and, therefore, line of fire onto Omaha beach. The problem: to get to the farmhouse, troops would have to cross a no man's land of a hundred yards of open beach and then climb nine stories worth of cliffs. Both objectives were given to the Rangers under the command of Lt. Col. James Earl Rudder. Gen. Omar Bradley said of Rudder, "Never has any commander been given a more desperate mission."[10]

On D-Day, Rangers from units of the 2nd Battalion conducted first-wave amphibious assaults. Rough seas and deadly enemy fire caused Ranger casualties and sunk some landing craft long before they could reach land. When the Rangers of C Company reached land at Pointe de la Percée, they faced decimation immediately, as they were met by automatic weapons, artillery and mortar fire before and after they hit the beach. Yet they fought their way across the sand and to the base of the cliff. As they attempted their ascent, sometimes forced to climb using their bayonets to gain a hold, the Germans fired automatic weapons and dropped grenades down onto the Rangers. Yet they reached the top and seized the farmhouse. The cost, however, was dear; of the thirty-seven Rangers assigned that mission, only nine made it to the top, and only two of those were unwounded.[11]

Meanwhile, Rudder was leading three companies at Pointe-du-Hoc. Landing on a narrow spit of sand, they immediately began their difficult and dangerous climb. As at Pointe de la Percée, the Germans fired automatic weapons and dropped grenades down onto the rope-climbing Rangers. Casualties suffered in getting to the summit were fifteen dead or wounded. But amazingly, Rangers reached the top of the cliff in ten minutes! Upon doing so, however, they discovered a major problem: the large guns were missing from their emplacements! Others may have been satisfied with such a turn of events, but the Rangers knew the intent and importance of their mission. First Sgt. Leonard Lomell and Sgt. Jack Huhn spotted tracks on the ground. Searching quickly while engaging German resistance, the Rangers located and destroyed the hidden artillery and the large stores of ammunition that had been positioned to repel the invasion force.

Meanwhile, the 5th Battalion and two companies of the 2nd Battalion moved to assault the beach east of Vierville. Intelligence for this area indicated that the German defense would be minimal, and once again Rangers would pay for poor intelligence. Unknown to the Allies, the Germans had moved an experienced infantry division into the location. When the two companies of the 2nd landed in lead of the 5th, they were met with devastating fire and were massacred. Maj. Max Schneider, commanding the 5th, saw he would be sending his Rangers into disaster if he stayed with the original plan. He immediately improvised a new landing plan that put the Rangers farther east, where they got ashore and helped to establish a very tentative beachhead.

As the day drew to a close, it looked as if the relatively small number of Allied soldiers, including the much-bloodied and isolated Rangers, would be repulsed. American troops clung to a very small beachhead, and to stay in place was to invite defeat. The assistant commander of the 29th Infantry Division, which had also put troops onto Omaha, was Brig. Gen. Norman D. Cota. Rallying troops and directing tactics, he attempted to consolidate the forces on D-Day+1. The Company C Rangers from Pointe de la Percée, now commanded by 1st Lt. Sid Salomon, linked with D, E, and F companies at Pointe-du-Hoc. Schneider's 5th Battalion was perched outside of Vierville when Cota approached the command post. The invasion and perhaps the war in Europe depended on a breakout from the beach. What happened next has become part of Ranger lore.

Cota gave orders to his commanders to break out of their tiny deathtrap. He turned to Schneider and gave the mandate, "Rangers lead the way!"[12] And they did. The 5th, with soldiers of the 116th Infantry Regiment, fought off the beach and captured the town of Vierville allowing passage for other Allied troops. The two Ranger battalions briefly linked and contributed to victories at Brest and on the Crozon and Le Conquet Peninsulas. They then separated, with the 2nd fighting in the "Bloody Heurtgen Forest," Hill 400, the Bulge, and Czechoslovakia. The 5th was directed to conduct several long-range patrols and then completed a daring battalion-sized Ranger infiltration of enemy forces at Zerf where the Rangers fought successfully in isolation for four days before being relieved. Both units were awarded Distinguished Unit Citations and the French Croix de Guerre. The 5th also received a Presidential Unit Citation.

FIRST SPECIAL SERVICE FORCE

After Cisterna, Darby's battalions were disbanded, but some of those Rangers soon joined another special operations unit. The First Special Service Force (FSSF) was a joint U.S. and Canadian unit, which, while not officially designated as a Ranger unit, very much fit the Ranger profile in terms of its training and utilization.[13] Their training included airborne and mountain operations, demolitions, hand-to-hand combat, and the use of a wide variety of weapons. Initially employed in the Aleutian Islands and Africa, the FSSF's first major engagement was near Naples in December 1944.

The "Forcemen" took on the challenge of climbing an "unclimbable" cliff. In fog, rain, and bitter cold, 600 Forcemen climbed the 200-foot sheer face of Mont de la Difensa and then launched a savage attack from behind German forces in the Liri Valley. What military planners thought would take days took the FSSF a few hours. The Forcemen next helped to break through the German Winter Line, allowing the Allied advance to Cassino; they later led in the breakout of the Anzio beachhead and the drive to Rome. Taking part in Operation Anvil, the invasion of southern France, the Force conducted an amphibious assault on three coastal islands, climbing dangerous cliffs to knock out enemy artillery and secure the islands. Known for their blackened faces and stiletto knives, the First Special Service Force was dubbed The Devil's Brigade.

MERRILL'S MARAUDERS

Not officially designated a Ranger unit, an infantry regiment with the ungainly name of the 5307th Composite Unit (Provisional) was Ranger in action and spirit and is honored as such to this day. Code-named Galahad, the unit is more popularly known as Merrill's Marauders in honor of its leader, Brig. Gen. Frank D. Merrill. Made up of volunteers trained in India, the Marauders were deployed as a long-range penetration unit in Burma (Myanmar).[14] Marching more than 1,000 arduous miles through the jungles, up and down the mountains, and across the rivers of Burma, they fought not only the Japanese, but oppressive heat and humidity, monsoons, and diseases such as typhus and malaria. They battled along the Ledo Road, fighting both major and minor engagements that culminated in the daring capture of the airfield at Myitkyina. Often unsupplied and unrelieved and fighting with very ill soldiers, the Marauders battled to exhaustion.

An interesting footnote involves the Marauders. In August 1944 they were consolidated into the 475th Infantry Regiment, whose designation was later abbreviated to the 75th Infantry Regiment. A further modification of that name and the adoption of the Marauders' unit insignia provide the heraldic lineage of today's premier Ranger unit, the 75th Ranger Regiment.

RESCUE OF THE GHOST SOLDIERS

Japanese forces attacked the Philippines at the onset of World War II and eventually overwhelmed the U.S. troops isolated by the surprise attack. The already depleted Americans and other Allied troops were then forced into the infamous Bataan Death March. Many died from illness and/or Japanese savagery. Those who endured were put into prisoner camps, where survival became a moment-to-moment challenge as they battled disease, malnourishment, and brutal conditions. Isolated and almost without hope, these survivors wasted away day by day, becoming "ghost soldiers." [15]

Meanwhile, at Port Moresby, New Guinea, the 6th Ranger Battalion was formed from volunteers from the 98th Field Artillery Battalion and trained rigorously for Ranger operations. Leading Allied forces to retake the Philippines, the Rangers landed three days before the main invasion of Leyte and knocked out enemy communications and gun emplacements. When they arrived on Luzon in January 1945, the American commander, Lt. Gen. Walter Krueger, was facing a worrisome situation. Thirty miles behind enemy lines at Cabanatuan was an Allied prisoner of war camp. Many feared that, as the invasion proceeded, the atrocities of the Death March would be revisited, perhaps culminating in the slaughter of the prisoners. Not only were distance and time crucial factors, but also the camp was located on a major Japanese troop and supply route, meaning that many Japanese in addition to the prison guards could be expected to be in the area at any one time.

One hundred twenty-one Rangers took on the challenge of rescuing the prisoners. Supported by two Filipino guerrilla units and two small Alamo Scout reconnaissance teams, the force would be led by Lt. Col. Henry "Hank" Mucci and Capt. Robert Price. Great planning and preparation went into this mission, and, before departing, Mucci required his Rangers to make a prayerful vow that they would rather die than let something happen to the prisoners who had suffered so much. At their base camp, the best available intelligence was provided to the Rangers, and it was updated en route by personal reconnaissance of the prison camp. It revealed that there were more than 200 enemy soldiers in the camp, another 200 to 300 just north of the camp, 800 troops with tanks in a nearby town, and at least a division of several thousand troops about four miles to the south.

The Rangers moved without cover through open areas such as grasslands and rice paddies and made dangerous crossings of the Talavera River and a major highway. Security was an overarching concern during the three days it took to silently approach the objective. But the storming of the compound and the rescue of the prisoners took only about forty-five minutes. Prisoners who could walk did so, while the most seriously ill were placed into carts that had been commandeered and positioned for the return trip. Although it would have seemed impossible, this raid has been called "one of the most well conceived and perfectly executed operations ever performed."[16] It freed 511 American and Allied prisoners and left the Japanese with more than 500 casualties. Yet, only two Rangers were killed and ten wounded. Gen. Douglas MacArthur called the operation "magnificent," and the 6th Battalion received the Presidential Unit Citation.

: : :

The World War II Ranger units reestablished the Ranger tradition. They more than once succeeded in accomplishing "impossible missions." They developed the tradition of rigorous training; successful amphibious, mountain, and jungle operations; and behind-the-lines commando-style warfare. They established the Ranger Buddy system and the tradition of Ranger commanders leading by example and sharing the hardships endured by their men.

Korea

Shortly after North Korea's massive infantry-armor attack into South Korea in 1950, the Army realized the need for an elite force for airborne raids and infiltration behind enemy lines. The Ranger units that had been disbanded after World War II were reincarnated first as Ranger, and then as Airborne Ranger, companies. Among the first volunteers were World War II veterans from the Ranger Battalions, the First Special Service Force, Merrill's Marauders and paratroopers from the 11th and 82nd Airborne Divisions. During

1950–1951, seventeen Airborne Ranger companies and one "leg" (non-airborne) Ranger company were formed. Among them was the 2nd Airborne Ranger Company, the only all-black Ranger unit ever formed. This company fought with distinction especially in the key battle of Hill 581, which the Rangers assaulted, seized, and held against a Chinese Army counterattack. The Rangers inflicted more than 210 casualties, while suffering only 16.

In general, the Ranger companies were used as assault forces, for capturing prisoners and for behind-the-lines patrols and blocking operations. The 2nd and 4th Companies are credited with making the first Ranger parachute assault, dropping behind and cutting off retreating North Korean forces.

Another noteworthy Ranger action was the bloody, subzero-degree fighting on Hill 205 by the 8th Ranger Company. The Ranger commander was recent West Point graduate Lt. Ralph Puckett. Puckett had trained his Rangers hard, insisting that they conduct in-depth after-action briefings, learn from their mistakes, and incorporate their learning by continually refining their Standard Operating Procedures (SOPs). The Rangers assaulted and captured Hill 205 from Chinese forces. They then successfully defended the hill against five human wave attacks by the Chinese. Having suffered heavy casualties and running out of ammunition, they were overwhelmed by the sixth human wave attack. But even then, Rangers left the hill only reluctantly, fighting with bayonets, going back to rescue fallen comrades and, in one case, fighting a suicide rear guard action that allowed other Rangers to move to safety. Leading, steadying, and directing the defense, Puckett himself was wounded three times, including multiple wounds by a mortar round that landed in his foxhole. Unable to move off the hill, he was rescued by two enlisted Rangers, David Pollock and Billy Walls, who fought their way back to him and carried him down the slope. When the badly wounded Puckett was asked if he was all right, his reply was, "Yes, I am all right! I'm a Ranger!"[17] For his great leadership against overwhelming odds, he was awarded the Distinguished Service Cross. Retiring from the Army as a colonel, he was inducted into the Ranger Hall of Fame and made an honorary colonel of the 75th Ranger Regiment.

The Ranger companies formed for Korean fighting required extensive, rigorous training. The first company was trained in Japan, but the remaining companies were trained at the newly established Ranger Training Center at Fort Benning, Georgia. The training given there was demanding and multifaceted: small unit tactics, land navigation, demolitions, domestic and foreign weapons, river crossings, parachute jumps, hand-to-hand combat, communications, and sabotage. The Georgia training was supplemented with cold-weather training and mountaineering at Camp Carson, Colorado, and some companies received jungle/swamp training at Eglin Air Force Base in Florida. When they graduated, the new Rangers were the first to be awarded the coveted Ranger Tab, a black and gold (originally yellow) arc to be worn on the left shoulder above their unit patches.

: : :

Thus, from the Korean Conflict came the established Ranger training program that exists today. It has changed names twice, first to the Ranger Department of the Infantry School, and later to the separate Ranger Training Brigade. The demanding, multifaceted training established in 1950 remains the core of Ranger training. Also a legacy of the Korean Conflict is the intense Ranger approach to learning, conducting after-action reviews and continual refinement of operating procedures.

Vietnam

The Ranger presence in the Vietnam War took three forms. The Army had returned to General Marshall's original concept to spread Ranger-qualified officers and noncommissioned officers (NCOs) throughout the units. The ideal was to have at least one Ranger officer per company and one Ranger NCO in each platoon. Within certain special infantry units such as the 82nd Airborne Division, even larger numbers of Rangers were assigned. This concept saw the Rangers filling three roles: they would set and model high standards within their units, they would act as instructors in Ranger tactics, and they would be available for leadership and advice when unusual missions or obstacles were encountered.

The second approach to Ranger utilization took the form of the Long Range Reconnaissance Patrol (LRRP). Each major independent unit of brigade size and up had a separate company designated for infiltration of enemy areas and concealed, long-term observation. (Included was the LRRP Company of the 82nd Airborne Division commanded by my Ranger Buddy, Bill Jones.) Generally operating in six-man independent teams, these patrols would be inserted by boat, helicopter, or on foot, and would last from five to seven days. Most of the time would be devoted to silent reconnaissance, but the patrol might culminate in setting up an ambush shortly before the team was due for extraction.

In 1969, most of these LRRP units were officially designated Ranger Companies and provided the lineage of Merrill's Marauders and the 475th Infantry Regiment. (Some LRRP units carried the designations of the 20th and 51st Infantry Regiments.) Now known as companies of the 75th Ranger Regiment, these units were assigned to separate infantry brigades, divisions, and field forces. They became the eyes and ears of their commanders, moving silently among enemy forces. But they also were fierce fighters whose many engagements cannot be treated adequately here.

A third U.S. Ranger utilization was in the form of advisors to military units of the Army of the Republic of Vietnam (ARVN). Particularly notable among these units were the Biêt-Dông-Quân (BDQ). Known as Vietnamese Ranger units, these specially trained forces were guided and supported by American Ranger advisors. The BDQ were considered to be among the best and hardest fighting ARVN forces, and their American Ranger advisors saw plenty of action including a pitched battle in Kontum Province in which Sergeant First Class Gary Littrell's outstanding heroism earned him the Medal of Honor.

One Ranger-style mission in particular deserves special note. In the early morning hours of November 21, 1970, a U.S. special operations force, which included several Rangers, daringly raided Son Tay deep within North Vietnam in an attempt to free U.S. prisoners of war. Air assaulting by helicopters, the force quickly killed 150 Chinese advisors. Unfortunately, undetected by intelligence, the prisoners had been moved. But the raid, led by such noteworthy warriors as Col. Arthur "Bull" Simmons and Dick Meadows, was a courageous parallel to the Cabanatuan raid in the Philippines. Although disappointing in that no prisoners were rescued, the raid lasted less than thirty minutes, involved no U.S. losses and was conducted only twenty-three miles from the North Vietnamese capital of Hanoi.

: : :

Vietnam returned Rangers to the tradition of Church and Rogers in the form of the LRRPs. It implemented Marshall's original concept of Rangers-as-yeast distributed among the Army's units to be standard setters, expert tacticians, and instructors. It added a new role for Rangers—that of advisors to allied forces. And it established for the first time the designation of the 75th Ranger Regiment, although the reorganization of that unit with a regimental headquarters would have to wait until 1984.

The Ranger Regiment

Concept for Contemporary Ranger Battalions:
The Ranger Battalion is to be an elite, light, and the most proficient infantry battalion in the world. It must be a battalion that can do things with its hands and weapons better than anyone. Wherever the battalion goes, it will be apparent that it is the best.

    —Gen. Creighton Abrams, U.S. Army Chief of Staff[18]

The 75th Ranger Regiment is the present-day successor of the Ranger units described above. It is the preeminent strike force, setting the standards not only for light infantry in the U.S. Army, but also for similar forces around the world. Today's Airborne Rangers are carefully selected, rigorously trained, and kept razor sharp to be able to deploy around the world in a matter of hours.

Comprising approximately 2,000 Rangers organized into three battalions and a Regimental Headquarters, the Regiment is capable of being deployed to any kind of terrain and can arrive by parachute assault, helicopter insertion, amphibious landing, or overland infiltration. The Regiment is equipped with some of the latest weaponry and technology, and it receives more ongoing training than any other Army unit. Its missions are in the true Ranger tradition updated for today's battlefields. Now truly regarded as a special operations force, today's Ranger units may be deployed for hostage rescue, seizing of airfields, prisoner snatches, strike-force assaults and other behind-the-lines operations. The Regiment's skill set, mobility, esprit, and firepower allow it to be the prime support for the Army's super-secret Delta Force.

Rangers of the 75th tend to stay out of the limelight, partly because as quiet professionals they tend not to seek public attention, but also because the nature of their missions requires secrecy. While some of their activities have become somewhat public, others remain classified.

DESERT ONE

In April 1980, the first collaboration of Delta and the Rangers took place in the attempt to rescue hostages taken from the American Embassy in Iran by militants. Delta commandos would have responsibility for assaulting the hostage location and evacuating the hostages. Rangers led by Capt. David L. Grange had responsibility to provide security at one landing site and to secure an airfield for transports to airlift the prisoners and the troops to safety. But this mission was ill fated. Plagued by dust storms and aircraft equipment problems that reduced the number of helicopters to below a critical number, the rescue attempt was called off. Unfortunately, before the forces could be extracted, a tragedy occurred at the initial insertion point in Iran known as Desert One. Swirling dust from helicopters and transports that were readying to leave soon denied visibility to some pilots. The crash of a Sea Stallion helicopter into a C-130 transport plane resulted in a fiery explosion that caused several deaths and injuries. The force was able to withdraw, and the hostages were released eight months later. Despite the heart-breaking failure, many lessons regarding special operations were learned and implemented.

GRENADA: OPERATION URGENT FURY

With so many things going wrong, operations on the Caribbean island of Grenada were a real test of Ranger discipline. The overall mission was to protect and evacuate Americans when the island nation erupted in political and military instability in 1983. Intelligence regarding both the enemy and the terrain was sadly lacking. Little time was available for planning. Initial missions and schedules of the various forces went through significant changes and became confused. There was a shortage of assault aircraft, and the aircraft available were not equipped with appropriate communications gear. Given the mission to seize the Point Salines airfield, Rangers were told to get into their parachutes while in flight on transports crowded with vehicles and helicopters. Some Rangers were erroneously told by the Air Force to take off their chutes, and, then, with only a few minutes to go, were told to put them back on. Meanwhile the runway had been blocked with heavy equipment and other obstacles by enemy forces. When the first Rangers did jump at Point Salines, it was daylight. Their transports came under antiaircraft fire, and some planes aborted their missions leaving just a few Rangers on the ground and under fire.

But those Rangers overcame the resistance at the airfield. Additional Rangers parachuted in and cleared the airfield, allowing transports to land with elements of the 82nd Airborne and other allied forces. The Rangers then secured a nearby medical school to rescue American students. After it was discovered that many of the students were in another location, the Rangers were tasked to rescue the remaining students. Flying Marine helicopters, the Rangers deployed to the second location and rescued those students.

Then, when given the mission to take the military camp at Calivigny, the Rangers found that their friendly artillery support had misplotted their firing position and sent almost every round into the sea; naval gunfire was about as ineffective. Close air support was better, but as the helicopters carrying the Rangers landed, three of them crashed. Then it was discovered that there were no enemy at the camp.

Ten Rangers were killed (five accidentally) and ten others wounded (five accidentally) during Operation Urgent Fury. Friendly snafus proved as dangerous as the armed enemy, but the Rangers accomplished their mission. Following Grenada, and in response to the need for better coordination and planning among the services, the United States Department of Defense established the Special Operations Command.

PANAMA: OPERATION JUST CAUSE

In mid-December 1989, the Ranger Regiment conducted a rare training exercise with the objective of seizing a large airfield. This rehearsal was unusual in terms of the high command level and large number of Rangers involved. Six days later, the Rangers realized the true nature and goal of their training. As part of the invasion of Panama to seize its drug-smuggling dictator, Manuel Noriega, the Rangers were tasked with capturing the Torrijos-Tocumen airport complex, a large civilian airport with an adjacent military airfield. Using the same names for objectives as in their training exercise, 1st Battalion Rangers supplemented with C Company of the 3rd Battalion conducted an airborne assault on the complex. They quickly took over both the military complex and the civilian airport with few casualties, although the action was harrowing and did involve a successful nose-to-nose hostage rescue. The Rangers then proceeded to take part in the successful assault of the Panamanian Defense Force (PDF) Headquarters, La Comandancia.

Simultaneous to the assault on the airport, the 2nd and 3rd Battalion Rangers conducted an airborne assault against the PDF's best fighting units at the coastal Rio Hato camp. Taking antiaircraft fire as they exited the airplane, the Rangers soon found themselves surrounded by PDF soldiers and in a major firefight. Taking control area by area, they soon dominated the situation, but at the cost of four Rangers killed and twenty-seven wounded. The PDF lost 34 KIA, an unknown number of wounded, and 362 taken prisoner. The Rangers finalized their actions in Just Cause with the airborne seizure of another airfield and a penal colony at Camp Machete.

DESERT STORM

The liberation of Kuwait from the clutches of Iraq's invading army was code-named Desert Storm. The operation began with seven days of intense bombing by American forces and their coalition partners from thirty-four nations. Following the bombardment was a large-scale infantry-armor assault on Iraqi forces designated Desert Saber. Lasting only about 100 hours, it was one of the most remarkable military victories in historical annals. The overwhelming firepower and technology of the coalition destroyed and overwhelmed Iraqi forces in large numbers. Rangers from the 1st Battalion were involved in Desert Saber. They knocked out border observation posts that facilitated the search for Scud missiles, and in a remarkable raid deep into Iraqi territory (details in chapter 10), destroyed an important communication facility that apparently controlled the launch of Scud missiles.

MOGADISHU

In the early 1990s, suffering from years of clan warfare and starvation, the East African country of Somalia was collapsing. With vivid images of starving children broadcast on international news networks such as CNN, the United Nations felt it had to offer some relief. But efforts to supply food failed, as warring clansman took the goods for themselves. In 1992, shortly before leaving office, President George Bush authorized that humanitarian aid be sent and that U.S. forces insure that it get to the people. Soon the clansmen, especially those led by Mohamed Farrah Aidid, directed vicious military attacks against UN forces. Determining that Aidid was a major obstacle to restoring peace and stability, the United Nations sought his apprehension, and military operations were directed against his forces. This, in turn, united many of the other clansmen and ordinary Somalis against the UN and U.S. forces seeking to help them.

Stirred to action, President Bill Clinton ordered a special operations task force composed of a Delta squadron, a reinforced Ranger company, and support helicopters from the 160th Special Operations Aviation Regiment (Night Stalkers). Their primary mission was to arrest Aidid and/or neutralize his ranking staff in order to help restore peace to the country. On October 3, 1993, the task force was given the mission of seizing some of Aidid's lieutenants. Delta was to conduct the actual "snatch" while the Rangers provided support and security. The Night Stalkers would deliver the troops and provide close air support, while an armed convoy would be used to evacuate the troops and their prisoners.[19]

Dropping by rope from the helicopters, forty Delta troopers and sixty Rangers went into action. They quickly secured the five-story target house and seized twenty-four prisoners. Unfortunately, the clansmen and the Somali people had witnessed similar previous operations, and this time they were prepared to react aggressively. Very large numbers of Aidid's militia and supportive civilians began to form into mobs and set up roadblocks with barricades and burning tires. Armed with semiautomatic weapons and stockpiles of rocket-propelled grenade launchers (RPGs), they brought heavy fire on the Rangers and Delta operators. Then, using massed RPG fire, they brought down first one and then another of the Black Hawk helicopters that were supporting the mission. The Ranger Creed demands that no comrade alive or dead be left behind, and the Rangers and Delta operators lived by that Creed. With large mobs forming around the target house and each of the crash sites, the ground troops sent units to secure the helicopter crews.

The Rangers in the convoy had to fight their way in through very heavy fire, and then, loaded with the prisoners and many wounded, tried to fight their way back to the base while their movements were hampered and confused by communications delays. The foot Rangers fought inch by inch through a hail of fire to reach and assist the downed helicopter crewmen, and then fought at close range to hold off the growing mobs. A second small convoy of volunteers fought their way to reinforce and assist the first beleaguered convoy back to the base. Other special operations troops including Air Force elite rescue Parajumpers and Navy SEALs roped down from helicopters. Two Delta Rangers, Gary Gordon and Randy Shughart, pleaded to be allowed to drop down to protect one helicopter crew that was about to be overrun. Finally receiving permission, they jumped from their helicopter and fought to their deaths to protect the downed crew against overwhelming numbers of enraged Somalis.

For approximately sixteen hours, as day turned into night and back to day, Rangers and Delta fought against thousands of Somalis, and brave Night Stalkers flew every moment that they could to provide cover and support to the surrounded ground troops. A third convoy led by soldiers of the 10th Mountain Division and augmented by volunteer cooks and clerks as well as already wounded Rangers attempted a rescue, but it was beaten back. Finally a fourth rescue attempt succeeded in a linkup. So many wounded were placed onboard that, amazingly, the Rangers and Delta who could still walk then had to fight their way back to the base on foot through the still deadly barrage of fire! Eighteen Americans and one Malaysian ally were killed. Seventy-three friendlies were wounded. Somali deaths were numbered at close to 1,000 with an additional 1,000 wounded. The mission was successful, but tragic beyond any expectation. Shortly thereafter, the President ordered the end to U.S. involvement in Somalia.

AFGHANISTAN: OPERATION ENDURING FREEDOM

September 11, 2001 brought terror to the heart of America with a tragedy that shocked the world. It was soon determined that the terrorists responsible were part of a worldwide Islamic militant organization known as al-Qaeda. Headquartered in Afghanistan and supported there by the ruling Taliban party, the terrorist and Taliban leaders bragged of how they would crush the Americans who might come seeking justice. Their bragging did not last.

On October 27, following two weeks of devastating air strikes, Rangers led the U.S. "up-close" response to terrorism with an airborne raid on the Taliban airfield and command-and-control facility at Kandahar.[20] The Rangers went on to fight in other battles of the war, including the fierce fight at Shah-i-Kot during Operation Anaconda. Instead of being devastated by the bragging terrorists and the harsh Afghan winter, America's warriors quickly destroyed and replaced Taliban control of the country, killed and captured numerous terrorists and their supporters, and forced still others to scatter to other countries.

OPERATION IRAQI FREEDOM

At the time of this writing, information of Ranger missions in Iraq is just becoming public. It is now known that Rangers operated in the northern and western regions of the country.[21] They were tasked to destroy Iraqi air defenses, and they took part in the attack on Republican Guard units at Tikrit. In one incident, three Rangers were killed by a suicide bomber as they rushed to the aid of a pregnant woman taken by terrorists.

Two assignments highlighted Ranger special tactics and abilities. On April 1, 2003, pulled from their other missions, U.S. Army Rangers and a team of Navy SEALs conducted a surprise commando assault on a hospital in Nasariyah. There they freed prisoner of war Pfc. Jessica Lynch and recovered the bodies of eight other Americans.[22] Later, as combat was drawing to a close, Rangers were involved in another high-profile event, the capture of international terrorist Abu Abbas, who was wanted for the hijacking of the *Achille Lauro.*

Into the Future

Rangers, as individuals and as a Regiment, continue to learn and build competencies. They are diligent in incorporating the lessons of Ranger operations from the early days to the latest action in the present day. Their tradition continues to grow, as does their pride. They are unswervingly dedicated to their country and keep themselves on the razor's edge of readiness to defend its people and its freedoms. They also know what recent events and operations portend: they will likely be deployed even more frequently in the future. War has changed, as has America's potential enemies. We are in an era in which battles and military actions take a different form. They must be conducted skillfully, fought fiercely, and won quickly. It would be nice if it were not so, but Rangers will be called upon again. And they will respond. Staying true to their Creed, a new generation of Ranger will lead the way.

2 Move Farther, Faster, and Fight Harder

Acknowledging the fact that a Ranger is a more elite soldier who
arrives at the cutting edge of a battle by land, sea or air, I accept
the fact that as a Ranger, my country expects me to move farther,
faster, and fight harder than any other soldier.

—Second Maxim, The Ranger Creed[1]

We have seen that Ranger units are special high-stakes teams that take on
challenges that others shy from or label impossible. As the second maxim of
The Ranger Creed states, Rangers are expected to accomplish more and
accomplish it faster than other military units. And they do, time and again.
There is much we can learn from their thinking and their mode of operation.

Rangers operate on the cutting edge, out "on the frontier." There are
also civilian teams and organizations that, while facing considerably less
danger, operate under very difficult and demanding circumstances as they
seek to respond to crucial challenges. Before we explore what those teams
can learn from the elite Rangers, let us consider why they exist and why they
are so valuable.

There are and have been many such teams. Some have even become
famous in their own right. One of the most notable was the original Skunk
Works at Lockheed Martin. Dating from World War II, this highly secretive
operation was officially known as Lockheed's Advanced Development Projects. Comprising approximately fifty engineers and designers supported by
about one hundred technicians, the Skunk Works was one of the finest

research and development (R&D) operations of all time.[2] Operating under the shroud of Cold War secrecy, this group produced a series of strategically important military aircraft including the P-80 (the first American jet fighter), the F-104 Starfighter (a supersonic attack jet), the famous U-2 spy plane, the SR-71 Blackbird (a Mach-3 spy plane), and their crowning jewel, the F-117 Stealth Tactical Fighter.

Another notable special projects team was the "Pirate" band at Apple that invented the Macintosh computer.[3] Operating almost defiantly within the Apple organization and flying a Jolly Roger over their team building, these technical wizards designed and developed a computer so small, fast, powerful, and user-friendly that it established, and to this day, shapes the concept of personal computing.

The Taurus teams at Ford also fit the description of high-stakes special teams. The first Taurus team designed "the car that saved Ford" in 1986. That first Taurus was so well engineered that it reversed Ford's losing economic trend and became the best-selling car in America. Operating in the early 1990s, the second Taurus team reformulated the original design and positioned Ford to compete well in the midsize car market against strong Japanese competitors.[4]

Other high-stakes teams are around all the time, even if they are not sufficiently recognized for their important contributions. Emergency medical technicians and medical trauma units are the first responders to critical health emergencies. Firefighting teams provide skillful and quick reaction to save lives and property. Emergency management teams at both local and federal levels are now in the spotlight as they deal with natural disasters and terrorist actions. Special law enforcement units such as SWAT teams, the FBI's Hostage Rescue Team, and the Joint Antiterrorism Task Force work under high pressure to deal with some of the most serious of challenges. Astronaut crews and NASA ground operations personnel come together to form high-intensity special teams. Meanwhile, numerous innovation teams and special task forces are responding to unusual and critical challenges in business, education, and government.

These teams activate and deploy for special missions. That is their function: to respond to specific, demanding, sometimes dangerous challenges that must be dealt with in a relatively short time. Often the circumstances, even for special teams in business and education, are dynamic and complex; sometimes they are chaotic.

Light Teams

Rangers are light infantry. Unburdened by either bureaucracy or heavy equipment (although a 100-pound rucksack can feel pretty heavy), they can move farther, faster. Made up of volunteers who are trained to razor sharpness and equipped with the latest weaponry, they can fight harder. Likewise, the civilian "light teams" are often made up of some of the most qualified and highly motivated individuals who have been formed into tight, mobile units. And there is a need for these light teams.

Most corporations, educational and health care institutions, and governmental agencies are "heavy" units. Like conventional armed forces, they are relatively slow to mobilize, and they are burdened by their own bureaucracy. They can be quite powerful and effective once they begin to move, and they can sustain operations indefinitely as they plow toward their goal. They can take on large conventional challenges, and the good ones have winning records to show for it. But they are not generally agile. They are more like military heavy divisions. While there is always one Ranger battalion standing ready and capable of deploying anywhere in the world within hours, an armored division could take weeks to move to a combat zone. Unfortunately, some businesses take months and sometimes years to deliver the newest automobile model or the next generation of software. They often take even longer to adjust to the challenges of changing markets and new technologies.

But in many cases, time is of the essence. Opportunities appear and disappear quickly; they are there for a moment, and then are lost. Sometimes crises demand immediate action. Organizations that can only lumber toward their goals are doomed to fail in the dynamic circumstances faced by today's businesses and institutions.

Some organizations are smart enough to recognize the nature of contemporary challenges and the constraints they put on themselves because of their size and bureaucracy. Often leaders cannot or may not choose to change the scale and structure of these large companies and agencies, but some recognize that parts of the organization must operate differently. Like Rangers, some small teams must be out on the edge doing "reconnaissance" for the company, some teams need to be agile enough to provide a "ready reaction force" in times of crisis, and some must be capable of taking on "special operations" for which the rest of the organization is not suited.

Accordingly, some organizations have established special high-stakes teams and task forces. They may go by different names, but the nature of the work and the challenges they respond to have a lot in common. Such teams will be relatively small—sometimes only a few people. They will be skillful, made up of some of the best and most highly motivated people in the organization—not necessarily the most senior, but the hardest charging individuals. Those individuals will be confident risk takers; they will be imaginative and decisive. They will have a bias for action coupled with a sense of urgency. That is, they will be naturally inclined to take the initiative and act in the face of difficulty. They do so because they understand that some challenges must be met head-on and quickly, and that crises require a ready, though thoughtful, response.

To maintain their agility, these teams will be relatively unencumbered by bureaucracy. This is not to say that they are rogue teams acting without regard for the organization's standards or procedures. In fact, they often govern themselves by the organization's deepest values and truest sense of mission. They may, in fact, exemplify higher than normal standards. But because they are often given special mandates and resources, they move at a pace and level different from the rest of the organization.

Because they are light teams with special mandates, they are capable of rapid and decisive responses to unusual challenges or changing circumstances. Sometimes, these teams are set up to respond to emergencies or crises. Sometimes, they are scouts on the frontier charged with helping the organization to keep pace or even gain ground in terms of technological, market, or community developments. Occasionally, empowered special teams are tasked to lead organizational reinvention and transformation. They may be given the mandate to challenge current thinking or at least to work toward a future using a very different set of assumptions and expectations. These roles in turn provide parent organizations with an agile, responsive, forward-looking capability. They also provide a model and a nudge to the more conventional elements of those organizations to better position themselves for the uncertainty and changeability that characterizes the world today.

These special teams often operate on an ad hoc basis. They are constituted for a special purpose. Some may be kept in a constant state of readiness and activated as needed; others may be formed for one-time special missions. They may not have permanent membership, or they may be made up of members who spend most of their time doing other work on other teams. These teams come together when needed, do their work, and disband until called upon again.

Special teams and task forces often represent the best and the brightest in their organizations. This book is focused on bringing them lessons and guidelines from the U.S. Army's elite. Beyond the focus on such teams, however, the lessons offered here have value for highly motivated individuals and leaders in general. Although they may not currently be members of special teams or they find themselves leading departments and organizations rather than teams, there are many individuals and managers in corporations, hospitals, and nonprofit organizations who must regularly deal with highly intense and challenging situations. The lessons of leadership and teamwork offered here would be helpful to them as well.

The Three Dimensions of High-Performing Teams

What are those lessons? What guidelines and standards do Rangers have to offer? Where are the principles of high-stakes leadership to be found?

At the most abstract level, the Ranger tradition outlined above points to three interconnected aspects or dimensions of high-performing special projects teams. First, such teams start with strong individuals. Team members must be carefully selected and well prepared. Second, teams must be carefully formed and well supported. Individual members must be forged into a high-functioning, high-spirit unit; and that unit must have adequate support and information from the larger organization. And, third, high-performance teams must be well led. Such teams require decisive leaders who bring a clear sense of direction, who earn the trust of team members, and who lead by example. We will explore these dimensions in depth in sections labeled *The Individual, The Team,* and *The Leader.*

Rogers' Standing Orders[5] and the Ranger Creed

For more specific guiding principles, we will look to Rogers' classic Standing Orders and to the Ranger Creed. The Standing Orders are among the first principles presented to prospective Rangers. As noted above, there were originally twenty-eight Rules of Discipline, which over time became restated as nineteen Standing Orders. Rogers' intention was to offer tactical guidance to his Rangers. For contemporary Rangers, updating the Orders is fairly simple; for example, "Have your musket clean as a whistle . . . ," easily becomes "Keep your rifle clean." Our intention, however, is to offer operating principles for civilian special teams. Analogy must then be our vehicle of translation. And while it is probably true that one can force an analogical connection between any two things, it is not my intention to do so. I will not be translating "Have your musket clean . . . ," to "Keep your computer clean." Those Orders or sections of Orders with applicability so specific and peculiar to military tactics will be omitted. There are, however, some of Rogers' Orders that provide closer analogies and that offer some important advice to high-stakes teams. Specifically, the first five orders or parts of them are quite relevant, and we will pay close attention to them. Staying true to their original phrasing, the Standing Orders are offered in their original, though nongrammatical form. They are:

1. Don't forget nothin'.
2. Be ready to march at a minute's warning.
3. See the enemy first.
4. Tell the truth about what you see and what you do.
5. Don't never take a chance you don't have to.

Additionally, there are some elements of the Ranger Creed that fairly easily convert to principles of high performance and great teamwork. The Creed is the Ranger's code of conduct. It is a values statement that establishes the Ranger way of life for the individual Ranger and a bond and brotherhood among Rangers. As we did at the beginning of this chapter, we will incorporate some of those guidelines as well. Rogers' Standing Orders and guidance from the Ranger Creed will be addressed in those chapters and sections where they are most relevant.

Principles of War[6]

Rangers also abide by overarching military precepts that make up the U.S. Army's Principles of War. Recognizing that we will not be attempting to equate civilian business operations with war, these principles still offer analogies that can be easily drawn and that will inform the efforts of high-stakes teams and organizations. Those principles, which also will be blended into the narrative at the most relevant points, include:

- Objective
- Offensive
- Mass
- Economy of Force
- Maneuver
- Unity of Command
- Security
- Surprise
- Simplicity

Supplemental Concepts and Guidelines

There are other concepts or prescriptions that will add significantly to our thinking about teamwork and leadership. Although they may have military roots, they may not be as codified as the above elements. Because of their value to our study, they will be included and reviewed. They include:

- Skills and Personal Traits
- Motivation
- Leadership
- Learning

We will now begin our study by looking at the first dimension of high-stakes teams: the individual.

Part II

THE INDIVIDUAL

3

Don't Forget Nothin'

Don't Forget Nothin'.
—Rogers' Rangers Standing Order Number 1

It is not grammatical, but it provides quite a challenge. Robert Rogers' first Standing Order has two potential meanings. One is the obvious: don't forget anything that you will need—data, equipment, and so forth. The other, for us, is the more crucial meaning. In line with much of today's emphasis on organizational learning, this Standing Order prompts individuals, teams, and organizations to learn continually and to keep the resultant knowledge readily accessible. With our emphasis in this section on the individual, there are two points to be made: what a person knows and what kind of person he is will contribute greatly to his being selected for special teams, and those same abilities and qualities will make him a valuable asset to those teams.

Good teams start with good people. It is often the case that the people chosen as members of high-stakes teams are among the best available at what they do. They are not necessarily *the* experts in their fields, but they have high levels of knowledge, skills, and abilities. They are not, however, just content-area specialists; they demonstrate the potential for good thinking, for being good team members, and for providing leadership as needed. They are highly motivated, and they have the character and personal traits that prompt their leaders to bank on them.

It might be nice to say that decent levels of competence and good intentions count, that if you do your job in a satisfactory manner, you are

41

automatically in the pool of candidates for special teams. That is often not the reality. Being "good" is not enough. An "average" surgeon is not chosen for the trauma unit. A "competent" engineer is not selected to do break-through work on the company's next generation of hardware or software. A "good" manager is not charged with the launch of a new product, nor is a mediocre scientist placed on a high priority R&D project. To be tapped for the biggest challenges, you have to be outstanding. You have to be better than most at what you do, you have to show yourself as a strong team player and reliable follower, *and* you have to manifest strong leadership qualities. That's saying a lot, so we need to spell out what it means.

Skill and Trait Clusters

One way to conceptualize the hallmarks of personal excellence is through *skill and trait clusters.* There are four such clusters. The three skill categories are domain skills, process skills, and interpersonal skills. We will examine those skill sets in this chapter. In the next chapter, we will look at the fourth cluster, which has to do with motivation and character traits.

DOMAIN SKILLS

> My mind's a computer,
> My fists are like steel.
> If one doesn't get you,
> The other one will.
>
> —Ranger Running Cadence[1]

We can describe domain skills fairly easily: they are the qualifying skills of a profession. They are what you must know or be able to do in order to get and hold a job in a particular field and at a particular level. They give a person what Rangers would refer to as *technical and tactical proficiency.* Domain skills comprise the knowledge and abilities of a particular job or profession. Accordingly, they vary from profession to profession and from job category to job category. The knowledge and skills of a business manager will vary greatly from those of a law enforcement officer, which in turn will vary from those of a surgeon. While there may be some overlap in the domain skill sets of a manufacturing manager and an R&D manager in the same company, there will also be skills that will be peculiar to each. Likewise, the knowledge and skills of an R&D manager in a computer technology firm will be somewhat different from those of an R&D manager in a chemical corporation.

One can also think of domain skills in terms of levels. As a person grows in the job and proceeds up the ranks of the organization and/or profession, higher level, more extensive, and more sophisticated knowledge and skill will be required. The experience and abilities required for promotion to senior research scientist or chief financial officer will far exceed those required for an entry-level position in research or accounting.

The point to be made here is that to be selected for the biggest challenges, to be allowed to work out on the frontier, you must continually acquire, develop, and extend your domain skills. You must engage in continual learning and competency building and must purposefully pursue higher levels and greater breadth of experience. It may help to think of domain skills in terms of concentric circles. There may be a core of knowledge and competence that allows a person to enter a profession. But growth in that profession comes with moving outward to larger concentric circles of knowledge, experience, and ability. And it is by acquiring and demonstrating increasingly sophisticated skill sets that one gains entrée to the next level of professional growth and opportunity.

TAKE PERSONAL RESPONSIBILITY FOR GROWTH

Most professions and many organizations have established cultures and programs that encourage and enable motivated individuals to move through ever-higher levels of achievement. These opportunities may take the form of in-house professional development courses, tuition reimbursement programs, professional certification requirements, even sabbaticals. Opportunities for growth also consist in job rotations, temporary assignments, transfers, and, of course, promotions.

It is nice when an organization puts the development of personnel high on its list of significant goals. But it is too frequently the case that other concerns supersede (or impede) professional development. Increased workload, heightened competition, economic downturns, and unexpected challenges often have the effect of keeping people busy with what they are doing now, rather than promoting their learning for the next phase of personal or organizational growth. Paradoxically, when an organization finds itself in tough times, some of the first things cut are the budget allocations for training and conference attendance. Yet it is in the development of individual and organizational competencies and in the up-to-date awareness of professional trends and new technologies that the organization's future may lie. (It is noteworthy that the Ranger Regiment, the unit most likely to be the first called upon for larger-scale special operations trains harder and more continually than any other unit in the Army.)

Since we cannot depend on organizations to usher us through a developmental regimen, it falls to each individual to take responsibility for his professional development. Seeking out and requesting the developmental opportunities that exist within the organization may open the doors to those opportunities—or, at least, will show the individual to be someone interested in growth and greater challenge. But even if such programs are not accessible or supported through the organization, the motivated individual needs to take steps for his personal development. Individuals can take enrichment and certification courses; pursue an advanced degree; and read journals, books, and articles within their field (and in other areas as well). If necessary and if affordable, people can enroll in external professional development courses and workshops at their own expense. Remember also the informal means to knowledge acquisition. Lunch conversations, visits to other areas of the organization, and participation in on-line "communities of practice" can not only enhance a person's knowledge and awareness, they can extend and strengthen professional networks—a particularly valuable asset these days.

In any case, if you aspire to be part of high-stakes teams, learning and competency building must be ongoing aspects of your professional life. The person whose abilities and value are evident is more likely to be chosen for significant challenges. It may be that such added personal value will be recognized and rewarded by one's current organization, or it may be that a person will "outgrow" the current situation and will move on to new levels of challenge at a new organization. But the desire and responsibility for personal growth lies with the individual.

WHAT TO LEARN

Within each career track or profession, what is involved for the next level of growth is usually apparent. There is often a set of competencies and a clear progression of expertise building. But the forward-looking individual must seek to go beyond the obvious. Besides progressing through the traditional skill ladder, look to your organization's future (even if others in the organization are not doing so). Besides building and refining your skills for current operations, ask: What will be my organization's key competencies in the future? What will my organization need to be capable of in order to gain and/or maintain a competitive advantage? What forms of leadership will we need? How might my job or my organization's products and services be transformed in the future? What is happening on the frontier of my field?

The answers to those questions provide the agenda for the highly motivated individual's professional development. The modern Army is very supportive of individual learning, and in Ranger history, individuals with the next generation of skills have been chosen to lead and/or instruct their units as they moved into the future. If you want to be a big part of your organization's future, if you are seeking to take on the toughest challenges, you would do well to think about what that future and those challenges will likely be. You can then develop a personal action plan on how to prepare for and position yourself for the next set of challenges—and the ones after that.

Another way to put yourself in line for exciting challenges is to think in terms of *niche talent*. High-challenge teams sometimes need specialists who have unusual talents or experience. (See the case study, Rocks on the Brain, below.) Sometimes, what is currently an uncommon or unique ability may represent the future of the organization. Take, for example, the situation of a company that has traditionally served the domestic American market. When projections indicate a great future if the company could provide its products or services to China, it may be that the one manager with Mandarin language skills or who had a year of study in Hong Kong as a graduate student will become an integral part of the organization's future team. Such was the case with Fred Walker. As a Ranger, he had been trained to take on extraordinary challenges at a moment's notice; as a Santa Clara University undergraduate, he had spent his junior year studying economics in Tokyo. When McNeil Pharmaceuticals wanted to launch its Tylenol brand in Japan, that leadership ability and experience with Japanese culture, together with his marketing background, made Fred a clear choice as the launch-team leader.

One of my former college students provides another example. Although only a recent graduate in nursing, she found herself working on a high-level task force charged with establishing a brain injury unit in her hospital. What helped give her entrée to that team was that she had learned forecasting and critical decision techniques as part of a unique nursing curriculum that was supported by my center.

This last example brings up an encouraging point for young go-getters. In some cases, only the most skilled and most senior professionals are selected for groundbreaking teams. But it is frequently the case that such teams also include bright, energetic young professionals who show great potential as team members. They must still demonstrate a threshold level of ability, but what they lack in experience, they may make up for in motivation, a desire to learn, or special talents. An individual's demonstrated drive and potential for greater responsibility may be what opens the opportunity for membership on a high-stakes team.

■ **CASE STUDY**

ROCKS ON THE BRAIN

In addition to the above, here are two other examples of how specialized knowledge or experience brought an individual to the foreground in unusual circumstances. During the hunt for Taliban and al-Qaeda fighters in Afghanistan following the 9/11 terrorist attack, U.S. commanders were sometimes frustrated with unsuccessful bombing runs against tunnels in mountainous regions. The militants seeing U.S. planes approaching could quickly run into deep tunnels, which protected them from lighter bomb loads. The U.S. Central Command developed a unique solution. A Navy reservist, whose civilian specialty was geology, was then on active duty. Using survey maps, the geologist pinpointed new bomb target positions. After bombing runs seemingly far from their positions, the militants would resume their activities only to shortly find themselves buried by rockslides started by the geologically selected targeting.[2]

On a more uplifting note, the mine collapse in western Pennsylvania in July 2002 provided another opportunity for someone with specialized knowledge to respond to an intensely challenging situation. Nine miners were quickly trapped 240 feet underground by a flood when a new excavation broke through to an old mine shaft filled with water. Volunteers were willing to dig out their colleagues and friends, but the rescue digging was itself a dangerous and difficult operation. On the one hand, because digging would take so long, an inaccurate path that might need to be corrected would leave the miners dead; on the other hand, with an underground gas line close to the potential excavation path, a slight miscalculation could be devastating for the miners and their rescuers. But after four exhausting days, all nine miners were rescued. They were considered heroes for banding together and supporting each other; so were the miners who worked tirelessly to dig them out. But out of the limelight was someone who deserved great credit. Called by CNN "the man behind the miracle," engineer technician Bob Long was the one whose background and knowledge provided the exact determination of where, and at what angle, the rescue shaft should be dug.[3] ■

HIGH STANDARDS

Technical and tactical domain skills, "knowing what" and "knowing how," are very significant; but it is important to remember that to be valuable, knowledge must be applied and applied well. If you seek membership on high-challenge teams, be clear about what counts as excellent and produce at that level. Determine what the standards of highest quality in your field are, and then reach for them. Identify what counts as the threshold to bigger challenges, greater responsibilities, and opportunities to work out on the edge. Then position yourself to take on work at those levels—and produce beyond expectation.

But be sure to let the quality of your work, not your mouth, tell your story. Don't talk more than others; do more. Don't put the spotlight on your own work; do work that calls attention to itself. Show yourself to be outstanding, not only at what you know, but at what you can do. And that brings us to the next skill set.

PROCESS SKILLS

Process skills are cognitive abilities. We can view them as our intellectual skills as critical and creative thinkers, or we can categorize them as our competencies in problem solving, decision making, and planning. While domain skills, generally speaking, *reside* in a particular content area, process skills cross boundaries. For example, marketers may leave their marketing-specific skills at the office when they go home in the evening, but they take with them their critical and creative thinking skills, which they can apply in their personal lives or in other areas of interest.

What has been said in terms of domain skills also applies in the area of process skills. Individuals must have the desire to enhance their skill levels, and they must take personal responsibility to do so. This may be more of a challenge with process skills than with domain skills, because our cognitive skills are so internalized and idiosyncratic that usually we are not aware of how or how well we are thinking. And since most people believe they already are good thinkers, they do not feel much of a need to improve.

The reality, however, is that most people learn problem solving, decision making, and planning incidentally; that is, they pick up those processes fairly early in life and usually from family members. Those basic processes *may* get modified somewhat through the years, depending on an individual's education and work experience. Unfortunately, most formal education at basic, secondary, and even college levels does not provide for substantial development of thinking skills per se. Rather, the emphasis is on learning content, and the hope is that in doing so people will become good thinkers. Research and daily experience indicate otherwise.

The question is: Do people normally think at an optimal level? The answer is easy. One does not have to look very far to find poor judgment, superstition, cognitive biases, unchallenged assumptions, and self-limiting thinking. My experience in the fields of cognition and leadership has shown that these weak spots are not to be found solely among the poorly educated or least experienced. Even top executives and individuals with advanced degrees can fall victim to poor reasoning.

LEARN HOW TO THINK, NOT WHAT TO THINK

Membership on high-performing teams requires optimal thinking: well-reasoned critical judgment, inventive idea generation, timely decision making, careful planning. Developing those process skills is a matter of learning how to think, not what to think. The challenge is to improve as a thinker per se, and it may help in conceptualizing this challenge to apply a martial arts analogy. Expert martial artists are on both offense and defense at all times. They are poised to strike, yet are ever ready to defend against an attack. Here it may help to see our goal as developing greater ability in terms of both offensive and defensive thinking. That is, we must do good purposeful thinking, while at the same time guarding against the cognitive biases and pitfalls that can so naturally and easily occur.[4]

We can improve our offensive or purposeful thinking by learning how to be better critical and creative thinkers. Specifically, I would recommend that individuals seeking to be members of high-challenge teams become very good at diagnostic problem solving (how to determine what *really* went wrong), creative problem solving (how to generate novel and effective ideas), decision making (how to make the best choices in a timely manner), and planning (how to turn ideas and decisions into reality). Test and apply those skills at every opportunity. Conduct self-assessments and also look for the feedback of people you respect.

■ **CASE STUDY**

BREAKING THE RULES

My first assignment as a second lieutenant was with the 82nd Airborne Division. Specifically, I was the antitank platoon leader for the Red Falcons, the 1st Battalion of the 325th Airborne Infantry. Despite my relative inexperience, the Ranger Tab on my shoulder often got me chosen for challenging assignments. One such assignment came during battalion maneuvers in Florida. I was designated as the leader of the opposing forces, a small handful of fighters cut out of the battalion and given the task of being an enemy guerrilla force for this extended training exercise.

Our first attack was scheduled for the first night. The three companies of the battalion had dug into defensive positions. We had been designated to probe the battalion lines. We were expected to conduct the probe shortly after dusk. The defenders would respond and repel our probe, and then everybody would get a good night's rest. I delayed well into the night until the defenders had gotten sleepy, and I instructed my troops in some of what I had learned in Ranger School about infiltrating enemy lines. Instead of a noisy frontal assault, which would have been silly and not how things would actually happen, I led them in a stealthy infiltration. Moving painstakingly slowly, we probed until we found a gap in the line of foxholes. We then slipped silently through the line and entered the center of the compound. We moved to a company commander's tent. In front of the tent, mounted on a staff, waved the company guidon, a small flag displaying the company's insignia. Taking the guidon, we slipped back through the lines and into the night without firing a shot. In the morning, there was great embarrassment on the part of the company whose lines we had penetrated, but considerable praise from the battalion commander for our tactics and skill.

That combination of authentic success and encouragement from the commander reinforced our inclination toward risk taking and creativity. For our little guerrilla group, the remainder of the training exercise was a run of one creative tactic and one broken rule after another. We were learning and being reinforced in the value of creative thinking. ■

It should be noted that to improve our thinking, we often have to unlearn bad thinking habits. Much as someone who wants to be better at tennis or golf has to change his swing in order to improve, we may have to become aware of, and then take steps to overcome, those approaches to problems or decisions that are weak or faulty. Learning and adopting strong and proven thinking strategies and techniques will greatly improve the offensive side of our thinking.

As to the defensive aspect, we need to begin by recognizing that the pitfalls to good thinking take many forms and usually occur unconsciously. Our thinking may be less than optimal because we do not challenge assumptions, or, worse, because we fail to recognize that we make decisions on the basis of assumptions. We may be the victims of self-imposed mental blocks because we fail to think beyond the current situation or current ways of doing things. We may make poor judgments because we do not understand probability or fail to recognize patterns over time. We may take simplistic approaches because we fail to perceive the complexity of the systems of which we are a part. To combat these pitfalls, we have to become—through study and reflection—aware of the forms they take and learn to guard against them.

INTERPERSONAL SKILLS

In our context, we can think of interpersonal skills as our ability to work well with and/or to lead others. To use contemporary terminology, they represent our *emotional intelligence.*[5] As with process skills, we are born with a degree of natural aptitude in this area, but we can take steps to improve and enhance our ability—and participation on special teams will require that we do so.

Human interactions present significant challenges. Simply as members of organizations, we are faced with myriad interpersonal challenges on a daily basis. Communication is lacking or breaks down. Misunderstandings occur. Differing perspectives often transform into arguments or prompt the formation of opposing groups. Misapprehensions prompt turfism and narrowed perspectives. Old, dormant prejudices are revived when we feel threatened. And manipulative attempts to "manage" others often backfire and result in downward spirals of aggressive reaction and counterreaction. Even when relationships seem to be going smoothly, substantial thought, tact, and effort are required to keep them so. When humans are thrown into the cauldrons of intense stress that surround high-stakes teams, the potential for team-destructive dynamics is greatly increased. Yet high-performing teams have found ways of dealing with and even avoiding interpersonal problems. In coming chapters, we will address interpersonal concepts and strategies that particularly apply to special teams. Here, with a focus on the level of individual skills and traits, let us consider some foundational concepts.

RESPECT

An essential aspect of any constructive relationship is respect for the other person. This is a matter of valuing others as persons, as individuals with the same moral worth that we give to ourselves. Respect begins with an awareness of our shared humanity: we all have thoughts and feelings, problems and sorrows, dreams and hopes. And when, by circumstance or design, we find ourselves joined with others in the face of difficult challenges, our relationships should begin with the recognition that the people around us deserve our respect. Unfortunately, we do not always value others as we should.

Sometimes, we make the determination that some of the people we have to work with are more trouble than they are worth. They do not seem to understand what is going on, or they do not seem to work hard enough. They seem disagreeable, even antagonistic. It is easy for us, especially when we are stressed, to characterize such people as incompetent, inept, irrational, or even malicious.

In fact, it is likely that they are behaving quite rationally and with good intentions—from their perspective. So, let us begin by adopting the constructive attitude that others have value, even if they think or behave differently from what we would want or expect. Now we can explore the nature and source of those differences.

UNDERSTANDING AND VALUING DIFFERENCE

Others, whether family members, friends or colleagues, think and act differently for a simple reason: they are different! It is a simple matter of fact that each individual is different from all others in important ways. Clearly it is the case that even siblings with similar genetics are individuals who behave differently from one another. Even identical twins with the same genes diverge from one another to become distinct persons. Of course, someone who has come from different social, geographical, educational, or professional circumstances will think and behave differently. And, with good upbringing and/or diversity training, we have been taught to accept and respect those differences. What I would like to address here, however, goes beyond a normal understanding of the concept of diversity.

It is important to recognize that even beyond differences of gender, age, race and ethnicity, people think differently because they must. Contemporary research and theory on the brain tells us that each person cannot help but see the world and circumstances slightly differently from everyone else. The differences in the structure of our individual brains and the differences in our life experiences shape how we interact with the world and with others. In fact, it would not be an exaggeration to say that we all perceive and experience (slightly or vastly) different worlds.[6]

And on high-stakes teams, that's immensely important! Even slight differences in experience, education, and thinking style can contribute to the success of teams facing important challenges. Depending on the nature of the challenge, it may well be that the broader the diversity among team members (to include, importantly, diversity in perception and thinking style), the greater the team's potential for adaptability, responsiveness, and higher quality productivity. Strength, for Rangers and for civilian special teams, comes from recognizing, valuing, and leveraging the differences among team members. Just as an alloy is stronger that its separate metals, teams are stronger when they value and forge the various perspectives and abilities of the members.

Beyond a respect for difference, Rangers have a deep and abiding value for each other. The creed that they live by dictates that they will not leave a fallen comrade behind. It is not a matter of whether they like the person or not, or even if they know the person, a comrade will not be left behind. Rangers have shown in both Somalia and Afghanistan that they are willing to give their lives for their brothers-in-arms. We would not expect to see such self-sacrifice on civilian teams, but it does not seem too much to ask of civilian team members that they respect and value one another. For the sake of good interpersonal relations and in service to the accomplishment of the mission, such attitudes are terrifically important.

Be the Best

It's not the resources; it's the man.

—Delta Force Saying

Given our initial look at personal competence, it is clear that to be chosen for and to excel on special teams, a person will have to bring a great deal of knowledge, skill, and ability. But while those things are needed in abundance, they are not sufficient to guarantee high-level individual performance. In fact, a person can have great potential, but without great motivation and the appropriate character traits to match the challenge, innate abilities will largely remain inert. It would be similar to someone having great natural athletic ability, but no desire or energy to train and compete.

The U.S. Army Leadership Framework, which we will investigate in detail in Chapter 9, has three major aspects or categories. They are: *Be, Know, Do.* The last chapter, with its emphasis on skills, knowledge, and experience, gave a first look at the Know dimension. Here we will begin our examination of the Be dimension, the affective or psychological aspects of the high-performing individual. We will look at the great importance that motivation, values, and character have at the individual level. In coming chapters we will see how this dimension continues to be crucial at the team and leadership levels.

CHARACTER

> Character gives you the courage to do what is right regardless
> of the circumstances or the consequences.
>
> —U.S. Army Field Manual FM 22–100

Character is not a principle of war, although it probably should be. A person's character can make the difference between success and failure in combat, in business, and in life in general. As a point of fact, Ranger School is designed to sternly test the character of potential Rangers, and the Ranger Regiment carefully scrutinizes a person's character before they are "hired" to serve in that unit.

Character is the inner nature or essential qualities of a person. It is a psychological disposition and a moral perspective; it is how we look at circumstances and how we see ourselves in those circumstances. It is the synthesis of our beliefs, values, and ideals, the fusion of how we perceive the world and how we think the world should be. In turn, that combination of beliefs, values, and ideals becomes the wellspring of our actions. Character, therefore, becomes a crucial criterion for selecting individuals to take on great challenges.

Although we talk about a person's character as though it were a single thing, it is actually a cluster of traits that bring forth and support one another. Since "taking on the impossible" is a real test of character, we need to examine those elements of character that would directly affect a person's ability to perform well on a high-stakes team.

CONFIDENCE

The first trait is confidence, but, for membership on high-challenge teams, it should be confidence born of testing. Confidence is not a matter of baseless ego, bravado, or even hope. It surely is not a matter of bluster or talking a good game. Rangers, as quiet professionals, generally look askance at anyone who swaggers and boasts; managers who have to select individuals for challenging tasks would do well to follow suit. Confidence is a matter of knowing one's capabilities and having had the experience of taking on and responding positively to demanding challenges. Past successes, lessons learned, and personal assessments at increasing levels of challenge are what build confidence, which in turn connects with and supports other traits.

PERSISTENCE

Persistence is perseverance or tenacity. It is staying at a task until it is successfully completed—an especially important trait when the stakes are high and the possibility of failure looms. If we look below the surface, we can see that persistence has deeper psychological aspects. Upon reflection, we can see that it derives from two things: high motivation based on the value of the task and a faith in oneself and those around you. We will talk about motivation shortly. Here let us note that persistence is, in part, a faith that develops and strengthens over time as an individual or a team experiences success through extended effort. When a person or a group succeeds because they have pushed a little bit further, held on a little longer, or applied a little more effort, they come to realize the value of and need for persistence. Then, rather than taking the form of a mindless pushing forward, persistence comes to represent a critical judgment and a trial-tested faith that success often comes to those who tenaciously persevere.

COURAGE

Another crucially important aspect of character for the high-achieving individual is courage. Courage is not fearlessness; rather, it is the ability to take action within a context of risk and uncertainty. And to achieve great things, to answer great challenges, you must take risks. Some civilian special teams, for example, law enforcement, firefighting, and other types of emergency response teams, require physical courage. Some teams, such as medical trauma teams and air traffic control operators, require great psychological courage and confidence. And many civilian teams in business, while they may not require physical courage, demand risk taking and the courage to take on important tasks that may fail (and, therefore, can make or break a career).

As with its cousin, confidence, courage can grow through experience. But for that to happen, you have to be willing to test yourself and/or be tested. In military special operations, the ultimate test is combat, but noncombat tests are found in the so-called Hooah Schools: the Army's Airborne, Ranger, Pathfinder, and Special Forces schools; Navy SEAL training and the Air Force's PJ (Parajumper) rescue training. These are schools that, beyond technical knowledge and skill, require physical and psychological courage. These are experiences that test a person's limits and, in the case of Ranger School, subject candidates to stresses that some say exceed those in a combat zone.

Testing one's limits is crucial for high achievement. Succeeding at increasingly demanding tasks promotes confidence and persistence and inspires courage. I found it noteworthy that even though I interviewed a number of Rangers separately, they provided an invariable response to the question of the most important thing they had learned in Ranger training. They reported that the greatest benefit they had derived was the knowledge that they were capable of responding to any challenge (see case study below). Alex Gorsky, Ranger, West Pointer and now CEO of Janssen Pharmaceutica, perhaps captured the Ranger imprint best: "There is no obstacle that you cannot get over, through or around. There is no such thing as an impossible task." Having been tested so severely and for so long, Rangers emerge from Ranger School ready to tackle any problem and confident that they will succeed in the effort. It follows that to grow as people and as professionals, highly motivated individuals must enter into situations that test their abilities and strengthen their character. It also follows that team leaders and mentors should provide such opportunities for their subordinates and should encourage them to respond to demanding challenges.

DISCIPLINE

The next aspect of character is discipline, a rather misunderstood attribute. Discipline is about mental control and self-possession. It is about dedication and strength of mind. Many feel that discipline means doing what you really do not want to do, subjecting yourself to something that is uncomfortable or bothersome. That is not the case. For me, discipline is living in accordance with nature and the circumstances in which I find myself. If I want to stay fit, for example, I have to maintain my physical condition through exercise and a healthy diet. That discipline is simply living in accordance with my human nature. When Rangers return from rigorous training, the first thing they do is clean their equipment, especially their weapons. It would be easier to throw that equipment aside and climb into bed, but the discipline of keeping equipment ready and operational prepares them for combat, where well-functioning equipment may mean the difference between life and death. They live by a discipline that simply is prudence for the long run. Most civilian special teams do not face threat at the level of life and death, but disciplined individuals—people who do what needs to be done for top performance—make good team members.

EXCELLENCE

"Doing the impossible" is a call to produce an outstanding result, to perform at an extraordinary level. It is a call to excellence, and it requires a commitment to the highest standards. It is a matter of demanding the highest level of achievement from one's self and challenging others on the team to produce at that level as well.

The urge or the need to excel is a key characteristic of the high-performing individual and of the high-performing team. If you want to be chosen for such teams, and if you want to succeed once chosen, you must be willing to prepare harder, work longer, and deliver the highest quality product—even when you don't have all the resources or time you would like. The orientation to excellence is something you must exemplify at all times.

Note, however, that the call to excel is not a call for perfectionism. High-stakes teams often have to perform under high stress and must produce within a short time. Such teams, generally speaking, are not a place for perfectionists, who tend to keep polishing their work and doing "just a little bit more." The result is that their work is never quite complete, although others may be waiting for it. High-challenge situations demand high standards, not perfection. The job has to get done successfully, but it has to get done before time runs out.

There is another point about superior standards that is worth noting: on high-stakes teams, you have to have the need to excel, not the need to be right or to be in the spotlight. Impossible challenges demand the highest level of teamwork. On great teams, individual egos are kept in check in favor of team cohesion and group success. Credit and responsibility are shared, as are successes and failures. Similarly, if one individual seeks the spotlight or attempts to dominate team processes, you can bet that the team's processes and outcomes will suffer.

HONOR

The capstone of character is honor. Honor is the fusion of integrity, honesty, and the acceptance of responsibility. The honorable person consistently lives by a clear set of values and beliefs. It is obvious where such a person stands, and his words and actions are consistent with his values. The honorable person is honest and fair in his dealings with others. He takes a stand that he believes in even when it is unpopular, and he can be counted upon to speak the truth. He can, in fact, be expected to "speak truth to power," that is, to tell a superior what he honestly believes even though his words might be unwelcome and might subject him to reprisal. As one Ranger, now a civilian, said of courageous honesty, "You have to go to work ready to be fired each day." Honorable people seek, rather than shirk responsibility, and they acknowledge responsibility for their actions or omissions. Rather than blame others or circumstances when something goes wrong, they make an honest assessment of their behavior and acknowledge what role they played.

Motivation and Commitment

You can have skills and good character; but to be effective in this world, you have to vigorously apply yourself to important tasks. And that means seeking out work and challenges that excite and motivate you. Motivation is the aspiration and willingness to bring about a desired future. In a sense, it is the product of how valuable something is for a person multiplied by the probability that it can be achieved. People are motivated differently because they place different value on a goal or they make different judgments about the chances of success.[1]

We can, however, easily generalize about the challenges and goals that high-stakes teams take on because, by definition, they will be especially valuable and at the same time difficult to accomplish. If, then, you are seeking to be a member of such teams, position yourself, if you can, to work at tasks that hold special value for you. You will be tapping into your intrinsic motivation.

Intrinsic motivation is that form of motivation in which the work, the mission, or the challenge itself has great value for the individual or the group. People who are intrinsically motivated are not focused on getting rewards or avoiding punishments; such things represent *extrinsic motivation*. Rather, they are focused on the essential value of the objective, the goal, or the process, whether it is to protect one's country, to make a scientific discovery, or to open doors to the company's future.[2]

Research has shown that intrinsic motivation promotes creativity; people tend to produce a more original and higher quality result when they feel the work or goal is valuable. This is because the motivation in such cases has a basis in personal values. Of course, not every task in every job, or even every task on a high-stakes team, will be exciting or crucial. Some tasks will be grunt work. But if the overall goal is a worthy one, and if you are genuinely committed to it, even such chores will provide an opportunity to contribute meaningfully.

Commitment is immensely important. Whether it is to the organization, a particular goal, an idea or the community served, with commitment comes an *ownership* of the project. Having a sense of ownership means having a heightened sense of *personal* responsibility for accomplishing the mission. When talented, motivated people feel that the success of an important project will depend, even to a small degree, on their personal contributions, they commit themselves to the task and are willing to put in extra effort. They seek to deliver the highest quality product. They take responsibility for solving problems, for supporting other team members, and, as necessary, they take on leadership roles. And the idea of a follower who can move easily into the role of leader matches nicely with the training and expectations regarding both Rangers and members of high-performing teams.

■ **CASE STUDY**

RANGER TRAINING

The Ranger Imprint[3]

Pride, confidence, self-determination and the ability to lead, endure and succeed regardless of the odds or obstacles of the enemy, weather and terrain.

— U.S. Army Field Manual 21–50

Ranger School has been modified through the years, but its core experiences remain the same.[4] Initially designated the Ranger Department of the Infantry School, it is now officially known as the Ranger Training Brigade. Its purpose since its inception in 1951 has been and remains "to develop combat skills of selected officers and enlisted men by requiring them to perform effectively as small unit leaders in a realistic tactical environment under mental and physical stress approaching that found in actual combat." That official mission statement hardly begins to describe the breadth and depth of this most demanding of military training experiences.

Rangers assigned to the Ranger Regiment will enhance and continuously hone their skills through the nearly constant training of the Regiment, but surviving and succeeding at Ranger School provides the essential experience that tests and stamps a soldier's character for life. It is that training experience that provides the foundation for the Ranger version of the four skills sets described in this chapter.

Already accomplished soldiers will enhance their domain skills in the areas of weapons, tactics, land navigation, communications, demolitions, airborne and airmobile operations, waterborne operations, military mountaineering, urban operations, reconnaissance and combat patrolling, insertion and extraction techniques, and hand-to-hand combat. There will be considerable development of the process skills of problem solving, creative thinking, timely decision making, and action planning. During Ranger training, they will be challenged to think well under extreme levels of physical stress and mental exhaustion while operating day and night in terrains and climates varying from below freezing temperatures in mountains to the depleting heat and humidity of swamps. Ranger training especially calls for growth in the interpersonal skills of teamwork and leadership. Rangers will frequently rotate, often with little notice, through a variety of challenging team member and leadership roles. And character and motivation will be tested beyond psychological limits that most people never approach. Military discipline, standards of excellence and personal honor will be constantly scrutinized and perseverance sorely tested, as Rangers must negotiate challenge after challenge in this dangerous and most demanding training.

Ranger training represents some of the best preparation for combat ever devised. Specifically, it prepares daring and skillful soldiers, not just for conventional fighting, but also particularly for special operations, the often secret, quick response, hard-hitting fighting that has gained more public awareness because of U.S. military operations since September 11, 2001. Yet at its core, Ranger School is about the development of leadership and character.

Prospective Rangers arrive for training hopefully in the best shape of their lives, but no level of conditioning will make for easy passage through what will come. Ranger training consists of approximately eight weeks of long, grueling training days that usually allow for only about three hours of sleep. And despite the fact that Rangers burn a tremendous number of calories in meeting what seems like never-ending physical demands, they receive only one or two meals a day—usually not hot meals, but Meals Ready to Eat (MREs), pre-packaged combat rations. With all rank and other insignia removed prior to arrival, soldiers undergo the training as lowly equals and are simply addressed as "Ranger (Surname)."

Traditionally, the first five days of training, the Ranger Assessment Phase (RAP), is conducted at Camp Rogers at Fort Benning, Georgia. Consisting of punishing physical training (including long Ranger Runs), hand-to-hand combat training, land navigation and battle drill/patrolling instruction, this phase is spiced with demanding obstacle courses and water confidence tests. RAP concludes with a twelve-mile march in full gear to Camp Darby, an isolated training area deep in the woods of Fort Benning. There, Rangers live and train in the field, learning classic commando tactics and techniques. Strong emphasis is placed on decision making and planning, and graded leadership challenges begin.

For those who successfully complete the Benning Phase, the Mountain Phase awaits, and the Rangers move to the mountains of the Tennessee Divide. Working from a base at Camp Merrill in Dahlonega, Georgia, Rangers learn military mountaineering, which includes rope handling, rappelling, belaying, and team rope climbs—all in weather so cold that frostbite is a serious ongoing concern. More confidence tests, including night cliff descents, must be successfully accomplished. Meanwhile, reconnaissance, raid, and ambush training is conducted, in addition to skill building in mountaineering.

The final phase takes place at Camp Rudder on Eglin Air Force Base in Florida. This Florida or Jungle Phase finds the now-depleted Rangers moving into swamp and jungle environments. Small-boat operations on rivers and in the Gulf of Mexico, crossing swollen streams using ropes, and slugging through sometimes chest-high swamps provide added challenge even as military operations continue at a high pace. In this phase as in the other phases, operations must be conducted against a feared OPFOR (opposing force) of seasoned Ranger Instructors determined to defeat, capture, or otherwise embarrass the trainees "on the battlefield."

Despite its harsh demands, physical endurance and courage are not the keys to success in Ranger School. They are necessary, but not sufficient. Rangering involves considerable knowledge, skills, and abilities. Rangers must receive positive leadership evaluations in each phase, must pass twelve critical tests, must receive at least two successful peer ratings out of the four conducted throughout the course, and must avoid an accumulation of negative special observation reports. Lying, cheating, or stealing results in immediate and permanent dismissal. Dropout rates have run as high as 65 percent. Fifty percent of those who start the course do not receive the Tab, and only 30 percent will complete the course with the class with which they began. Being awarded the coveted black-and-gold Ranger Tab at graduation and knowing what it took to earn it imprints a Ranger for life.

Some who earn the Ranger Tab will volunteer for and be accepted into the Ranger Regiment. Others return to their original units, where they take on the role of "yeast." It is expected that their presence and example will raise the standards of their home units, their skills and abilities will add to their units' knowledge base, and their units will be provided with soldiers who can be tapped to lead and/or advise when extraordinary circumstances arise. ∎

SUMMARY

As we complete part 2, let us summarize that to be selected for teams that take on the impossible and to do well as a member of such teams, you have to know your stuff, you have to be an outstanding thinker, and you have to be willing and able to work well with others even when stress levels rise. You will need to be motivated and committed to the task. You will be expected to demonstrate initiative, resourcefulness, and imagination; to be an independent thinker who maintains a positive attitude; and to be a person of integrity and good character. Having these attributes and qualities *self-nominates* a person as a good candidate for high-challenge teams. Exemplifying these traits as a member of such teams contributes to both individual and team success.

Part III

THE TEAM

5

Select the Best

Careful team leader and member selection is crucial for team success. In part 2, we saw that to be selected for and to add value to special teams, a person must demonstrate a powerful synthesis of domain knowledge and talent, strong creative and critical thinking ability, finely attuned interpersonal skills, good character, and high motivation. A good approach to selecting individuals for high-stakes teams is to return to those chapters and convert those desired individual characteristics into qualification criteria. There are, in addition, some further guidelines that pertain to the selection of special team leaders and members.

The Right Match

Individuals should be matched to the task. For that to happen, however, the person or group charged with the formation of a high-stakes team first needs to be very clear about that team's mission and the circumstances in which it will be expected to operate. For individual selection to directly affect team success, a number of important questions will require thoughtful answers. Will the team be taking the place of another team, or will this be the first team of its kind? Are the operating rules for this team in place, or will this team be breaking new ground and establishing precedents? What are the management or leadership team's expectations regarding this special team? Are those expectations based in experience, or are they hopes about the future? Can the team's mandate and desired outcomes be clearly delineated, or will the team be expected to explore the situation and create its own mandate? Has management decided on reasonable, yet challenging, criteria for success, or will the team be expected to establish and live up to its own standards? Will the team be adequately supported by available resources, or will it be expected "to live off the land," scrounging for time, people, and materiel?

The answers to such questions have serious import. They can serve to guide a management group in its selection of both the leader and the members of high-challenge teams. Consider the following examples. Teams that are scheduled to rotate with, replace, or further the work of other teams should have members whose skills at least match those of their predecessors. Teams that will be asked to face novel challenges or to break new ground will probably benefit from having leaders whose style is more democratic and members who are very independent thinkers and high-risk takers. Strategically oriented teams will require individuals capable of turning complexity and unconnected data points into clear and coherent plans. Teams charged with program development and implementation will need to bring great operational competence, analytical abilities, and project management skills to bear. Those teams asked to work in very ill-defined or chaotic circumstances will require leaders and members with a strong mix of expertise, creativity, and decisiveness.

Team composition is not easy as, ideally, three key elements should be matched to each other. Leaders and team members should be suited to each other and, in turn, should fit the task and its peculiar circumstances. This three-way challenge is a difficult one to wrangle with, as all elements must be considered at once; the fact of the matter is that matches on paper may not connect in real life. But those forming high-stakes teams should do their best to get the right people into the right circumstances, while recognizing that once they are there they will still have to gel as a team and adjust to the circumstances. Here, we will look at the first of those challenges, team composition. Next chapter will focus on forging the team, and the following chapters will deal with team operations.

Domain Skills

For specific advice about team member selection, we can return to our model of the four skill clusters. Beginning with domain skills, it is important that team members as individuals have the appropriate knowledge and skills to fulfill their roles. They do not have to be the top experts in the field, but they will require a certain threshold level of ability. For some high-stakes teams, those that will be required to perform at full speed from the first moment (e.g., a hospital trauma team), all members should be highly qualified and capable of performing their tasks without negotiating much of a learning curve. For other teams, those for which learning will be crucial to success and some (small amount of) time for learning will be available, members will require a core of strong basic skills in the field and the ability and motivation to learn quickly.

Beyond selecting individuals who meet domain skills criteria, it is also important that the mix or repertoire of skills *among* all team members appropriately match the requirements of the task and situation. Here we are looking to put the team "puzzle" together. To begin with, team members should be selected to fill task roles and to add value to the team. But beyond that, the knowledge and talents of individual members should complement and reinforce one another so that taken together the skills and abilities of the team as a whole will match the demands of the task.

Tough challenges demand highly capable and highly diverse team members. Today's business teams are often cross-functional in their makeup. It is the variety of perspectives that allows for a fuller rendering of the total picture; it is the medley of skills that enables a team to be agile and responsive to changing situations. In selecting team members, management should therefore seek not only balance and complementarity, but also the diversity (as exemplified in the case study, Rocks on the Brain) that may position a high-challenge team to deal with the unknown or with unexpected challenges. That diversity may be in gender, age, education, professional experiences, ethnicity, or travel experiences. In any case, senior management should guard against what Ranger Lt. Col. Mark Meadows figuratively refers to as "choosing twelve guys that look alike."

It is important to note here that it would be nice if choosing highly qualified individuals would insure the strong formation and high performance of the team. The reality, however, is that often a team members' credentials on paper may not be sufficient to meet the demands of the situation. Sports all-star teams are often not good *teams*. A collection of knowledgeable and capable individuals is not enough to guarantee success. To deal with the greatest challenges, a strong synthesis or integration of those individual talents and abilities will be required. We will address this concern shortly.

Returning to team composition, if the task requires specialized knowledge or ability not found among the line team members, management should arrange and ensure ongoing support for the team. One form of such support may be *adjunct* team members, specialists who are on call and ready to join the team for a short time and then leave. The support could also be found in normal organizational support networks—provided that the team's priority has been well established and recognized. And occasionally, some or all team members will have to go through training prior to team activation in order to pick up the skills necessary for their success.

Process Skills

The selection of members on the basis of their process skills can be approached in similar fashion. First, management should look at the challenge to determine what thinking skills will be required for success. Will there be high demand for creative thinking, as would be the case in new product development? Will team members have to bring strong exploratory techniques and critical thinking to bear, as for such situations as accident or criminal investigations? Will decisions be made quickly and in the midst of chaos or will time allow for reflection and strategic study? Will the team control a project from beginning to end, or will it be responsible for only one key phase or aspect? In the first case, the mix of skills must be both broad and deep to ensure success in all the phases of the project. In the latter case, specialized knowledge mixed with a strong sense of the bigger picture will be required to deal successfully with the team's part of a larger initiative.

Ideally, team members will contribute strong critical and creative thinking abilities; they will be good problem solvers, decision makers, strategists, and planners. But again reality cannot be ignored. Strong content-area specialists do not necessarily bring the requisite process skills for special teams, and even good thinkers vary in thinking ability. Some may be great at decision making, but weak innovators. Others may have strong creative problem-solving skills, but lack critical judgment. Some may be facile problem solvers and decision makers, but may lack the planning and implementation skills needed to bring a project to completion. So once more it falls to higher levels of management to ensure appropriate team makeup.

Of course, we should try to find people with strong process skills across the board. This will be especially important in choosing team leaders. But once again, what the individual may lack, the team as a whole may provide. In forming special teams, seek to meld individual cognitive strengths into powerhouse team thinking. Insure that curiosity and creativity are balanced with critical judgment, that hard-nosed investigative skills work hand in hand with imagination, and that idealized goals are made feasible through pragmatic planning.

As with domain skills, if necessary, provide the adjunct specialists to supplement the team's inherent abilities. Depending on circumstances, advice from senior managers may serve to guide the special team. Often teams and task forces benefit from having an internal or external process leader assigned to them to facilitate their work (and to concurrently enhance and develop their process skills).

STYLES

Thinking style adds another aspect to the topic of process skills. Using the Whole Brain Model developed by Ned Herrmann,[1] we can talk about four major style orientations. Some thinkers are theory oriented. They tend to be strong logical problem solvers and critical analysts. They are good at processing data and are comfortable with technical and technological challenges. They may, however, be low on compassion and insensitive to the needs of others. Some thinkers are tradition oriented. Highly organized and reliable, people with this style know how to get things done. They are great at planning and implementation. But their orientation to what has worked in the past tends to blind them to new possibilities and keeps them from being strong risk takers. The third style is people oriented. These individuals are very empathetic, collaborative, and supportive. They are sensitive to human needs and ensure that the people-dimension is addressed in the work situation. Their strong feeling orientation, however, may challenge them when it comes to making objective decisions. The final style is future oriented—a visionary, adventurous approach to life and work. People in this group seek to understand the big picture and have a preference for change and experimentation. They are open-minded and inventive, but their provocative approach can run afoul of current organizational culture and established procedures.

Everyone is an individual mix of these four styles. Some, but relatively few, lean almost solely on one style. Most people have strengths in two of the styles, and a little more than a quarter of a population can blend three or all four styles. The study of people who rise to the tops of organizations suggests that they can be comfortable and can "converse" in every style. But what do we need to think about with regard to style when it comes to assembling high-stakes teams?

BLENDING STYLES

Thinking styles are another form of diversity, and in this regard, as is usually the case, diversity is a source of strength. Generally speaking, we will want to build special teams that are balanced in their style makeup. We will need to tap the strengths of each style while mitigating its weaknesses. The way to do that is configure teams so that they are *whole-brained*, that is, they have strengths in each of the style orientations. But simply selecting members with diverse styles does not insure balance; the different orientations can tend to pull away from one another. Team leadership must insure that the differences in styles are seen and respected as complementary strengths. Team leaders must also structure assignments and processes so that individual strengths will be tapped, but weaknesses will be neutralized by the other styles. This will be an important concern in the initial forging of the team to be discussed below.

Interpersonal Skills

Assembling a team with an eye to interpersonal skills can be an even trickier proposition. Because of our complexity as human beings and the unpredictability of human dynamics, choosing friendly and likable individuals does not guarantee a well-bonded team; in fact, it does not even guarantee that a team will form. When it comes to the interpersonal dimension, assessment and selection of individuals is not, and should not be, a matter of identifying a group of jovial extroverts. But here, unlike in the previous skill sets, team balance is not what is sought. We are not looking for a mix of introverts and extroverts, loners and party animals. As noted earlier, when it comes to selection with the interpersonal dimension in mind, *every individual* must value the other members of the team and must respect and honor their skills and differences. If we have hopes of assembling a high-performing team, we have to begin with that requirement.

Unfortunately, even beginning with respect does not guarantee that individuals will bond. Personalities vary too greatly, and the mixes and matches of individuals often result in very challenging dynamics. But the good news is that the bonding of members of a high-performing team does not generally result from psychological matching at the time of team formation. Rather it comes from the good intentions and hard work that each team member invests in the forging of the team. And it comes from strong team leadership—leadership that insures that attention will be paid not only to getting the job done, but also to the importance of developing and maintaining constructive team norms and dynamics. We will address this issue in the next chapter.

Character and Motivation

The high stress of difficult challenges can easily test the character and motivation of team members, and, in most fields, there is no civilian equivalent of a Ranger Tab to signify who has the potential to take on the toughest tasks. So management will have to look to previous behavior to spot individuals with high motivation and deep strength of character. From our day-to-day dealings with people, we do get a sense of whether or not they are honest, can handle pressure, or have high standards. And, of course, we can look at past performance assessments. Maybe more important, we can survey present and past supervisors and coworkers in order to develop a fuller picture of a person's character and motivation to excel.

THAT EXTRA SOMETHING

We may want to look for people who have ruffled feathers on conventional teams because they were not satisfied with the level of achievement or the pace of those teams. We will especially want to discover those people who continually look to learn, who get excited about new challenges, and who have emerged as leaders in assignments in which they did not have a formal leadership role. We want to find those individuals who are committed to the organization's goals, values, and future, and who have shown a willingness to do more than was asked of them.

Some sponsors and leaders of high-stakes teams look for that special something. Insurance executive Betsy Scarcelli says that she looks for *heart* when selecting people for high-stakes challenges, and she says that trait is especially important in the person of the leader. Her experience tells her that the key to success is a never-say-die, stick-with-it attitude. But she also looks for "human doers"—curious, highly motivated individuals, who are willing to cross the boundaries of their roles in order to fill in gaps and help others.

Ranger Fred Walker, now a marketing executive, looks for "battle scars." He seeks out people who have been through a lot and who have been in situations that have not gone well, and yet have come out stronger for their experience. He notes, "When everything is fine and there are plenty of resources and everybody's motivated and there's lots of money and there's lots of time . . . most people can do a very good job and look like a very good team player or leader. I like to find the person . . . who's been in business situations where you don't have enough money and you don't have enough time and you don't have enough people and you don't have enough information, yet they still dove in with both feet and gave it everything they had." He wants to tap that experience of being a good team member/leader and accomplishing the mission when the odds were stacked against the team. He thinks back to his days as a Ranger and remembers being cold, wet, tired, hungry, and miserable and having to lead or cooperate with others who were feeling the same. And he notes that it was not a time for complaining; it was matter of accomplishing the mission despite what you didn't have. That, he feels, is how Rangers win wars and business teams succeed. He says straight to the point: "You've got what you got. Make the best of it. Accomplish the mission."

INTRINSIC MOTIVATION[2]

Now let us say that management is lucky enough to have a pool of sharp, dedicated, hard-charging individuals; the actual assignments for any one team may come back to the concept of intrinsic motivation. You may recall that intrinsically motivated people have a passion for what they do. They deeply value the work and/or the goal and are likely to invest themselves much more than people who are doing it simply for a paycheck. They are likely to work harder and longer, persist through difficult times and produce higher quality outcomes. If we can match people to teams and tasks based on intrinsic motivation, we can greatly enhance the probability of success. If we find people who love the challenge and who feel that they are doing something good by contributing to a project, we stack the deck in favor of success.

6

Forge the Team

Initial Challenges

Once team members have been selected and assembled, the team leader must begin the process of molding a high-performance unit. Generally for special teams, two tasks must be accomplished quickly. First, the mission must be spelled out in the clearest terms. Second, as expeditiously as possible, the assembled group of individuals must be transformed into a true team.

FIRST WHY, THEN WHAT AND HOW

PRINCIPLE OF WAR: OBJECTIVE

Direct every military operation towards a clearly defined, decisive and attainable objective.[1]

—U.S. Army Field Manual 3–0

The special teams that are the subject of this book often work in circumstances that are highly fluid, risky, and sometimes chaotic. It is very important that team members have a very clear picture of their objective. But—and this may seem surprising—as a team assembles, the leader should put emphasis not on the *What* of the mission, but on the *Why*.

A special team's mandate, or at least its form, may undergo dramatic change once work and learning begin. What may seem to be a clear objective at the launching of a team may become relatively unimportant, or even irrelevant, as the team begins its operations out on the frontier. Once the team digs into its work, new information, new discoveries, new perspectives, or changing circumstances may prompt a drastic reassessment of what the goal should be. Consider, for example, a team that is charged with developing a new technology for a company. As the team members proceed with their work, if they discover that a competitor is ready to launch that same technology in a proprietary form or that an even better alternative could be developed, they would be mistaken if they blindly followed orders and proceeded to the original objective. In such cases, we would expect that the parent organization would want team members to rapidly report what they discovered and then shift their emphasis appropriately.

We would trust that team leaders and members chosen with the characteristics outlined previously would have the independence of thought and courage to question, or even challenge, a mandate that seems wrongheaded. But, because in certain circumstances a team may need to shift its efforts on the fly, it would be even better if team members felt empowered from the start to put their efforts where they would count the most. A key first step in that empowerment process is to make clear to all team members what *really* must be accomplished, what constitutes the *essential purpose* of the team. And the goal statement that better constitutes the essential purpose is the answer to the question, Why?

TASK VERSUS PURPOSE

> Don't get wedded to the plan; get wedded to the objective.
>
> —Fred Walker, U.S. Army Ranger

It is both important and appropriate to provide a team with an initial sense of direction for its work. The team needs to have some sense of currently anticipated products or desired outcomes. This represents the *Task* or *What* of their work. Organizations generally do not form teams and tell them to do whatever they please. In fact, there is research that indicates that a more focused approach to team goals tends to produce higher quality creativity. Thus, a task statement, which points to the desired products of the team's work, can be helpful. But for high-stakes teams that will be asked to work in very fluid circumstances or to break new ground, that statement of currently anticipated deliverables should be provided in outline or general form; it should serve primarily to point the team in a *general direction*. Accordingly, it could, maybe should, be a somewhat fuzzy statement.

But what must be crystal clear to all involved is the essential end for which the team exists or the crucial function it must fulfill. *Purpose*, the *Why* of the work, focuses on benefits and needs rather than on products. It provides a team with a clear rationale for its efforts and delineates the role and value of the work. For these reasons, a clear and shared understanding of the team's essential purpose greatly facilitates the team's decision making and guides its efforts. It helps to avoid the dissipation of resources, especially time and energy. And, if the goal is worthy, it sparks motivation and encourages persistence.

Continuing with the technology team example above, the difference between a task and a purpose would be as follows: the initial task of the mission may be stated as, develop the next generation of a laptop computer. The purpose of the mission, however, might be: provide consumers with enhanced individual computing power, and, in doing so, move the company toward its vision as the producer of the most powerful personal computing technology on the market. Note in this case that the team could deliver a better laptop and thus fulfill its objectives. But also consider that a creative team might discover and/or invent ways and means other than "the next generation laptop" that might better achieve the company's overarching goals and vision.

TACTICAL FREEDOM

To deal with fuzzy and fluid situations, Army commanders issue what are known as *mission-type orders*. These are orders that assign tasks, but without providing specific directions as to how those tasks are to be accomplished. Such orders, while providing a clear sense of direction and rationale for what must be accomplished, encourage initiative and aggressiveness on the part of subordinates. For special action teams, mission-type orders may be the most appropriate way of providing direction. When a team is clear about the purpose of its mission and empowered to achieve that purpose as a primary objective, the tasks of the work can be addressed creatively and fashioned to fit changing circumstances and/or future needs. Likewise, once everyone is clear about the essential purpose, management can feel more confident to leave decisions about the team's work processes, the *How* part of the equation, to the team itself. While senior management should set the strategic agenda, research and current systems theory indicate that there are considerable benefits to be derived from empowering a team with *tactical freedom*.[2] When faced with complex and dynamic situations, decentralized decision making coupled with a strong sense of vision and purpose seems to be the combination that benefits both teams and their parent organizations. This combination allows decisions to be made on the spot by those most in touch with the current reality, which, in turn, promotes great agility and responsiveness—traits crucial to the twenty-first century organization.

We will discuss this matter further in the section on Commander's Intent, but here let us say that in the early stages of team formation the concern of first importance to a team leader is to clearly specify the mission and essential purpose of the team. And it should be further noted that verbally providing this information, perhaps during an initial team meeting, may not be sufficient. Depending on circumstances, it may be that the mission and purpose of the team's efforts should be put into a clear written statement and discussed among team members until the team leader is confident that everyone understands and is committed to what must happen and why.

A TEAM, NOT A GROUP

The team leader's second major concern is the formation of the team. As quickly as possible, the leader will need to fuse the individual members with their particular talents, knowledge, skills, and styles into a consolidated, well-synthesized team.

There is a clear difference between a group of individuals and a true team. A group, even if it is labeled a team, is a collection of individuals. Those individuals may lack a shared, explicit sense of the goal and/or they may be pursuing personal agendas and possibly competing goals. Their "support" for each may range from conflict and manipulation to a coexistence with clearly marked boundaries; if they are lucky, they may experience a modicum of professional cooperation.

A team is a band of individuals mutually supporting one another while striving to achieve a shared goal. True teams have a strong, shared purpose and a clear sense of identity. Individual goals and team goals are consistent and aligned with each other. Team members aggressively work at accomplishing their tasks, while at the same time assisting and encouraging each other. Rather than taking personal credit when things go well or placing the blame when things go awry, they demonstrate a shared sense of responsibility. The members of true teams have a shared ownership of everything the team does—both its processes and its products. The very best teams, the high performing champions, not only have a strong respect for individual differences, but they have figured out how to tap the strength that comes from diversity of talent and style. They forge individual abilities into a powerful, positive synergy that allows them to operate beyond everyone's expectation. And, importantly, they come to care about one another and have fun being together.

BECOMING A TEAM

One of the informal tenets of Ranger School is "cooperate and graduate." There, the only way to succeed as an individual is to succeed as a fully committed member of a team. But neither wishing nor good intentions will be sufficient to turn an assembly of individuals into a team. Yet doing so is a crucial challenge for both the leader and the members of special teams. To deal with high-stakes situations successfully, the team must be forged through purposeful, dedicated effort and maintained through constant support and shared leadership. But what does it take to meld and maintain a strong team?

INCLUSION AND CONNECTION

There are three initial tasks that should be accomplished. The first of these is inclusion and unification of all team members. This should be common sense, but it does not always happen. Some groups begin their work so quickly that members do not get to know each other's names. Team members need to connect; they need to get to know one another. I do not recommend touchy-feely exercises, but something beyond quick introductions of each member is in order.

When new teams form, just about everybody is in a deferential mode. People tend to be polite and unassertive. This is because most people are feeling a little bit insecure as to whether or not they belong on this high-stakes team. The leader or facilitator needs to break the ice. It may be as simple as a get-together over coffee, but the emphasis should be on getting to know one another beyond learning names. Discovering similarities and shared experiences helps to connect members quickly; so does humor. Learning something about each other's professional background and experiences helps to build mutual respect and credibility; it also adds to the team's sense of itself and its capabilities. The kickoff activities or event should not be forced or uncomfortable; people need to feel secure and to maintain a sense of privacy and, of course, dignity. But the leader should arrange an informal experience that begins the process of team members getting to know one another as persons and as professionals.

Socialization contributes to team cohesion. Informal get-togethers help team members to see each other, not in their roles, but as other humans with similar hopes and needs. Beyond the initial kickoff, the leader should seek as many opportunities as possible for team members to be together in social circumstances other than work. These could be as simple as having lunch together or going for beer after work. These shared times and get-togethers can be powerful in forging good team relationships, and yet it is amazing to me that some leaders and teams are so reluctant to enjoy them. Even if personal schedules are difficult to arrange, the team leader should work to get the team together socially.

A UNIQUE IDENTITY

The second task is to establish a unique team identity. My experience is that teams that see themselves as special and that enjoy a distinctive identity tend to outperform other teams. Sometimes the team's official designation serves to accomplish this well. Larger military units often have a long tradition complete with heraldry, motto, and nickname. Smaller units sometimes adopt a nickname or a motto that all team members can buy into and be proud of—even if it is a rather colorful designation or description. As part of the integration process for civilian teams, I often challenge team members to reach consensus on a logo and/or motto. I encourage them to choose a metaphorical symbol that encompasses their task, their goals, and their values. This is not an easy challenge, especially for teams that are just forming; but that is why it is especially worthwhile. The process takes the focus off of individuals as separate entities and places it on the team, its goals, and the hoped-for connections among members. It initiates a dialogue and decision process on important questions such as the following: Are we clear about our challenge and task? What are our hopes for this team? What do we see as our role or function? How do we want others to see us? How do we want to live and work together? What standards should we adopt?

A CREED TO LIVE BY

The process of answering these questions connects with the third challenge facing new teams: establishing team values, norms of behavior, and standards. Rangers commit to live by the Ranger Creed;[3] it provides them with a clear set of norms and standards. Through the Creed they know what is expected of them as individual Rangers. They know what is expected of their unit. And they know what they can expect from each other. Such clarity regarding interpersonal behavior and team standards is terrifically important, and civilian teams would do well to address these concerns early in their existence. In fact, as we will see shortly, until such norms are established formally or informally, groups do not perform as teams.

Composing and committing to standards of behavior is one of the most important team milestones. There are really two interconnected sets of standards that should be addressed: process norms and interpersonal norms. Process norms establish how the work will get done. They may include administrative requirements such as expectations regarding attendance, promptness, or communication. Importantly, they should clarify team member responsibilities and key task processes such as decision making. This latter element is a very important concern on special teams. As we will see, in military units there is a well-established decision process, and responsibility for decisions at different levels fall to the senior person at each level. On civilian teams, such clarity is not always obvious. The nature of team composition and the varieties of leadership style may leave the process of decision making fuzzy in the minds of team members. Depending on circumstances of individual teams, the leader and/or the team as a whole should clearly establish who will make decisions and what level of agreement will be required. Will decisions be made by the leader on his own authority or by the team members as a body? If group decisions will be made, what level of agreement will be required: unanimity, consensus, majority rule? I have seen serious problems regarding this issue develop even in well-established organizations; but for special teams operating in intense short-term situations, loss of time and energy over such concerns could be very damaging.

The second set of norms focuses on standards for interpersonal behavior. These norms, in effect, constitute a social contract among team members. As such, they should delineate expectations based on a foundation of mutual respect. Because they set standards for team member interactions, they should be both high-minded and pragmatic. They should call on team members to treat each other with consideration and dignity, and they should set forth team values such as honesty, trust, and personal accountability. They may also stipulate how to handle common, yet important, occurrences such as conflict resolution or the giving and receiving of feedback.

The following are examples of actual process and interpersonal norms culled from several teams. Note that while there are stylistic differences as to how they are worded, each provides a clear sense of how team members are expected to behave and perform.

- Build relationships through brave, open, and honest dialogue.
- I will strive for continuous improvements.
- I will give timely and constructive feedback and accept it in a positive manner.
- Feel free to debate and disagree.
- Be willing to be a minority of one.
- I will promote an atmosphere of achievement, enthusiasm, and pride.
- Think as a team (about the big picture), rather than as individuals.
- All ideas belong to the whole team.
- Be aware of and challenge assumptions.

Ideally, both the process and interpersonal norms should be established early and clearly set forth in a written pact or statement of team values. Let us examine why this is important.

Team Cycles

There is a kind of predictability to human teams. It is not that one can predict what a particular team will do and when it will do it; rather it is that teams can generally be expected to move through certain foreseeable phases during their life cycle. Theorists have developed more than twenty versions of what a team life cycle looks like, but one of the best known is the one developed by Bruce Tuckman.[4] In fact, if you take many of the others and array them parallel to Tuckman's model, you would see that they largely say similar things even if they use slightly different wording.

Tuckman's model outlines four stages of team development. First there is *forming*, the stage in which team members get to know one another and get an initial sense of the task. This is the stage we are addressing in this chapter. The forming stage is often characterized by excitement, anxiety, and confusion. Individuals are feeling challenged by the task ahead, although they may be unsure as to what will be required. At the same time, they are seeking to be included as full-fledged members and are concerned about how to conduct themselves. It is for these reasons that I recommended above that leaders/facilitators conduct some activities that establish personal connection while at the same time delivering a very clear statement of the team's purpose and role.

The second phase is *storming*, a rather emotion-laden phase in which the team struggles with issues of power and control. Arguments may occur when some of the first important decisions come due. This often happens because the team has not explicitly discussed decision-making rules or other operating norms. Even if control of the team is not being debated, team leadership often comes under attack in one form or another. The storming phase causes a significant dip in team productivity and endangers overall team success. This is why team processes and interpersonal norms should be discussed, agreed upon, and made explicit as early as possible. Doing so helps to expedite a team through the storming phase and reduces the distractions that accompany that phase. (See The Hyena Pack below.)

If the team survives storming—and that is sometimes a very big *if*—it starts to get its act together. The team moves into the *norming* phase, as members figure out how to go about their work efficiently and develop a respect for the differences among themselves. If they have not been developed previously, the process and interpersonal ground rules now take shape, and the team becomes functional again. Norming is what most teams shoot for because it allows them to operate at about the level of expectation that team members and management have for the team.

But some teams go beyond norming and grow into a new phase, *performing*. This is the phase reached by high-performance teams. Day-to-day problem solving is replaced with proactive problem finding and future-oriented inventive thinking. Collaboration evolves into interdependence and high levels of mutual support. Respect among team members is surpassed by trust, friendship, and loyalty. Relatively few teams will reach the high-performance level.

■ CASE STUDY

SHARED HARDSHIPS—A KEY INGREDIENT

Just as fire tempers iron into fine steel, so does adversity temper one's character into firmness, tolerance and determination.[5]

—Margaret Chase Smith, U.S. Senator and
Lieutenant Colonel, U.S. Air Force Reserve

In the Rangers, teamwork is built by awareness, discipline, practice, feedback, and group challenge. Rangers work together until they can read each other's minds and can execute flawlessly. They learn to depend on one another literally for their lives, and that's just in training.

Consider, for example, the mountain phase of Ranger School. During their time in the mountains, Rangers are trained to high levels of competence in mountain climbing. They learn rope skills, rappelling and belaying, team climbing on sheer cliffs, negotiating overhangs, climbing at night in subfreezing weather, and more. And all of this training is mixed with the continuing challenge of surviving in the wild while conducting military operations against the dreaded opposing force.

As I underwent this training phase, it struck me that in terms of falls and other mishaps while climbing, other Rangers were saving my life everyday. And I was regularly being called upon to save their lives as well. We were learning to come together as a true team as we dealt with the cold weather, the mountains, the lack of food and sleep, the opposing force, and the ever-aggressive Ranger Instructors. Those shared hardships were forging in us a deep trust and sense of teamwork that we needed to tap daily as we physically and mentally supported one another on the sheer cliffs and in the frigid cold. We began to feel the interdependence and esprit that our instructors were breeding us for—the kind that would serve us well when facing an armed enemy. ■

In today's corporations, the danger is not as great, but there is an ever-growing need for teamwork. It is helpful for teams to know about the team life cycle, and, when I advise teams, I generally tell them about it early on so that they get a sense of what they will go through and also so they can set their sights on becoming a high-performing team. I have found that it is helpful for teams to expect storming. If they don't, when the arguments start, they feel that something is very wrong with their particular team, rather than recognizing that what they are going through is normal and predictable.

The model of the team life cycle implies an important message: Grow or fail. If a team does not manage to move through each level successfully, its growth will be stunted and its potential for accomplishment weakened. On the other hand, if team members invest energy into their team processes and do what is required in the early stages, their potential for becoming a great team is strongly enhanced.

■ CASE STUDY

THE HYENA PACK

One high-intensity team that I was advising hit the storming phase fairly quickly, and when it did, the team members turned their sights on me in my role as process leader. The team was given a high-stakes assignment to come up with new product concepts in a very short time. The team had done a good job of bonding. Team members had followed my suggestions about developing team norms upfront and also had developed a strong and distinctive team identity. They had designated themselves The Hyena Pack because, operating as a tight team, they felt that they could bring down both big game (innovations) and small. They also planned to do a lot of laughing as they went about their work.

And work had actually been proceeding well. But a couple of weeks into the process, the team leader approached me to say that the team thought I was moving them too slowly toward the creative solutions they were tasked to invent or discover. They were probably ready to dump me if they could.

I was moving them slowly because they were in a crucial phase of the creative process, problem formulation. Most people, and the members of this team were quite normal in this regard, try to move as quickly as possible to the solution of problems. But in the search for substantially creative answers, jumping to solutions is usually a quick way of coming up with mediocre ideas. Creative experts, like good military tacticians, take time to understand the problem deeply and to assess the most promising routes to the objective. I was keeping this team in this fuzzy and uncomfortable phase on purpose because I wanted them to get beyond standard thinking. But something else was going on here, and, in any case, their impatience had to be addressed.

Without defensiveness, I pointed out to the team that I had predicted that we would get to this point. I referred them to the Tuckman model that I had shared with them a couple of weeks earlier. There almost seemed to be a general sigh of relief. If storming was that predictable, maybe they weren't on a bad team after all, and now they just had to figure out how to get beyond it. We stopped our inventive work and started a dialogue about what was going on. Then the truth emerged.

This was a high-intensity team that met once a week to develop the company's next generation of products. During the rest of the week, team members worked on normal tasks in their regular teams. They now reported that they were getting a lot of static about leaving their regular teams each week. Their regular team leaders were pressuring them about ongoing tasks and derogating their work on this special team. Now it became clear what was going on. Because of the pressure being applied from outside of the team by their regular supervisors, team members were becoming anxious about the process and its ultimate success. When the leader of this special team realized what the real problem was, he took no time in confronting the regular supervisors and assuring that the mandate given to the team by senior management was seen as a priority. With their supervisors off their backs, the team members settled comfortably back into our creative strategy. They produced strong results in a very short time and became one of the highest-performing teams with which I have worked. Their storming became the springboard for their higher-level achievement. ■

This team made it to the highest level of Tuckman's model. Most teams do not, and there is no guarantee that any one team, to include a carefully chosen special team, will do so. That is why moving a team through its life cycle should be a matter of great concern and continuous attention on the part of the team leader.

Unity of Command

PRINCIPLE OF WAR: UNITY OF COMMAND

For every objective, ensure unity of effort under one responsible commander.[6]

—U.S. Army Field Manual 3–0

In addition to the challenges of the team life cycle, there are other concerns that require serious attention. One of these has to do with chains of command and competing priorities.

CHAINS OF COMMAND

We usually think of chains of command as linkages between higher-level and lower-level individuals. We need to remember that those chains bind, constrain, and exert pull.

I cringe whenever I hear of someone reporting to two people. Things go wrong when people are working for two people at the same time. Each supervisor naturally feels that hers is the more important work and will demand the subordinate's time accordingly. The Hyena Pack had its brush with failure because each team member was reporting to two different leaders who were following two different mandates. It prompted a *ghost conflict* within the team that fortunately was dealt with expeditiously. The problem is that their experience is not uncommon, so some guidelines on how to handle the situation are in order.

While generally it is best to have individuals and teams report to only person, sometimes it is necessary to attach a person to another group for operational purposes. In such cases, reporting lines should be manifestly clear. Also, the allocated percentages of time or the actual scheduling of the person's time should be understood and agreed upon from the beginning.

If a conflict is still likely to ensue, senior management needs to establish which mandate will have priority and how efforts should be shifted. It is also best to look ahead to see what impacts may have to be addressed when a person is lifted from his normal duties, whether for a continuous stretch or for part of the work week over an extended period of time. This concern rightly falls to senior management where priorities are set and workforce allocations are made. But the leader of a special team should address these concerns with team members, their normal supervisors, and senior management before team operations begin. Although they may seem like distractions, such issues can fester and cause a team trouble down the line if they are not handled up front.

Individual performance reviews should also be addressed. Time and effort put into special task forces need to be included in professional assessments. Whether through a special assessment, a letter for the personnel file, or by means of input into the normal review process, a person's performance on a special team needs to be spotlighted and given appropriate weight. If it is not, the organization sends a message that special team duty doesn't count officially.

THE ROLE OF ADVISOR

Because of their unusual expertise, Rangers often serve as internal consultants within more conventional units, sometimes advising individuals of superior rank. Additionally, many of the U.S. Army's Special Forces (Green Berets), whose primary role is to live with and advise foreign military and paramilitary forces, are Rangers. I experienced the internal consultant role while serving with the 82nd Airborne Division, and, although not a Green Beret, I received intense advisor training at Fort Bragg's John F. Kennedy Special Warfare Center before being assigned to the Military Assistance Command Vietnam (MACV), where I lived with and advised Vietnamese forces. In civilian life, I have served as both an internal and external consultant, advising superiors or facilitating the work of special teams and task forces. It is relative to that latter role as a process leader/facilitator that some special notes regarding Unity of Command may be helpful.

The principle of Unity of Command calls for clarity with regard to authority, responsibility, and accountability. Even in cases in which team leadership is shared by a formal leader and a process leader/facilitator, the boundaries of their responsibilities should be clear to each other and to all team members. Generally, the formal team leader has overall authority and responsibility. The process leader's functions are, through coordination with the team leader, to provide the team's strategy and scheduling, to lead work sessions, and to focus on establishing and maintaining constructive interpersonal dynamics. In doing so, the process leader lifts some of the day-to-day concerns from the team leader, allowing that person to put her primary focus on the challenge at hand. But the team leader and process leader must be in sync at all times. Continual coordination is a must, and the authority of the team leader should never come into question. Again, these concerns are well worth the time invested and should be addressed before formal team operations begin.

My training at the Special Warfare Center (SWC) required that I learn about Vietnamese culture, politics, and religions. Additionally, I had to learn the Vietnamese language. I have found that to function well as an external consultant requires the same kind of preparation. Since there are no special schools like the SWC to prepare an advisor to work with specific corporations or even specific industries, that preparation falls on the consultant personally.

Technical consultants from within a field will not have to learn the content of the problem area, but they may still have to learn about the culture of the organization they are advising. As a cognitive scientist and someone who is not a subject-area specialist, and in order to function in such diverse areas as chemistry, pharmaceuticals, insurance, education, and social services, I have had to take responsibility for my own education in the content, culture, and language of my clients in those fields. My preparation starts by seeking a detailed briefing from the client when first taking on the assignment. I want to know a lot about not only the task to which I will be assigned, but also the general culture and current state of the organization. When appropriate, I try to gather that information from several sources within the client organization through in-depth interviews. Besides what I am told, I seek additional information in whatever forms seem appropriate: annual reports, strategic planning documents, special mandates, even newsletters. If there are materials such as guidelines, surveys, focus group reports, and such that especially pertain to the challenge, I ask to view or learn about them. In addition to what the organization provides, the Internet and other media sources are quite helpful in developing a total picture of the industry, the client organization, and the specific challenge.

A facilitator from outside a client's field has to guard against ignorance slowing a team down, or prompting a loss of credibility. Once work with a team begins, I seek to be as informed on the topic as the team members I am serving. For example, I will request a copy of all the articles that they are reading and researching, and I apply myself to understanding as much of those materials as I can. If the topic is technical, I will, on my own, get outside references and textbooks and put myself through a crash course so that I can understand the concepts better and talk the language of my team members. While sensitive about slowing the team down during work sessions, I generally do not hesitate to ask about concepts or items that I do not understand, even if I have to do so during breaks or outside of sessions. Overall, I attempt to clearly demonstrate that I am eager to learn and want to understand what they understand.

If a process leader can get somewhat up to speed with the team they are facilitating, it may provide the team with an additional bonus: the facilitator can act as a *wild card*. A wild card is someone from outside the field of the problem. Since the wild card's thinking is not colored by the tradition and precedents of the field, that person brings a different point of view and, by doing so, can potentially contribute to the team's creative process. If process leaders become knowledgeable enough to have a working understanding of the problem area, they are better equipped to offer the team an occasional idea or feedback without their remarks seeming to come from out of left field. The different perspective may be helpful to the team, although the facilitator must guard against interfering with the team's thinking or imposing ideas.

DEALING WITH EGOS

There is a special challenge regarding Unity of Command that can come up in situations in which the membership of a special team includes several equally high-ranking members of the same organization or of different organizations. In such cases, it is easy for power plays to occur or turf issues to arise. I have dealt with both kinds of situations, and they can be tricky.

One suggestion for working with teams comprising high-level people (who usually come with high-level egos) is, make the challenge very big. The task has to exceed the ego wattage of the people involved. If it is a smaller, more routine task or if it is a matter of polishing something that already exists, buy-in will be less and/or parochial interests will kick in; team members will focus on what's best for their division or organization. But presented with a big challenge that potentially could fail, good people who have risen to the top of their organizations are likely to respond with drive and determination. If their personal reputation is at stake and if their joint efforts are facilitated well, the results can be powerful. Two examples come to mind. One was a challenge to "reinvent higher education," and the special task force involved the deans of each of the schools of a college. Another was to conduct strategic planning for a newly formed *value chain* made up of four separate companies and the powerful client organization they were to serve. Both situations involved a lot of hard work, but both were quite successful. Both called on task force members to represent their constituencies well, but they also demanded that they contribute their experience and best thinking. Motivated by great challenges, members could "forget" about how and what they were currently doing in order to think way beyond the present. Such challenges tend to tap intrinsic motivation and creativity. They help to keep egos in check, rather than at odds; and they pull good minds into the future, rather than miring them in the present.

Shared Ownership and Responsibility

> Never shall I fail my comrades. I will always keep myself mentally alert, physically strong and morally straight, and I will shoulder more than my share of the task, whatever it may be. One hundred percent and then some.
>
> — Ranger Creed, Maxim Three

In situations in which there is a team leader and a process leader, it naturally falls to those individuals to direct the team's strategies and to accept joint responsibility for the team's progress (or lack thereof). But in reality, on every high-intensity special team, all team members must share ownership and responsibility for everything the team does.

The hardships of Ranger training and Ranger fighting and the clear demands of the Ranger Creed serve to forge units willing to take on the impossible because each individual accepts responsibility for the whole mission. You will not hear individuals in those units talk of how they did their part, but the other guys fouled up. Rangers operate as high-performance teams, and that means every individual Ranger feels responsible for the accomplishment of the mission. From the commander to the lowest rank-ing enlisted man, everyone has a part to play—but, even as you go about your assignment, you must remain ready to pitch in and help others who may be having trouble accomplishing theirs. It doesn't count to accomplish part of a mission; nobody succeeds unless the total mission is accomplished. There can be no meaningful talk of winning your part of a battle or fulfilling your part of a team's assignment. Special teams succeed or fail as a unit. The team leader needs to send this message early, constantly, and consistently. It is the responsibility of each individual to do his part, and sometimes more. *Shared ownership of everything* must be the maxim of high-stakes teams. And no one must be left behind.

Trust

> Surrender is not a Ranger word. I will never leave a fallen comrade
> to fall into the hands of the enemy, and under no circumstances
> will I ever embarrass my country.
>
> —Ranger Creed, Maxim Five, excerpt

■ CASE STUDY

I WILL NEVER LEAVE A FALLEN COMRADE

Combat veteran Lt. Col. Dave Anders, reflecting on the Ranger Creed and the self-sacrifice that it may demand, declares, "It is unimaginable to leave soldiers behind." The following instances sub-stantiate that fidelity to fellow warriors. They express the vibrancy of the Creed and the loyalty and constancy it instills.

In the battle of Mogadishu in Somalia, the Ranger assignment was to provide security and support for Delta Force as the Delta operators pursued their objective of capturing a warlord group. Those assignments were already successfully completed when the first Black Hawk helicopter went down. The Rangers and "D-Boys" didn't claim that their part of the mission was over. Without hesita-tion and facing extreme danger from warlord militia and large armed mobs, they moved through the streets to rescue the downed helicopter crew. And when a second helicopter went down in an even more distant location, they moved again and fought a pitched battle in an effort to save that crew as well. Meanwhile, back at the base camp, Ranger cooks and support personnel who weren't even assigned to the mission, were volunteering and getting ready to go into battle to support their comrades.

This brave loyalty to an endangered comrade was repeated in Operation Enduring Freedom in Afghanistan. During a fierce battle against Taliban and al-Qaeda forces in the Shah-i-Kot mountains, a Navy SEAL was accidentally thrown from a helicopter when it came under fire and veered away from its landing zone. Learning that he was alive but in great danger, Rangers requested and received permission to mount a rescue attempt. They quickly made a helicopter insertion into the battle against a large entrenched enemy force. Fighting lasted through the rest of the day. The SEAL and six of his rescuers were killed before the troops could be withdrawn that night, but no one would be left behind.

A more fortunate outcome occurred on April 1, 2003, when Rangers and SEALs accomplished the rescue of POW Jessica Lynch in Iraq. In a lightning-fast raid supported by Marines, the special operations troops secured the hospital where she was being held and brought her to safety. They also recovered the bodies of several other Americans who had been killed. ■

Special operations troops develop great trust in each other. Through their intense training, shared experiences, and examples such as those above, they learn to count on one another. They know they will complete their mission together and no one will be left behind.

Trust is a field that binds and provides security to team members. It is an energy that reinforces itself through each good act and one that dissipates rapidly in the face of one act of betrayal or disappointment. Trust takes a while to form and take hold. New teams often have the benefit of beginning with a clean state and may move to a trusting atmosphere fairly quickly. Ongoing teams that have been experiencing trust issues will likely take a much longer time to overcome the disappointments and insecurities that haunt them. Composing the team's creed or social contract of norms is a good first step in the development of trust. It would be nice if that were all that was required, but thinking so is naïve. Trust forms after repeated experiences of people meaning what they say and doing what they are supposed to do.

While trust, or the lack thereof, is a key leadership concern even early in a team's formation, it is not a responsibility of the leader alone. Nor is it a consideration that can be addressed and put swiftly aside. All members of the team, like nodes in an energy field, must continually give and receive; they must learn to trust and be trustworthy. Deep, enduring trust will form and develop as individuals do their jobs and support each other, especially as they do so through difficult times. But for a team to reach the level of high performance, a level characterized by high trust among team members, every individual must live up to his responsibilities and be willing to go beyond those responsibilities, if necessary. Trust and shared ownership are critical characteristics of high-performing teams because they contribute so much to a team's performance and working relationships. As such, these qualities must become goals to which special teams aspire.

Team Mind Power

It is a major challenge to meld the diverse personalities of individual team members into a tight, well-functioning unit. Yet there is a second, related challenge that has a direct impact on the accomplishment of the mission: connecting the knowledge, skills, and talents of individuals into a *team mind*.

Sometimes, the knowledge and skills brought to the team by highly capable individuals are sufficient for team productivity. Such might be the case, for example, with a medical trauma team. In such circumstances, the blending of expertise and skills may require only a briefing on the particular task and an organizing of assignments. Bringing together people with considerable knowledge and great skill is not, however, always sufficient. In today's world, it is often the case that tasks are too big for any one individual and even for a group. Bigger challenges can be taken on only by bigger minds in the form of the synthesized experience and abilities of all the individuals on the team. But how does a team leader go about forming a team mind?

Two tasks must be accomplished. The team needs to develop a common core of understanding shared by all team members, and the team's total knowledge base must continually grow, be maintained, and be accessible. How these things are accomplished will vary from team to team.

The first challenge is that with so much knowledge and data available through today's technology, it is usually impossible for any one individual to store it or even to make sense of it all. This is not an insurmountable problem, however. It is not necessary that every member of a team know everything that the team needs to know. If that were the case, we wouldn't need teams except to share the implementation workload. What is important is that team members share a core of general understanding that is updated on an ongoing basis.

One method of providing this common core would be by means of a comprehensive mission and "intelligence" briefing given to all team members. The team leader, a knowledgeable team member, or experts from outside the team could present the briefing, which would provide essential knowledge and updated information on the situation. Another approach would be to require team members to take a crash course on the subject area by undergoing some training and/or by doing some in-depth reading of important articles and documents. In either case, the team leader must ensure that all members do what is required to gain a strong understanding of key principles and data.

Sometimes, all the important information has not been consolidated or is not readily available. Perhaps no one person has, or is available to provide, sufficient information to enable the team to begin its work. Teams and task forces commissioned to develop substantially new programs or products typically find themselves in such circumstances. In these situations, the challenge falls to the team members themselves to pool what they know. If the knowledge and experience currently exists among the members, even if in unconnected form, they can be organized to brief each other and to construct a shared knowledge base.

Often, however, a challenge involves new learning that must be completed before the team can effectively begin its work. While this may slow final production, it may be quite desirable and may serve to enhance the result. Nothing stimulates a person to learn more than the need to know. Since at this point team members would have a general sense of the challenge before them, they would be motivated to discover and learn what will be important for their success. Additionally, I have found that teams that feel they do not already know all there is to know will look deeply and broadly for new information. This often results in making discoveries and connections that previously may have gone unnoticed.

In some cases, a team must learn very rapidly or must digest an abundance of difficult material. In such situations, a jigsaw approach may be helpful. The learning workload can be divided among team members with subteams given responsibility to cover and report on assigned areas. If the team includes subject-area specialists, they would be given roles on the appropriate subteams. If the team is made up of generalists, subteam assignments may be made on the basis of personal interest, motivation, or potential. Each subteam would be expected to gain and/or provide in-depth understanding of one area of team responsibility. Then, by sharing and interlocking these pieces of the puzzle, the total team can develop general understanding and shared meaning. While no one member would be expected to know every detail of every matter, the team as a whole would have an abundance of readily available knowledge and experience.

The jigsaw approach can help with the second objective of maintaining and expanding the knowledge base. The specialist subteams can be kept operational even after initial learning has taken place. They can be charged with staying abreast of developments in their areas and with conducting deeper investigations to gain greater understanding. As a result of such activity, the team's total knowledge base would grow and stay current. The team leader must then ensure that ongoing information sharing becomes second nature for all team members so that everyone stays as aware and up-to-date as possible.

Notice that the call here is for subteams of area specialists. If knowledge or ability in a particular area will be important for overall team success, redundancy will be required. It is necessary that more than one person be capable of providing crucial information and skills. Just as Rangers incorporate the concept of Ranger Buddies and "never send just one Ranger to do something," high-stakes civilian teams need to have more than one person capable of providing a necessary skill. People get sick, they leave, they have to deal with outside emergencies. For teams working in intense circumstances, the need for backup is crucial. Depending on its mandate and initial composition, it may even be necessary to initiate and maintain a program of cross-training in order to insure that knowledge and skill sets are well distributed among team members.

New Members = New Teams

Many special teams are formed with a specific mission in mind and a relatively short time in which to accomplish that mission. The team members selected for the task operate as a unit until it is time to disband the team. Some special teams, however, are given critical tasks that will take a somewhat longer time to complete. For them, there is a good chance that team membership will undergo changes; someone will leave and/or someone new will join.

While the preceding material was offered within the context of forming a new team, it remains relevant for ongoing teams for an important reason: whenever even one person leaves or one person joins a team, a new team comes into existence. The team life cycle begins anew; all team-oriented tasks may be readdressed.

The reason for this is that the team's internal dynamics shift whenever someone leaves or joins. A team is a *particular* group of individuals who have turned themselves into a well-functioning unit. Especially on high-performing teams, a strong bond among members forms, and roles and work processes are executed in a well-understood and expected manner. People learn to read each other's minds. When someone leaves a team, all those elements have to be renegotiated. The flow of energies will shift and, therefore, must be adjusted accordingly.

Perhaps an even more challenging situation comes about when one or more new people join a team. These "strangers" are not part of the team mind. Continuing team members do not have immediate trust for them. The mutual trust and support that team members had been experiencing came about through shared times and hardships, because of repeated instances in which people did what needed to be done and offered support to each other. The new members did not participate in those events and are, therefore, unknown variables. Insecurity around existing team values may even take shape, in that the new people may not know about those values or be committed to them.

Meanwhile the new members are reliving what the current members went through, but may have forgotten. The new people are insecure about whether or not they will be included and welcomed. They are concerned about fitting in and picking up acceptable behaviors. They need to know more about the goals, the tasks ahead, and how they will be accomplished. And, added to all of those things, they may be concerned about joining a team that has been together for a while and has gelled without them.

For the team to not suffer unduly because of change of personnel, movement through the first phases of the life cycle must be expedited. The leader, and, hopefully, the continuing team members, must ensure that the new members are warmly welcomed and brought up to speed as quickly as possible. Taking care of both the human and professional needs of the new people should be addressed as quickly as possible. A briefing should be provided to get new members actively involved and sufficiently in sync with the rest of the team. The team's task and purpose must be clearly presented, and the team's operating procedures carefully explained. Beyond that, the team's values and norms should be explicitly described, and the new person(s) invited to sign up to honor them. Sometimes teams will take the arrival of new members as an opportunity to reexamine and recommit to their norms and values. That renewal with the new members involved becomes an important step taken together.

While teams with membership changes must renegotiate the life cycle learning curve, there is nothing that requires that they stumble through it or take a great deal of time to get to higher levels. On the other hand, there is no guarantee that what might have gone well the first time will play out as well now. What are required to expedite the journey, however, are awareness and consideration on the part of the team leader and continuing members and good intentions and a willingness to do what needs to be done by everyone.

7 Be Agile, Versatile, and Responsive

... be ready to march at a minute's notice.

—Rogers' Rangers Standing Order Number 2

Success comes to those who have prepared for it. It comes to those who have the ability to respond expeditiously and decisively when opportunity presents itself or when necessity demands.

As part of its overall readiness strategy, the U.S. Army maintains a rapid deployment force. Units within the Ranger Regiment and the 82nd Airborne Division, for example, take turns serving in rapid deployment mode. Fit, trained, and ready, they prepare and position themselves and their equipment for deployment anywhere in the world at a moment's notice. They give the United States a rapid response ability to deal with crises that may develop quickly.

The need for agility, versatility, and responsiveness is one that must be seriously addressed by the contemporary corporation. The world does not stand still; neither do industries and markets. New discoveries are made every day, and new patents follow quickly behind. Start-up companies, capitalizing on their small size and quickness, invade niches left unattended by lumbering market incumbents, sometimes exploiting the incumbents' weaknesses or inertia to become the new big players in the marketplace. A small trend or movement builds momentum quickly and becomes a major opportunity or threat. An unfortunate accident, even in a distant part of the world, can shock organizations that are only remotely and indirectly connected to it. On the other hand, a small serendipitous event can provide a major opportunity, if it is noticed and taken advantage of promptly.

But in the above types of circumstances, it is almost never the case that the organization as a whole responds to do what is necessary. If such situations are addressed successfully, it will likely be that at least the initial reaction, and sometimes the total effort, will be the work of a nimble, responsive team. In circumstances of opportunity or emergency, special teams must be prepared to represent and fulfill the mission of the entire organization.

In some of the types of circumstances outlined above, the onset of events may be so rapid that initiating the formation of a special team may be ineffectual. Rather, such teams will need to be already in place or, because of previous training and positioning, capable of activating immediately. And while a rapid response situation may prompt creativity, it is not a time to invent operational procedures and doctrine. In this chapter, therefore, we will investigate how the Principles of War inform the employment and operations of special action teams.

Principles of War

Just as they are applied in military thinking, the following principles are offered as general guidelines for senior managers and team leaders to consider in envisioning and directing team operations. Although proven over time, they do not comprise a checklist per se, and their single or combined application may vary according to the type of team and situation. These nine principles and the accompanying tenets may serve best as analytical tools or schemas to be considered in forming and operating special teams.

OBJECTIVE

PRINCIPLE OF WAR: OBJECTIVE

Direct every military operation toward a clearly defined, decisive, and attainable objective.

This principle has already been addressed in some depth. The point was made that a team's goal needs to be abundantly clear in terms of both the mission and the purpose of the undertaking. Here we can add that the selection and setting forth of a high-stakes goal should be a matter of careful consideration by senior management. Decisions that are put into motion usually have the effect of closing down other options. Senior management, therefore, would be prudent to select and sponsor those special team missions that would contribute most decisively to current organizational vision and strategy.

At the team level, the objective should guide and motivate every action. The mission and purpose of the special action team should remain uppermost in the minds of all team members. In fact, it will likely be one of the team leader's principal roles to maintain team member focus on the objective. And the leader, using Objective in conjunction with the other principles, should direct operations in such a manner that the focus stays steady on the accomplishment of the most important objectives. Clear priority must be established and maintained unless appropriately changed. The effect of this should be seen in everything from efficient team meetings to streamlined team operations.

OFFENSIVE

PRINCIPLE OF WAR: OFFENSIVE

Seize, retain, and exploit the initiative.

Organizations and their special teams should always be in a proactive stance. Leaders should maintain a bias toward action. Above all, they must guard against complacency. They should never be satisfied with current status, market share, technology, processes, products, and services. Since the world is in fluid state, contemporary organizations and their high-stakes teams must be also.

SENSE OF URGENCY

To employ the principle of Offensive well demands the utmost in adept decision making and implementation. On the battlefield or in the marketplace, seizing, retaining, and exploiting the initiative requires great efficiency and speed. These are hot-button issues for high-stakes teams, whether they are involved in responding to emergencies or inventing new technologies. Efficiency and speed are key aspects of Offensive, and they require that all members of the team and the supporting administration work with a great sense of urgency.

A *sense of urgency* is the feeling that something is not only important, but that it must be accomplished *now*. Great achievements do not come from procrastination or lackadaisical efforts. They result from serious effort mixed with the sense that there may be limited opportunity for successful completion.

When I asked Betsy Scarcelli, who has significant experience in leading and supporting special teams within the insurance industry, what distinguished high-performing teams, her answer was a sense of urgency. Betsy, who seeks to merge a sense of urgency with clarity about the task (Offensive and Objective), said: "I have seen other teams spend millions of dollars. They didn't have a particular sense of urgency. They didn't have a clear focus on what they were going to do. And they floundered and spent a lot money, and . . . it was not a very good deliverable." Others that I interviewed shared this attitude. These people had strong feelings that a sense of urgency made a big difference in how a team operated and in the quality of the work that it produced.

Having a sense of urgency may be a key distinction between a normal team or committee and a high-performing task force. Normal teams and committees are fine for routine and relatively low-priority matters. Such groups plug away at their work. They are often structured for occasional meetings, relatively slow deliberations, and lots of political input. They take plenty of time and the results are usually in the form of routine products, reports, or recommendations. Members of high-stakes teams, on the other hand, see their challenges as unusual, maybe even unique. They see them as opportunities that are extraordinarily important, yet compressed into a relatively short timeline. I remember, for example, one high-stakes team leader saying that his special action team experience felt like being with the Blues Brothers—the team was on a "mission from God." Team members felt that their work represented the future of the company, and they recognized that they had only a relatively few days to accomplish their task. Driving hard, they crystallized into a great team and produced high-quality results.

DECENTRALIZED DECISION MAKING

But even with a hard-driving attitude, high-stakes teams must be well supported by senior management if they are to seize and maintain the initiative. One of the best ways in which management can support such teams is to empower them through decentralized decision making.

The best executive is the one who has sense enough
to pick good men to do what he wants done, and self-
restraint enough to keep from meddling with them
while they do it.[1]

—Theodore Roosevelt

Requiring that decision making go up and down several bureaucratic
levels greatly impedes a special team's ability to function, and in dynamic
situations, could be disastrous. What, especially, should be avoided are
micromanagement and what some in the Army refer to as *stovepiping*.
Micromanagement is a heavily directive and untrusting approach to management. Because it creates a downward spiral of people standing over the
shoulders of other people nitpicking, it usually has the effect of replicating
itself at succeeding levels. Stovepiping got its name because all of a unit's
broadly distributed energy is forced to flow up and down a narrow flue to
and from a commander. While more lumbering conventional army units
may be able to struggle along with such approaches, they would be devastating to high-stakes special operation troops. Such approaches are too slow,
inefficient, and wasteful. And they are generally so unresponsive to a fluid
environment that they ensure failure and lost opportunity.

Rangers and other special ops troops recognize that decision making
and planning must be decentralized if the mission is to be successful. High-
stakes situations demand initiative, quick reaction, and agility. It was
announced, for example, that the rescue of POW Jessica Lynch during
Operation Iraqi Freedom was executed by special operations forces (including Rangers) that were pulled from other assignments and quickly put to
work on the rescue raid. That kind of agility and versatility does not happen
easily with teams used to micromanagement and centralized control.

But decentralized decision making and action requires more than permission to make local decisions. When I asked Ranger Lt. Col. Dave Anders
how to develop initiative in troops, I got a surprising, but insightful answer.
I had somewhat expected that he would talk about special training or other
kinds of preparation. What Dave offered as an answer was: "The confidence
and trust of the next higher headquarters." He reinforced this statement by
saying that when a higher-level leader learns of a motivated team's initiative,
the appropriate response should be, "How can I help you?" This makes great
sense. If teams and subordinate leaders have felt over time that they have the

trust, confidence, and support of their senior leaders, they will feel empowered and enabled to proceed according to their own discretion.

But for decentralized control to be effective, the staunch support of senior managers must be palpable and enduring. People must know, for example, that if they make an honest mistake, they will not be hung out to dry. When individuals feel, with or without good reason, that their seniors will not back them up, they will become fearful of making decisions, and they will stop making decisions. An indecisive team in a high-stakes situation may as well not exist; such a team may only make matters worse. On the other hand, a confident, empowered team will be willing and able to take decisive action. Ranger Nick Panagakos used to tell his troops that he would be angrier "if they did not make a decision, than if they made a decision that turned out wrong." Today, as an FBI Special Agent, Nick's feeling is, "If you know your superior is going to support you, you'll go ahead and make those (important) decisions." In both the military and in civilian life, trusted subordinate leaders must be allowed to make crucial decisions on the spot to press for a win or to avoid serious loss. In either world, micromanagement and stovepiping serve only to promote inefficiency, missed opportunities, and insecurity. They also have the effect of killing initiative and leadership. In today's competitive environment, they must be avoided.

■ **CASE STUDY**

HIRE WELL, THEN TRUST

Nordstrom is a $1.9-billion upscale department store with world-renowned customer service that is the envy of its competitors.[2] It has a host of loyal customers who value the quality of Nordstrom's offerings, but also the treatment they receive from the sales staff. Nordstrom management is selective in its hiring procedures, bringing on board intelligent people with good interpersonal skills. These individuals are trained well in their tasks and the manner in which customer relations are to be conducted. Managers then trust and allow their sales staff to do their jobs as they see fit, but stand ready to support their efforts as needed. A deficiency or complaint, should one occur, is not answered by management; it is dealt with directly by the salesperson who is face-to-face with the customer. And it is dealt with constructively while maintaining a long-term perspective regarding the customer's value to the store. Should a mistake be made, it is not unheard of for a customer to receive a corrected or substituted item, an additional (relatively expensive) thank-you gift, and a handwritten note from the sales representative.

Nordstrom is highly profitable, with a large and loyal following. Yet its customer service policy manual is perhaps the smallest on record. It is one line only, and it reads: *Use your own best judgment at all times.* ∎

Careful hiring, good training, clear direction, and trust, not micromanagement and stovepiping, are the keys to Nordstrom's success—and the success of special operations troops. The Army encourages commanders to delegate decision authority to the "lowest practical level" and to give subordinates "the greatest possible freedom to act." The Nordstrom lesson and the military tenet of initiative are especially appropriate with regard to special action teams. In high-challenge situations, the *decision cycle* must often be speeded up. This means that whether going against an enemy, a competitor, or nature itself, offensive-minded leaders must seek and be able to make decisions proactively, rather than find themselves always reacting to circumstances. Decentralized decision making, then, is a key to implementing the principle of Offense.[3]

MASS

PRINCIPLE OF WAR: MASS

Concentrate the effects of combat power at the decisive place and time.

This principle prompts leaders to concentrate resources and efforts in areas that are most important and where the most good can be done. It challenges both management and teams to be decisive about when and where energy should be concentrated. Senior managers observing this principle may see in it the exhortation to establish strategic initiatives carefully and to build them around core, even unique, competencies. Leveraging an organization's distinctive capabilities may be crucial to success in crowded and ever-changing markets. Some research shows that companies that have established themselves as great organizations have done so by focusing strongly on products and services that could make them world class. Having made those determinations, those companies also sold off or shelved products and services that drained resources from their main efforts.[4]

In similar fashion, small teams need to direct their efforts to what is crucial for success. New product development teams or special education task forces, for example, can and should consider many ideas upfront, but they should fairly quickly narrow their area of investigation in order to do the highest quality work in the shortest time. Rather than scatter their efforts and potentially dilute their effectiveness, such teams should scan the horizon for objectives with high success potential and then invest themselves in achieving those objectives. This is especially the case in situations in which time is short. This helps to avoid a misunderstanding regarding the creative process. Rather than generate a great many ideas and offer some or all of them in relatively undeveloped form, it is better to seek a small number of key insights and develop those insights into the fullest form possible. This does not mean that teams should key in on easy successes; incremental improvements usually only provide marginal payoffs. The special teams that are the topic of this book are designed to take on the high challenges, the ones that may require considerable effort but have the potential to produce extraordinary benefit and success. This is another reason to guard against dilution of effort and to mass energy at the best place and time.

MANEUVER

PRINCIPLE OF WAR: MANEUVER

Place the enemy in a disadvantageous position through the flexible application of combat power.

The principle of Maneuver has to do with the disposition of resources. All these principles are related to each other, and Maneuver is especially related to Mass. While Mass deals with the concentration of effort, Maneuver focuses on the movement and realignment of resources. Maneuver counsels leaders to stay alert in order to focus their energies where they can have the most telling and beneficial effects. This may mean, for example, keeping a competitor at a disadvantage by sustaining a strong pace of new-product introductions that brings products to the market just before the competitor does.[5] It may also mean going around a competitor's strength to affect a market or industry in new ways. (See Mass versus Maneuver below.) Maneuver suggests that even if they can't control circumstances (and that is almost always the case), leaders can position their organizations and teams to substantially affect outcomes.

■ **CASE STUDY**

MASS VERSUS MANEUVER: A BATTLE IN THE COLA WARS[6]

Never go up against a competitor's strength. If a battle involves an equal number of troops on both sides, and the offensive action is a frontal attack on an established position, the result won't even be close. The defender will win. Likewise, if you are trying to introduce a new product designed to go head-to-head with an established brand, think in terms of Proctor and Gamble's time-tested formula: the new product must be preferred by customers by at least a two-to-one margin. The marketers at Pepsi had some difficulty learning this lesson, but they learned it well.

For many years, Pepsi-Cola and Coca-Cola have vied aggressively for slightly larger shares of the relatively stable soft drink market. Over the years, these cola wars have taken many forms. One battle of particular interest was fought in the 1960s and 1970s. At the time, Coke dominated the market, and Pepsi, while second, was far behind. Pepsi managers came to feel that one of Coke's best advantages was its distinctive hourglass bottle. They were probably correct. That bottle had become one of the most recognized advertising symbols in the world; it had, in effect, become a second logo for Coca-Cola and an American icon as well. And beyond brand recognition, it had good functionality in that it could be gripped comfortably and was durable enough to easily withstand the drop within vending machines.

Pepsi executives supported several expensive efforts to study and develop new bottle designs that would compete with Coke. They partially succeeded with the development of a swirl bottle for Pepsi, which reportedly had cost millions of dollars; but that bottle never achieved the immediate recognition of the classic Coke bottle. They were trying a frontal assault on a well-entrenched position.

The situation changed when John Sculley, who had become Pepsi's vice president of marketing, modified the approach to the problem. Sculley came to recognize that attempting to imitate Coke by developing yet another bottle was solving the wrong problem. His perspective is, "Usually, you can only nullify a competitor's strength by changing the ground rules of competition, not simply meeting a competitor on the same field, with his rules." He determined that Pepsi probably did not know enough about consumer needs to make proper marketing decisions. He ordered tests with 350 families to learn how consumers actually consumed soft drinks. The test families were allowed to order as much Pepsi as they wanted, and their ordering patterns provided the data that Sculley needed. He noticed that regardless of the amount requested the families consumed all the drinks that they ordered. This intelligence would soon become almost a law of marketing snack foods—as much as consumers could be persuaded to buy, they would likely consume. Sculley realized that the challenge for Pepsi was not to come up with a distinctive container; it was to come up with packaging that would *get more soft drinks into consumers' homes.* When Pepsi began developing larger-sized packages of cans and larger, generic-shaped bottles for easier refrigerator storage, its sales grew tremendously. Pepsi became a fierce competitor to Coca-Cola, and its new packaging pushed Coke's classic bottle to virtual extinction. ∎

Rangers avoid attacking enemy strongholds head-on. They surely don't attack in accordance with the enemy's defensive arrangements. They prefer to drop silently from the sky with parachutes, come in from the sea on small boats, or infiltrate silently through enemy lines. Such approaches and the case study above provide a number of lessons for us. Don't let a competitor establish the rules of the game. Don't waste time and resources going against a competitor's strengths unless there is a good chance that what you are developing will disrupt the market in your favor. Gather intelligence about what customers *really want* or how they *really operate.* Then maneuver *around* your competition to meet customer needs in a manner that exceeds expectations.

ECONOMY OF FORCE

PRINCIPLE OF WAR: ECONOMY OF FORCE

Allocate minimum essential combat power to secondary efforts.

Related to Mass and Maneuver, this guideline actually offers a rationale for special teams. Because small, highly qualified, well-led, high-energy teams can accomplish so much so quickly, they provide senior management with an efficient and economical means for completing important tasks. Whether for organizational reconnaissance, high-stakes special projects, or rapid response, the special action team may be the best bet. Senior management would do well to plan for, prepare, develop, and support the utilization of these high-capability units.

Within the special action team, this principle applies to the leader's allocation of operational resources. Depending on the mission and nature of the team, it may be appropriate to have the whole team engaged as a unit in accomplishing one activity at a time. But in many circumstances, that would be an inefficient manner of operation. When a division of labor is appropriate, the team leader should subdivide the team so that smaller action teams take responsibility for pieces of the total project. It is recommended that the Ranger Buddy approach be applied here. For any important area of concern or for any task whose completion is critical to overall team success, more than one team member should be assigned. This backing up of efforts provides the team with important redundancy and helps to ensure timely achievement of the goal. Coordination and communication become more important in such a scheme, but the efficiency gained may more than offset the time devoted to those efforts.

UNITY OF COMMAND

PRINCIPLE OF WAR: UNITY OF COMMAND

For every objective, ensure unity of effort under one responsible commander.

This principle was treated in chapter 6. There are two ways in which this guideline may apply to high-stakes teams, one that pertains to individual members and one that relates to the team itself. Individual team members should not be distracted or deterred from their team efforts by the pull of authority from other parts of the organization. There are two methods of assuring unity of command that immediately present themselves; which one applies best will depend on the nature of the special team and how it will conduct operations. For teams that require ongoing, active membership, individuals can be given a definite (temporary) assignment to the team. Such an assignment should establish that the individuals are assigned to the team for the run of the project and that coverage of their normal responsibilities should be dealt with by their regular supervisor with the support of senior management. For those teams that meet regularly, but for only a portion of the workweek, the special team should be given clear priority. The allocation and timing of team member participation should be worked out, if appropriate, between the special team leader and the normal supervisor with senior management ready to step in if agreement cannot readily be reached.

As to oversight responsibility for the team itself, it again makes sense to have only one person responsible. Even if it is by special arrangement, the team leader should report to one member of senior management who will serve as the team's sponsor, champion, supervisor, and liaison to higher levels. See below for an elaboration of these roles.

SECURITY

PRINCIPLE OF WAR: SECURITY

Never permit the enemy to acquire an unexpected advantage.

EXTERNAL SECURITY

This guideline can be interpreted to include the protection of personnel and facilities, but it may also apply to the protection of ideas and plans. In a world in which terrorism is a real threat, even civilian institutions cannot ignore the former, and given highly competitive markets, most business firms cannot ignore the latter. A comprehensive treatment of physical security and the protection of intellectual property is not appropriate to this work. Chapter 11, however, which deals with mitigation of risk and operations in the face of uncertainty, will offer guidelines that can be applied even to those areas of concern.

Here we can note one aspect of Security with regard to the active means that a team may take to protect what it is doing, including plans and new ideas. This concern especially applies to those teams engaged in new-product development. There are, of course, serious concerns that new ideas can be discovered and either snatched or blunted by a competitor. Internal security programs and confidentiality agreements with external personnel should help in this area, but they must be viable and well enforced. Teams working on proprietary ideas should never get complacent in their guarding of those concepts.

INTERNAL SECURITY

But there is another, and perhaps trickier, concern that confronts teams working on new concepts and programs: how might they keep those ideas from being killed prematurely by individuals and groups within the organization?

Creativity has a funny effect on people, including the people within our own organizations. While everyone generally claims that creativity and innovation are necessary in the modern corporation or institution, the reality is that many people are fairly quick to shoot down new ideas, especially ideas in the early stages of development. It has been facetiously noted that new ideas cause the corporate "immune system" to activate so that the ideas can be overcome before they become too dangerous to the status quo. There is probably a whole range of motivations for such negativity, and that range may span from a lack of understanding to turfism and envy.

Bringing a new idea into being requires that lots of thought be given to the process of gaining acceptance, not only from prospective customers and clients, but also from those internal decision makers and support groups whose approval will be necessary to the team's success. And care must be taken in introducing budding ideas for two reasons: they often have not been developed enough to have the bugs worked out, nor do they yet have sufficient internal support to keep them from being easily quashed. This is why burgeoning concepts are so vulnerable to even the slightest criticism.

We will address the notion of Acceptance Planning in chapter 10, but here let us consider why security is a tricky concern when it comes to new ideas. Even compelling new concepts require time and effort to develop to the point of being viable and worthy. They do need to be strengthened and polished. The problem is that often a new-product development team or new-program task force requires resources from outside itself to help with that effort. Legally binding confidentiality agreements provide an easy answer when working with experts from outside the organization; the internal resources may provide the greater challenge. Such resources may also have to be sworn to confidence and/or directed by higher management to refrain from discussing the new ideas until the wraps are officially off. What also may help is including such individuals as important parts of the project or giving them a stake in its success. When they too want the ideas to come to fruition, they will more likely be willing to protect them.

There is another aspect to this concern regarding internal security: while it may be beneficial to the development of a new concept to keep it under wraps until it is fully ready, springing a new idea on colleagues or senior management can be perilous. Presenting them with a fully formed idea, especially one that may represent the need for significant change and adjustment, is like introducing a complete stranger as a new member of the family. The answer to this dilemma may be found in the team's supervisor/sponsor mentioned above in Unity of Command. Since that person operates at least one level up in terms of authority and has direct access to yet another level higher, they may be in the best position to deal with the tension of security versus approval finding. This champion can provide the team with advice regarding how and when to introduce and/or market the concept to others. This individual's political astuteness in this area may be very valuable, especially to teams not used to operating in the rarified levels of the organization's bureaucracy. But the champion can also personally help set the stage for the unveiling of the idea by letting colleagues and senior managers know that something good is in the works, perhaps leaking little bits of information at her discretion so that senior decision makers will not be completely surprised by the new idea. They may even succeed in getting others to enthusiastically anticipate it.

Note: The team's champion may, however, need to be prepared to support the idea over a long run, especially if a good idea is met with initial resistance. The champion may have to advocate for the idea and spend some political capital to slowly gain allies and backers. This concern, by the way, does not represent an unusual or worse-case scenario; it represents the norm in most organizations. New concepts live or die on the basis of how well they are championed internally. Even 3M's wildly successful Post-it Notes required a good deal of internal political advocacy to get them out the door.

RESPONSE AND ANTICIPATION

Despite our efforts at security, we are sometimes surprised. A competitor gains an advantage through a new patent or product launch. Nature throws us a curve in the form of a natural disaster. Regional or world circumstances converge to disrupt our plans or our industry. What advice do Army tactics offer in such cases?

■ **CASE STUDY**

AMBUSH IN RANGER SCHOOL

The Ranger Instructor called me aside and told me to take charge of the patrol and to move to the next tactical objective. We had known since the early days of our training at Fort Benning that we faced an aggressive Opposing Force. We had even heard rumors of authentic torture that this force had visited on captured Rangers. The rumors held that the OPFOR troops physically and mentally tested Rangers who had been captured, and anyone who did not fully resist was dropped from the program. Whether the rumor was true or not, we did not want to be captured.

As our patrol moved through an area that was open except for tall grass, the treeline to our right erupted in fire. True, the OPFOR troops were firing blanks, but the stressful reality of Ranger School made this ambush seem quite real. Without conscious thought, but on the basis of trained reaction, I shouted to the patrol to veer to the right, form a skirmish line, and attack the ambush straight on. This was going to be a case of firepower against firepower. The team reacted immediately, firing on automatic as we charged our ambushers. We quickly overcame them without anyone being designated a casualty. We proceeded to search the ambush site and to examine the enemy "bodies" for intelligence, equipment, and anything else of use to us.

During my debriefing, the Ranger Instructor pointed out that I had had an option. I could have dropped my troops into the tall grass, returned fire, and maneuvered a squad to attack the enemy from their right flank. But the immediate return of fire by my skirmish line of Rangers was also a quick reaction and accepted procedure. He pointed out that there was more than one way to respond, and what counted was accomplishing the mission. I got a "Go" rating for this leadership challenge. ■

■ **CASE STUDY**

AMBUSH PREVENTION—VIETNAM

Our District Advisory Team operated in the Mekong Delta. The Mekong, which bordered our district to the west and southwest, is one of the world's great rivers, and its delta, which included our location in the Plain of Reeds, is an immense lowland region. During the rainy season, the river rises twenty feet or more, overflowing its banks and flooding the delta's rice paddies. In addition to the waterway of the river, a network of small- to medium-sized canals traversed the district, so, even during the dry season, travel by small boat was a frequent occurrence. While in some areas the banks of the canals were free of vegetation and opened onto rice paddies, in many areas the banks had thick vegetation and tall trees—perfect for ambushes that allowed a hidden enemy to fire almost unseen, sometimes downward, into a passing boat or sampan.

My training in Ranger School made me quite careful about ambushes. My awareness was heightened when we received intelligence that the Viet Cong were specifically seeking to ambush our team during our travels through the canals. Knowing this, it became a team SOP to keep our Boston Whaler in superb running condition. The 35-horsepower Evinrude engine was kept in top form, and we bragged that in terms of speed our boat was second only to the Province Senior Advisor's boat with its twin 40-hp engines. Beyond the speed and maneuver capability of our boat, we also sought to stay on constant alert with one team member often in the bow armed with an automatic or semiautomatic weapon and other team members scanning the banks ahead and to the sides.

We knew that there were spies among the Vietnamese forces with whom we worked. (In a previous assignment, I worked for three months alongside a Viet Cong spy until he was uncovered.) We also knew that within the local population there were spies observing our movements. Yet protocol required that we coordinate our movements with our Vietnamese counterparts, as they expressed an ongoing concern for our safety as we traveled. Therefore, in addition to the above precautions, I employed a tactic learned from my study of military history, specifically from Gen. William Tecumseh Sherman's March to the Sea during the Civil War. It was said that Sherman kept all his options open until the last minute. So I adopted that approach with regard to our travels through the canals. Knowing our destination, I would develop two or three alternative routes in my head, but in order to not even unconsciously signal what route we would take, I actually kept myself from deciding on a route until the last minute. As we boarded our boat, I would make a spontaneous decision and then inform the Vietnamese soldiers at dockside. We would be well on our way before the information even got back to district headquarters. For the return trip, we observed Rogers' Standing Order Number 11: "Don't ever march home the same way. Take a different route so you won't be ambushed." We never were. ∎

These case studies offer two suggestions. The first says that if surprised, our reactions to protect our interests must be purposeful, decisive, and unhesitating. The second says it is better to not be surprised. Regarding the former, civilian leaders generally have a great deal more time to respond to a surprise than soldiers caught in an ambush, and the nature of most business surprises, for example, a competitor's new product that threatens market share, are potentially far less devastating. But even given longer reaction time and less consequence, some surprises can be greatly troubling, and a decisive, well-considered response will be required. And in those times of real catastrophe, strong leadership—such as that displayed by Mayor Rudy Giuliani and the rescue and medical staff leaders of New York on September 11—must take charge and fill the breach quickly.

As to the latter guideline, organizational security should incorporate an interconnected, three-pronged approach to security concerns: develop an information-gathering process that continually scouts the potential for worrisome developments; incorporate creative thinking, scenario development, and competency building into all strategic thinking; and develop a culture that values both anticipation of, and quick and agile reaction to, problems and opportunities. The nature and timing of disruptive events may not be predictable, but the probability that they will occur is.

SURPRISE

PRINCIPLE OF WAR: SURPRISE

Strike the enemy in a time or place or in a manner for which he is unprepared.

While we may occasionally be surprised, it is better if we do the surprising. We can begin our reflection on this principle by considering how it relates to the concept of timing in general. Timing, with regard to surprise, means executing an action at an unexpected point in time or achieving a pace of execution that is faster than expected by competitors. Timing can be everything. Ideas will get accepted, initiatives will succeed, and products will sell on the basis of good timing. Things that are too far ahead or behind their time will either fail or struggle to survive. In fact, efforts and resources may be squandered if timing is not right; even if you succeed, your gain may be minimal and too costly. Therefore, special action teams, especially those involved in new-product or new-program development should make timing an important criterion in their planning and decision-making processes.

DISRUPTION

Surprise also equates to disruption, especially with regard to competitive or adversarial situations. In business situations, disruption may, for example, take the form of employing a new technology or being the first to deliver the next generation of products.

Nature teaches us that there is an occasional need for disruption. Forest fires started by lightning strikes, for example, burn away old growth that strangles vegetation, thus allowing the forest to rejuvenate itself. Organizations, too, need occasional rejuvenation, and the special action team may be a great vehicle for prompting and directing that change. But to help bring about new perspectives and new ideas, the special team has to venture out to the edge, to the frontier of the industry—in effect, into the future.

The literature on complex systems is clear on this point: great creativity emanates from a physical or psychological state that is far from equilibrium. It comes when members of a system or organization find themselves on the edge of chaos—not safe and stable, but not spinning out of control yet. The stakes are high; the future is uncertain. One thing is apparent: success and even survival will depend on innovative thinking and constructive change.

■ CASE STUDY

CREATIVITY UNDER THE GUN

Ingenuity has long been and continues to be one of the distinguishing characteristics of the American soldier. The ability to think clearly and creatively under enemy fire is, however, a remarkable attribute. The Ranger mission to seize the airfield at Point Salines in Grenada during Operation Urgent Fury provides a great example of that ability.

The original plan called for Rangers from B Company of the 1st Ranger Battalion to parachute onto the airfield. They were to seize and secure it so that Rangers from the 2nd Battalion, along with their gun jeeps and other equipment, could land by C-130 aircraft and then proceed onto other missions. But the airlift had been delayed, and the Cubans who were constructing the runway had learned of the approach of American forces. They positioned construction vehicles, trucks, fifty-five-gallon drums and concertina wire on the runway; they also drove heavy steel bars into the runway—all to preclude the landing of U.S. aircraft.

As the C-130 transports carrying the first Rangers approached the drop zone, they came under heavy antiaircraft fire. The planes were being badly damaged, so only the first two aircraft were able to drop the Rangers. The other planes veered off. As they descended and landed, the Rangers came under fire. There were fewer Rangers on the ground than planned, and they were under fire. The mission was endangered.

But those Rangers on the airfield quickly went to work to complete their assignment. One Ranger spotted a bulldozer and hot-wired it. Raising its blade to deflect enemy fire, he drove the bulldozer toward the main enemy resistance with his fellow Rangers on foot behind it. With bullets bouncing off the blade, the Rangers breached through the obstacles and pushed the enemy out their defensive positions.

Meanwhile, it was determined that with the runway filled with obstacles the 2nd Battalion would have to jump in, rather than land. They rigged their parachutes in the close confines of their aircraft, but their planes still faced the potential of withering antiaircraft fire.

The biggest worry was a powerful four-barreled 23-mm antiaircraft weapon positioned on a ridge that overlooked the airfield. In flight, a Ranger planner and an Air Force navigator studied the situation and determined that the gun could only depress its barrels so far. If the planes came in low, they would be safe. Descending to 500 feet, the C-130s began their run, and the calculations held true. The 2nd Battalion exited the aircraft with little room to spare, as military parachutes require 400 feet to fully open. Securing the area, hot-wiring more vehicles, and manhandling the obstacles, the Rangers cleared the runway to allow both their vehicles and a larger following force from the 82nd Airborne Division to land safely.[7] ■

■ **CASE STUDY**

CHAOS PROMPTS CREATIVITY

The successful rescue of Apollo 13 provides a great example of how a strong team pulling together can succeed in the face of great challenge and almost sure failure. I had the opportunity to gain insight into the rescue of Apollo 13 from astronaut Edgar Mitchell. Edgar, who would go on to become the sixth man to walk on the moon during the successful moon landing on Apollo 14, was scheduled to be on Apollo 13. When his crewmate Alan Shepherd developed an ear infection, their team was rescheduled for Apollo 14 and replaced by the crew of James Lovell, John Swigert, and Fred Haise. After the explosion occurred upon Apollo 13, Edgar, with little sleep, spent the next three days in a lunar module simulator at NASA. With his background in aeronautics, Edgar had been involved in the design of the module, which had now become a lifeboat in space, and he worked feverishly with NASA engineers on a rescue plan.

Apollo 13 was, of course, rescued. Applying powerful creative thought, the NASA team directed the rigging of a makeshift carbon dioxide filter out of found objects aboard the spacecraft. After three heart-stopping days, the spacecraft returned safely to earth.

These events were dramatic in themselves, but what I learned from Edgar Mitchell many years later heightened the impact of the rescue for me. It turns out that NASA engineers had studied the possibility of such an event aboard an Apollo spacecraft. After working hard to develop a solution, they came to the fatalistic conclusion that should such an event occur, the craft and its crew would be lost! I found this information astounding, and, knowing the successful conclusion of the real-life scenario, I asked Edgar about what had happened and why things had changed. His reply: "We needed more chaos in the system." Although the scientists had previously done their best to prepare the lunar missions, when the extraordinary challenge aboard Apollo 13 presented itself, it pushed their minds to greater creativity and ultimate success.[8] ∎

These two episodes underscore two important points. They affirm that the source of great creativity is found on the edge of chaos. They show that a sense of urgency about a matter of great importance can move high performers to extraordinary levels—even when failure seems imminent.

On a larger scale, we have seen that circumstances sometimes conspire to move a whole organization or industry to the edge of chaos. Such is the case, for example, of the terror attacks of September 11, 2001, followed first by an economic recession, then by the Severe Acute Respiratory Syndrome (SARS) outbreak, and the Iraqi War in 2003, which have landed a series of body blows to many industries, most notably, the airlines. When a system or an organization moves into such disequilibrium, incremental change will not suffice; only transformational creativity will save the day. Only when an organization reinvents itself will it have a chance at a new and brighter future.

RECON OF THE FUTURE

Sometimes, organizations seem stable, but forward-looking leaders realize that change is inevitable. Such leaders may be prudent to not move their whole organization to the edge of chaos ahead of schedule, but they can use the special action team in a forward reconnaissance role. A number of organizations have derived great benefit from doing so.

A special action team composed of imaginative, well-motivated team members, provided with access to ample information and, perhaps, some technological support, can invent and/or discover the future. Just as Rangers or a Long Range Surveillance patrol provides a division or corps commander with crucial information about what to expect and how to proceed, a special task force can provide a CEO with a glimpse into the future.

But to be successful in inventing or discovering the future, the high-stakes team must, in their thinking, leave the present behind. Purposeful disruption derives from original thought. Therefore, the suggestion for special action teams seeking to employ the principle of Surprise is this: the best way to disrupt a competitor, a market, an entire field, or a stodgy organization is to disrupt yourself. Surprise yourself. Be provocative in your approach to a challenge. Disrupt your own thinking. Begin by challenging your current assumptions and paradigms, then rewrite the rules. Seek insights. Search for anomalies, undiscovered trends, new connections, and surprising patterns. Be especially on the alert for weak signals—those little bits of data that, when put together, portend a significant change or event. Use scenario thinking and wargaming to provoke new perspectives and to pry minds loose from the present and the status quo. (For more on weak signals, scenarios, and wargaming, see chapter 11.)

It is only by challenging current thinking and paying attention to what would ordinarily go unnoticed that a team can initiate true innovation and transformation. And since most of the major players in a field do things in similar fashion, it is only by disrupting one's own organization first that one can have hopes of disrupting a competitor or an industry.

A particularly effective use of special action teams to move organizations forward is in the form of an Invention/Discovery (I/D) team. Sometimes known as Innovation Teams, these are small teams and task forces made up of carefully selected, usually cross-functional professionals assisted by a creativity specialist. They work under intense conditions for a relatively short period of time. Sometimes they are put into a full-time designated skunk works; often they will meet for a half day or full day per week for two or three months. They are generally well supported by senior management, which commissions them, sets their general areas of investigation, and establishes their priority. They are often given mandates that are out of whack with normal expectations either in terms of their focus or their desired results. For example, rather than being asked to enhance sales or improve educational experiences, they may be asked to design the sales force or college of the future. Rather than being tapped to develop product line extensions, they may be commissioned to generate highly innovative, new-generation product concepts. I have worked with several I/D teams and have personally witnessed how much they can accomplish in very short periods of time. One team, working about a day per week for twelve weeks, submitted six invention disclosures (the first step to patent application) and several significant recommendations at the conclusion of its work. Another team, working under similar circumstances, submitted twelve invention disclosures.

I/D teams do the impossible. They are so extraordinarily productive because they follow the guidelines offered here. The people on these teams are selected because they have proven their worth, and they bring with them the skill clusters and diverse backgrounds necessary for high-performance task forces. The team leaders are chosen for their domain knowledge but, more important, for their ability to lead and to get things done. They, in turn, are often paired with a process leader who brings a strong strategy and an arsenal of creative problem-solving and critical decision-making techniques. The teams are well supported and empowered by management. And, just as in a Ranger operation, higher management sets overall strategic direction, but the tactical decisions of what to do and how to do it are left to the team leader and members "on the ground." The result is that high-quality initiatives can be generated, investigated and moved up the chain of command faster than would be achieved by ordinary processes.

THE CREATIVITY CONNECTION

Whether involved in crisis response or invention of the future, high-stakes teams facing uncertain or unique circumstances need to bring creative thinking to bear in order to prevail in challenging circumstances. Accordingly, creativity is a competency that should be purposefully developed. Creativity is a natural power of the human mind, but it is one that can be enhanced by education and practice. For some special teams, all members may need to be creative from the outset, and creativity training should precede team operations. For other groups, for example, the I/D teams, it may be beneficial to add a creativity specialist as a member or facilitator of the team in order to provide the just-in-time techniques and tactics needed. In some cases, however, it will be team members' natural ingenuity that will save the day.

■ CASE STUDY

CALLING HOME FOR FIREPOWER

In an effort to protect American citizens endangered by political and military events in Grenada, Joint Task Force 120 invaded that island in October 1983. Paratroopers from the 82nd Airborne Division were part of that force. The mission of the "All-Americans" was to push eastward and to clear successive areas of enemy forces. The mission was proceeding successfully. But runway problems at the airfield in Point Salinas delayed the arrival of a crucial element, the attack helicopters that were to provide fire support for the ground troops. The only alternative was to make use of U.S. Navy planes and supporting fire from Navy ships, but the paratroopers' tactical radios were not compatible with the Navy's communications systems. What did they do?

The paratroopers used commercial telephone cards and the local telephone system to call their home base at Fort Bragg, North Carolina. The headquarters there then relayed the fire requests by satellite to the Navy, which provided the close air and naval gun support. In this case, All-American ingenuity provided an effective, creative solution and prompted correction of the incompatibility of the communication systems.[9] ∎

SIMPLICITY

PRINCIPLE OF WAR: SIMPLICITY

Prepare clear, uncomplicated plans and clear, concise orders
to ensure thorough understanding.

I grew up in the Germantown section of Philadelphia, pretty close to where the Revolutionary War battle of that name took place. One of the first lessons in my study of military history was that the Battle of Germantown was lost because the planning for it was too complicated.

∎ CASE STUDY

SUCCESS TURNS INTO PANIC

On October 4, 1777, two weeks after suffering a massacre at the hands of British forces at Paoli, General Washington decided to go on the offensive. His objective was the village of Germantown, then located about six miles from the Continental capitol, Philadelphia, which had recently fallen to the British.

On that day, the fog of war was not just figurative; it was literal, as the region was enclosed in a blindingly thick mass of moisture. Finally outnumbering the British (11,000 to 9,000), Washington set in motion a four-pronged attack to smash Gen. William Howe's army. He directed Pennsylvania militia to attack Howe from the west. Washington moved with a second column to the southeast, while the third and largest column under Gen. Nathanael Greene attacked to the south. A fourth column of Maryland and New Jersey militia moved to attack the British from the east. Incredibly, all four columns were to attack at the same time in the fog after an all-night march of 14 miles! And this was long before satellite imaging, Global Positioning System (GPS), and radio communication.

First, Greene's column fell behind schedule when one of its elements got lost. Then the second column came under fire from six companies of British infantry that had moved through the fog into a defensive position. Despite the advice of Alexander Hamilton to bypass the house where the British were emplaced and move on to the main objective, Washington engaged the British stronghold. Then Continental soldiers under a drunken Gen. Adam Steven crossed paths in the fog with Gen. Anthony Wayne's unit and began firing on these friendly troops.

While the battle had begun with Continental troops forcing the British to retreat and had continued, despite setbacks, with Washington's army moving into the center of the objective, it ended with Continental troops in full and inglorious retreat. The battle plan was just too complicated. When one considers that the much larger-scaled attack on Baghdad during Operation Iraqi Freedom was basically a two-pronged plan guided by GPS satellites, air surveillance, and abundant real-time communication, a four-pronged attack in the fog without communication was pretty much doomed from the start.[10] ■

Special team strategy in high-challenge situations must generally be clear and straightforward. Leaders should seek to develop elegant solutions—solutions that accomplish the goal directly, efficiently, simply. This is not a matter of dumbing down plans; the people on high-stakes teams are intelligent and capable. But things do go wrong, and people can become confused, especially in times of great stress. Special team leaders should keep assignments clear and conduct status checks frequently. Communication should flow freely, and expectations for each person should be clearly understood. If actions, especially those along the team's critical path, get out of sequence or timing gets out of phase, the team should make immediate adjustments. Leaders should keep their plans simple, their team's focus on the objective, and their activities integrated.

Senior Support

The above interpretations of the Principles of War offer guidance for special team operations, but there is another key element that must be put into in place to ensure the success: High-stakes teams must have the unswerving support of senior management.

This support will take several forms. First, senior management should make a judicious decision about the goals and area of operations for special teams. Since these task forces represent important resources, they should not be squandered, misused, or burned out. We have already noted that motivation is a key element in special team success and that the people selected for those teams are generally strongly motivated to take on important work and to do a good job. But these individuals must have a definite sense that they are taking on important work. Motivation can be dampened by repeated efforts to take on more and more "priorities," only to see one's efforts pushed to the back burner. I have seen that even the most motivated of individuals and teams can lose their edge if they work for an organization in which everything is a high priority. Worse still are situations in which teams deliver quality results in response to priority challenges only to see them put aside, criticized to death, or put into the maybe-later pile. Leaders must decide on true priorities and build a sense of urgency around them. The first aspect of support from senior management is a contract that teams asked to do the impossible will be used well and on missions worthy of them.

The second aspect of support is one of empowerment. Empowerment is not a license to do anything; rather it is latitude granted to teams and individuals by senior management to operate freely within established boundaries. For example, CEO Alex Gorsky works to maintain the culture at Janssen as a place where there is sufficient process and structure to run the company professionally, but also "where people feel empowered, feel that when they walk in the door in the morning, they can make a difference . . . and influence events." This is an example of leading from above that also involves pushing authority and responsibility down—an approach that is very appropriate to special action teams. As noted earlier, once a team has been formed and given its mandate, senior management should allow the team tactical freedom to get the job done as best it sees fit. It should now be left to action team members to develop their own plans and to take operational control of the mission.

This does not mean that senior management's job is done once a mandate has been given to the special team. There is a third crucial leadership task that requires fulfillment. Senior leaders should ensure that resources are expeditiously made available to the team. These resources may include facilities, equipment, funding, information and technology assets, internal or external experts, and, perhaps, even food service. It may also be the case that backup resources may need to be engaged to cover the team members' normal work in order to free them to tackle the higher-priority special task. Senior leaders should also ensure that supporting functions are made aware of the priority of the project and that assistance is provided readily and in good faith.

Beyond careful utilization, allowing operational latitude, and providing teams with sufficient resources, senior leaders must remain on standby to provide whatever else is needed. For a priority project, the special team leader should have fairly easy access to the sponsoring senior manager in order to get further guidance, direction, formative evaluations, and intermediate decisions. The senior leader's role is to stay informed of the team's activities and to provide the strategic perspective that will guide the team to successful completion of its work. As noted above, it is also the leader's role to protect the team and its efforts from internal interference and to provide active championing of the team's products once they are ready for unveiling.

Be Elite

The issue of elite forces and elite teams often comes up and can be a troublesome one. For a long time, Rangers were the stepchildren of the Army. When conflict arose, as in World War II, Korea, and even Vietnam, Ranger units were fairly quickly established. Then, almost as soon as those conflicts were resolved, the units were disbanded. The conventional Army maintained a kind of distrust regarding elite units. Whether it was out of fear that these units would draw the best soldiers to them or out of a sense of envy, conventional senior officers were reluctant to accept the elitism of the Rangers. Now, all that has changed. Rangers have served effectively and honorably in every major conflict since Vietnam. Even without the spotlight on them, it has become known that Rangers and other special operations forces have become key pieces in contemporary U.S. military strategy. Ranger units take on the impossible and deliver time after time. Meanwhile, Ranger officers and NCOs spread throughout the Army act as yeast, setting the standards, raising overall organizational performance, and enhancing the general morale of those units.

Civilian special teams may also feel the sting of the elitism worry. They should ignore it. Special action teams chosen for high challenges have too much on their minds to be distracted with others' concerns for equalitarianism. People have to work extra hard to qualify for and get onto high-challenge teams. These special teams are given more difficult and more important challenges because they are best suited to respond to them. And like Rangers, these highly competent and strongly motivated individuals have and accept the additional responsibilities of setting organizational standards and enhancing overall performance.

Elite teams motivate people to do a better job, and they contribute directly to organizational traditions and myths. Consider, for example, the contributions to organizational esprit that came from the skunk works at Lockheed and Apple that resulted in the F-117 Stealth Fighter and the Macintosh computer. By such demonstrations of organizations at their finest, special teams have an internal and external positive reinforcing effect. Internally, they help to invigorate and fortify an organization's sense of itself, and they reinforce the willingness to take on tougher challenges. Externally, they draw others to the organization as potential clients, customers, and employees. And, further, as one Ranger noted with regard to the fretting over elitism, maybe we shouldn't worry about everybody having a warm and fuzzy feeling.

SUMMARY

It has become very obvious that today's organizations and, in particular, their special action teams, must be characterized by mindfulness and vigilance, by readiness and prowess, by flexibility and ingenuity. They must be agile, versatile, and ready to act.

The Army defines agility as the "ability to move and adjust quickly and easily," and versatility as "the ability . . . to meet the global, diverse requirements of full spectrum operations."[11] For our purposes, agility and versatility involve quick comprehension of even unfamiliar situations, creative thinking, timely decision making, and a substantial repertoire of well-developed competencies that can be readily engaged. We will address specific thought processes and learning approaches that contribute to these abilities in coming chapters. Here we simply note that whether in the form of responsiveness, as in the Apollo 13 and Grenada incidents, or in the form of proactive initiative, as is the case of I/D teams, agility and versatility are crucial to success. Today's leaders and special teams have to be able to think and move faster than the circumstances developing around them.

8 Create Positive Synergy

Best Team/Worst Team

When I begin work with a new team, I often ask the team members to independently record their thoughts about the best and worst teams to which they have belonged. Perhaps because of our shared human nature, there is generally a lot of agreement about the characteristics of best and worst teams even though the individuals involved remember different teams. In fact, I find a lot of shared characteristics even as I go from team to team and organization to organization.

The worst team experiences are characterized by a serious lack of trust, direction, and shared values. People were out for themselves, people were treated unfairly, strong leadership was lacking. People did not feel supported, and communication into the team and among team members was poor or almost completely lacking. Talents and skills were wasted for lack of a cooperative spirit. People hated the experience and could not wait to get out of it.

The best teams were just the opposite. People shared a vision and values and were committed to both. They supported one another and took on responsibilities freely. They grew to understand, trust, and care for each other. Leadership was strong, respected, and shared. Communication flowed freely. Everyone nudged everyone else to perform at high levels. People looked back on the experience fondly, to include remembering a kind of sadness when the team had to disband.

We have discussed many of these elements already and have more to consider. Here I would like to focus on the connectivity of teams. Specifically, I would like to address the concept of synergy and the related issues of communication and feedback.

INTERCONNECTION AND SYNERGY

Team members are highly interconnected whether they realize it or not—and whether they want to be or not. Such connectivity is simply a characteristic of sophisticated, highly adaptive systems, and that is what organizations and special teams are. On special teams facing difficult challenges, each person's contributions or negligence has an impact, direct or indirect, on everyone else on the team. Not only do their efforts or neglect ripple through the team, they are often amplified for better or worse. This synthesis of all team members' contributions produces a *synergy*, an effect greater than those efforts counted separately.

There are two forms of synergy. Positive team synergy can produce results that far exceed expectations, while negative synergy can undo teams made up of even the brightest stars. The 1980 U.S. Olympic Hockey Team was a no-name group of competent individuals. But when those individuals combined and interlocked their moderate talents, they beat the best teams in international competition—including teams that were considered professionals—to win the Olympic Gold Medal. In Super Bowl XXXVI, the underdog New England Patriots chose not to be introduced as individuals at the start of the game. They had gotten to the Super Bowl as a team, not as a group of stars, and that is how they wanted to approach the big game. With strong teamwork, they went on to decisively beat the star-studded, heavily favored Saint Louis Rams.

Unfortunately, for any example of positive team synergy, whether in sports or in business, one can find many examples of teams that do not live up to their potential. Athletic all-star games are generally mildly entertaining, but often lack excitement. Although the best athletes are assembled, they have not formed true teams and generally do not feel the sense of urgency to put out their best efforts. When a group delivers a mediocre performance and fails to live up to its potential, it is generally a disappointing experience for all concerned. Negative synergy, however, is worse. Like drugs that should not be taken together because of their negative interaction, some groups actually perform worse when their members come together than they would have if they had been kept as separate individuals.

If a group does not produce positive synergy, it is a team in name only, and it surely is not a high-performing team. Positive fusion and interdependence of individuals is, however, a considerable challenge to establish and maintain. Yet exceptional teamwork is both the goal and the means for high-performing task forces. This is why I so strongly stress the need to fuse the knowledge, talents, styles, and personalities of individual team members—and to do so as early in a team's life cycle as possible. This is why shared experiences, especially hardships, can serve to bond team members to one another. This is also why there is a terrific need for mission clarity, shared understanding, and free-flowing communication. When all team members understand the importance and intent of their mandate, when they understand their individual roles and how their roles affect one another, when they provide each other with support and encouragement, and when they maintain open and honest communication channels, they stack the deck in their favor. They greatly enhance the probability that they will be a successful, high-performance team. The team takes on a palpable integrity and identity.

Special teams facing great challenges and operating under the gun will almost always succeed or fail based on the degree of mutual support and interdependence among team members. These characteristics, in turn, are built on trust and honesty. If there is even the slightest crack in either, it must be dealt with and repaired quickly.

■ CASE STUDY

IT'S ABOUT THE TEAM—CAMBODIAN BORDER, SOUTH VIETNAM

You join the military to serve your country, but in combat or training what you do is for the people on either side of you. You join a business, hospital, university, or other organization because what they do serves the greater community, but day to day what you do is for the people around you.

Our five-person advisory team was living on the Mekong River about six kilometers south of the Cambodian border. The closest Americans were the crew of the USS *Benewa*, a Navy LST (Landing Ship Transport) anchored in the middle of the river a few kilometers farther south. They represented our lifeline and closest hope for support if things ever got really bad.

I was the commanding officer of the team and the only Ranger, but the other team members, except for a young radio operator, were seasoned NCOs. And, I found out the hard way, one of the NCOs had a drinking problem.

He must have generally kept it pretty much under control, maybe tossing a couple before going to sleep. But one day, he hit the bottle early in the day and then left with another sergeant to make a supply run to the ship. His judgment was off, and our team's small Boston Whaler overturned while attempting to dock with the LST. Both soldiers were rescued from the river's treacherous current, but some important equipment, including their M-16 rifles, was lost. The sergeant's condition onboard ship after the rescue was a pain to the Navy, and it wasn't long before I was hearing it directly from my boss, the Province Senior Advisor, a full colonel.

A day or so following the incident when things were settling down, I asked the sergeant to talk to me in private outside our team house. I didn't punish him. I didn't rant or rave. I don't think I even raised my voice, and he took the dressing down in silence. Soon, however, tears came to the eyes and started down the cheeks of this veteran soldier. The reason: I had accused him of something far worse than the embarrassing incident and the loss of equipment. I told him he had let the team down. ∎

In combat or in the boardroom, it is the people around you who count. Every person is connected directly or indirectly with everyone else. Everyone affects everyone else. A team survives and succeeds on the basis of team synergy. It also survives and succeeds to the degree that team members are honest with, care about, and take care of each other.

Sometimes on teams that I am advising, something goes wrong. Somebody doesn't show up or doesn't complete his work. But another team member quickly takes responsibility for covering for that person and for working with him to get him back up to speed. I get the sense that I am working with a good team. Sometimes on other teams, a team member will approach me in private and begin to tell me about how so-and-so isn't pulling his share of the load. I cringe a little inside; I know I am working with a group, not a true team. I don't take sides, and I tactfully advise them to deal directly with the team member about whom they are complaining.

I also recognize that even a symptom as slight as this signals the need for some serious team building. I sometimes remember an incident in which a new person joined a very good team and started to gossip to some team members about some of the other people on the team. The veteran team members stopped the new person straightaway. Without hostility they simply said, "On this team, we don't gossip about each other."

That kind of straight talk treated the new person with respect. It also affirmed the team norms that had been established and that had brought the team its success. Team standards are team standards. Lowering them a little is like telling your body's immune system not to worry about that virus that is creeping into the bloodstream.

Information Flow

For individuals to come together and perform well together as a team, they must connect and align their energies. Sometimes, that means physically working together in such a fashion to leverage their individual strengths and talents. It definitely means exchanging information in an open, honest, and timely manner.

Information is the lifeblood of special teams. It must flow into the team, among team members, and out from the team. Special teams operating in high-challenge situations need the right information at the right time. Their parent organization should be pushing important information to them, and they should have easy access to any data that may be crucial to their success. Just as combat intelligence and a communication plan are crucial parts of military special operations, civilian special teams must also be provided with up-to-date data and solid communication links that provide information on demand.

The infrastructure and means for strong communication exist. Computer technology and the World Wide Web allow for an overabundance of accessible data. Some corporations and organizations have dedicated information centers staffed by highly qualified information specialists. Most modern professionals are computer literate and have relatively free access to computer stations. What is important is that before a team begins its work senior management must ensure that these portals, personnel, and support systems are made available to team members on a priority basis. I have worked with some teams in which a dedicated information specialist was assigned to the team as a full-time member. Other teams have enjoyed priority, or at least easy, access to information centers, libraries, and other internal data sources. If senior management is giving a team a high-stakes mandate, it must provide the team with appropriate resources, and in today's world, one crucial resource is data.

Presuming a team has access to sufficient data from external sources, it is the responsibility of each team member to access that data and turn it into meaningful information. This requires constant monitoring of the situation and an aggressive intelligence-gathering plan. We will discuss intelligence requirements later, but for now it is important to note that even when there is a designated information specialist assigned to a team, every team member remains responsible for continuous accessing and processing of crucial data.

A crucial part of data processing is information exchange. Special teams and task forces are usually small enough that information flow should not be a problem. That is especially the case with today's cyber technology. But team members must be aware of the need to provide key communication on a timely basis. For interdependence to result in positive synergy, the real-time flow of meaningful information is crucial. It is the team leader's responsibility to establish internal communication processes and to ensure that crucial information flows freely.

What data should members of a high priority team be able to access? The answer is easy: anything they need. Given my perspective that information is the lifeblood of the modern organization, and therefore of its special teams, I suggest that any organizational data short of confidential personnel files should be made available to teams with the need to know. All members of high-stakes teams should be as aware of the total situation as possible. It is in that manner that the team's probability of success is enhanced.

Special teams must, however, be ready to reciprocate. On the modern battlefield, it is entirely possible that an individual Ranger or a small Ranger team in the midst of the fray may have a better sense of the operational status of the mission than a commanding general back in headquarters. The special team bears responsibility not only to access and share information among its members, but also to output it to others who may need it. Most often, this is senior management, but sometimes other teams or organizational elements may need the information to successfully complete their part of the overall mission. Thus, I suggest that vertical and horizontal communication must flow easily, and that information must move smoothly from peer to peer as well as up, down, and across levels. We have seen the horror that resulted because the intelligence data available before the September 11 terrorist attacks did not make its way to all concerned in a timely and effective manner.

Not only is the open flow of information within organizations and teams one of the best means of supporting the accomplishment of the mission and preventing disaster, it is one of the best ways of developing trust and interdependence. Individuals at all levels must develop an awareness of the value of information and must do their part to ensure its easy access and flow.

Feedback

> Tell the truth about what you see and what you do. There is an army depending on us for correct information. You can lie all you please when you tell other folks about the Rangers, but don't ever lie to a Ranger or an officer.
>
> —Rogers' Rangers Standing Order Number 4

The shorter, contemporary version of Rogers' Standing Order Number 4 is the guideline, "A Ranger never lies to another Ranger." This is not to be interpreted as permission to lie to others; it is simply a strong statement that in Ranger units, whether in garrison, in training, or in combat operations, whether you are describing an enemy position, or providing personal feedback, truth is paramount.

Rangers speak very frankly to each other—sometimes colorfully so. They tell each other the truth, and they give straightforward feedback. While the civilian version, appropriately, is feedback, Rangers talk of brutal honesty. Ranger Instructors are not known for hemming and hawing, and Ranger units don't operate successfully by telling *approximately* how things are. To a man, the Ranger leaders interviewed for this book, whether on active duty or now in civilian roles, agreed on the great value of honest and straightforward feedback. They do not want to deal with yes-men, and they take steps to ensure they get the truth. They seek honest feedback from their superiors *and from their subordinates*. Whether in combat or in business, too much depends on truthful communication.

■ **CASE STUDY**

STRAIGHT TALK

The place was called An Long, and I was on another special assignment. I was the only American in the area, and I had arrived accompanied only by an interpreter. I connected with my Vietnamese counterpart late in the day. Almost immediately, we went on a raid to locate and root out Viet Cong spies in a nearby village.

Amazingly to my mind, the raid would be conducted on motorbikes! When darkness fell, we boarded the motorbikes. It was quickly established that I definitely should not drive, but should ride on a backseat. We crossed over the canal and into the village—going house-to-house in search of the enemy. No enemy was found, but the whole process made for an exciting evening.

It was a bit lonely being the only American, but that changed at daybreak. In came the engineers, a platoon whose job it was to construct an airfield that could serve as a potential staging area for airmobile operations. I had been chosen for this mission for two reasons: one, I was, in my mind, one of the toughest first lieutenants in the United States Army, and two, I outranked the engineer officer. This was to be my show.

As the engineers arrived, it was clear that they had a happy-go-lucky attitude regarding what lay before them. They offloaded their equipment and began the first task, which was to construct a fort. Now this fort was basically going to be a triangle of mud walls pushed together by bulldozers. The fort was to be constructed facing the canal to our front with a village approximately 500 meters to our west or left. The canal that lay to our front was relatively clear of vegetation on both sides—a good place to put in an airstrip, but one that offered clear shooting to the enemy we knew to be on the other side of the canal.

The bulldozers began construction and the fort took shape. During this phase, my job was general supervision since a lot of the work was technical in terms of the use of engineer equipment. As the walls were put into position, a helicopter came overhead and landed; it was my commander, the Province Senior Advisor. I reported to him in military fashion; my greeting was cordial. But things turned sour quickly.

Among his first questions was, "Where is your defense plan?" Although the fort was just recently constructed, it was my job to quickly establish the defenses for the perimeter of this makeshift base of operations. While not derelict, I had been a beat too slow, and the colonel laid into me. And he was right. The first thing that I should have been thinking about—probably before the walls were even constructed—was how to defend this remote encampment. It was still bright daylight, and I had some time before evening would fall, but I should have been doing it.

There was no excuse. The colonel left; I went to work. The next day, a helicopter again appeared. It was the operations officer sent on a mission by the colonel to check on what was going on at An Long. But when the major arrived, the gun emplacements had been established, automatic weapons placed with overlapping fields of fire, people knew where to go in case of attack, and there was even the best-looking defense plan that could be constructed with a couple of colored markers and a found piece of cardboard. The major was obviously pleased, offered no criticism, and, I am confident, went back and reported to the colonel that all was well.

The point was: the colonel was right. He had downloaded a bunch of negative feedback on me, and he had done so appropriately. The first thing I should have been thinking about, and probably a little earlier than I had been, was how to defend this remote location. I wasn't mad at the colonel, I didn't talk about the colonel. I didn't offer excuses. I simply got to work and corrected myself. The negative feedback had put me back on course. ■

The concept of feedback dates back to the eighteenth century with James Watt's invention of the steam engine governor, a clever mechanical device that slowed the engine when it started to go too quickly and increased its speed when it slowed below a certain point.[1] But the designation probably derives from World War II and the development of the field known as cybernetics. Norman Weiner and others were assigned the task of improving the accuracy of antiaircraft guns to be used against enemy planes during the war. What they developed was a system that, in effect, corrected itself. It did so on the basis of what was labeled feedback. The output of the system was fed back as new data into the system; the new data was then used for correction.[2]

There are basically two kinds of feedback. There is negative feedback and positive feedback. The first is the (self-)corrective kind. When the data from the output of the system (which could be the quality of a product or a service or the behavior of a person or group) is fed back to the agent body, an analysis takes place that determines whether the result or behavior is on target. Any deviation in any direction is corrected as quickly as possible. This results in targeted behavior that keeps the system on course. Such course corrections should be viewed as constructive. This form of feedback is negative, not because it is bad or critical, but because it negates change in an undesirable direction and points the system back toward the goal. The feedback in the An Long anecdote was negative; it was also appropriate and constructive.

The second form of feedback is positive feedback. This kind of feedback tells the system (person) to continue to do what is currently being done. Some people equate positive feedback to praise, but that is not necessarily so. Positive feedback is simply data that reinforces or provides motivation to continue the current activity or behavior. For that reason, positive feedback tends to produce either vicious or virtuous cycles. For example, credit card debt that is not paid off promptly leads to increased debt once the interest is added to the original debt. When that vicious cycle repeats itself a number of times, people can find themselves in very bad straits. On the other hand, a nice savings plan in which interest is added to principal and then compounded can result in a virtuous cycle of ever-growing savings. Both are examples of positive feedback. Thus, we can see that negative feedback, given and received properly, is almost always a good thing for mechanical systems and for people. Positive feedback, on the other hand, is helpful when the system or person is heading in the right direction and harmful if not.

Things can get sticky when providing feedback to people for a number of reasons. Some individuals are reluctant to give negative feedback. For whatever reason, they are uncomfortable about offering negative criticism to their subordinates or colleagues. Sometimes, they refrain completely from telling someone about an error or deficiency that they spot. At other times, they attempt to provide feedback, but do so in such a roundabout and fuzzy manner that the message is not understood (although both sides may believe that it has been). What some people do not realize is that no feedback, even in circumstances in which something has gone wrong, can be taken as positive feedback. And negative feedback delivered so "tactfully" as to not be clearly comprehended can also be taken to be positive feedback. In either case, the person receiving the feedback may feel justified in continuing what they have been doing. To get a sense of how bad things can get when feedback is not given or is misinterpreted, consider the following case study:

■ CASE STUDY

DISHONESTY EQUALS DISRESPECT

I once took part in a workshop group of managers discussing employee management. The disturbing case that one member of the group was working on had been brewing for some time and was about to come to a head. The manager worked for a very large consumer goods corporation and had responsibility for such things as facilities construction and engineering at several corporate sites. He had been told to fire one of his technical professionals, and he was at the workshop as a last ditch effort to come up with something that might change senior management's mind.

The employee in question was responsible for site drawings and plans for new construction. His work had been generally satisfactory, but had been slipping lately. In the past when mistakes were made, the manager gave his subordinate feedback. But the employee had recently lost his wife, and the manager, being sensitive about how hard he was taking that loss, sought to keep him from any further discomfort. Even though the drawings were often inaccurate, the manager quietly gave them to junior employees for correction without providing the senior designer with feedback.

Meanwhile, the manager and top management had also learned that the employee was doing substantial complaining about his supervisors as he traveled from site to site. The people at the sites listened to him and did not deter him, but then passed the word back to his manager. The manager, having learned about his subordinate's vociferous discontent confidentially didn't feel he could address the problem with him. Meanwhile, the combination of inaccurate work and frequent complaining had gotten to the point where senior management wanted the designer out.

Who is responsible here? Clearly, the designer was turning in unsatisfactory work and was doing a lot of complaining. But what feedback was he getting? His manager did not let him know about the inaccurate drawings. Doing work that is being checked yet with no correction forthcoming, would he not think his drawings must be passing muster? The lack of feedback in this case could easily be construed as positive feedback, that is, that no problem existed. As for the complaining, the people he was complaining to were listening and, thus, encouraging his behavior. Then they would sell him down the river after binding his manager not to say where the information came from. The designer had lost his spouse and things were plenty tough for him, but no one treated him with enough respect to level with him, to tell him that his work was slipping, or that his complaining was getting to be too much. And now, because people were trying to spare his feelings, he was about to lose his job.

I don't know the outcome of this situation. Our discussion group was only together for a couple of days, and the manager returned to work in another part of the country. But it is pretty clear that unless the manager owned up to a lot of responsibility, thereby getting himself into trouble, the employee was on his way out. ■

As the above examples show, telling colleagues, a boss, or subordinates the truth is a sign that you respect them. You think enough of them as professionals that you can offer your thoughts and feelings without sugarcoating or circumlocution. You tell them what is happening, not what they want to hear, because you believe they have enough strength and character to accept reality—or at least your perception of reality. This, of course, means that you should be using your critical judgment in determining and reporting the nature of the situation well. But, as one of the quirky songs from the forgettable movie *Ishtar* notes, "Telling the truth can be dangerous business. Honest and popular don't go hand-in-hand." And most people seem to prefer popularity over honesty, even when very important things are at stake.

Most often I see disrespect in the deference given to senior managers. That sounds paradoxical, in that deference is often seen as an indication of respect. But given our context of developing high-performance teams and great organizations, deference can also be seen as *avoidance behavior*. People are often so intimidated that they choose not to disagree with a senior manager or press their point even if it is a good one. I have seen teams work for weeks to develop new ideas only to cave in as soon as a senior manager asks a challenging question or points to a difficulty. Instead of championing their own idea and showing that they are willing to work out the bugs, they roll over rather than appear to disagree with the all-knowing boss.

And some of this problem is because many managers do not want disagreement. Having yes-people around them feeds their egos. Their day goes smoother if no one disagrees with them, and they have enough influence to let others know to keep quiet and nod along with their proclamations.

These can be seen as examples of what Chris Argyris, James B. Conant Professor in Harvard's graduate schools of business and education, calls "communication that blocks learning." Out of loyalty and good intentions or because of an atmosphere of politics and insecurity, team members become afraid to talk honestly to each other, let alone to team leaders and senior managers. They communicate, but they kowtow, downplay reality, or talk around problems. Their communication is ambiguous, and their feedback is fuzzed to the point of being meaningless.[3]

But that is not how high-performance teams operate. I have already suggested that information is the lifeblood of teams and that honest communication and feedback are signs of respect. These are elements that contribute to individual and team learning, and therefore to team success. They are definitely required for teams attempting the most difficult challenges.

Team members on very good, high-powered teams are quite willing to be honest even to the point of challenging one another. They even tend to fight a lot among themselves and often with the team leader. But, if one observes carefully, one notices that their fighting is not personal and is not taken personally. The discussions and debates are about the best way to reach their goal. They respect one another enough to share their thoughts and feelings openly, and they expect that others will respect them enough to do likewise. Since it is not a matter of attacking persons or egos, the discussions can be frank and to the point. The team benefits from such honesty and mutual respect: the quality of its work increases, and the team atmosphere is a positive one. Honest, straightforward communication helps greatly to build trust, mutual respect, and reliance among all team members.

Holding back on direct and honest communication is like limiting the flow of fuel to the engine of a high-speed racecar. Racecars perform best when their fuel systems are open and fuel is flowing freely; teams perform best when their communication channels are open and what is said is honest and straightforward. If you are a team member, share your perceptions and concerns honestly. Be tactful, but don't talk around an issue so much that your message is misconstrued. If you are a senior manager or a team leader, encourage, even demand, honesty and straight talk from subordinates. If you don't want to know the truth, you don't belong in a supervisory role. If you withhold the truth, you and your organization will pay down the line.

Closing the Feedback Loop

Feedback is data returned to a system or person. In the case of interpersonal feedback, one person is transmitting to a second how she views the second person's actions or products. In a sense, feedback represents a closed loop. A person does something, and the data about its impact is returned to the point of origin. There it should be read, evaluated, and incorporated into the next iteration or sequence of action.

I would suggest that another step is important in closing the loop. Provide those giving the feedback with some sense of how their feedback was used. At An Long, when the operations officer came out to check on whether I had acted on the colonel's feedback, he found a completed and implemented defense plan. In fact, the plan had been developed and put into effect shortly after the colonel had departed the day before. The defenses at An Long showed that I had received, understood, and complied with the feedback. I had closed the loop to everyone's satisfaction. The suggestion here is that in cases in which a person agrees with the feedback they have received, it benefits everyone involved to know that there is agreement and that action has been or will be taken.

The trickier situation occurs when a person does not agree with the feedback received. I still suggest closing the loop, but it would obviously take a different turn. In such cases, it does not hurt to thank the person for the feedback. Then, depending on the situation, the parties involved may enter into a discussion to share perspectives. Sometimes, one or the other may be persuaded to change his point of view. Sometimes, a compromise agreement may be reached, a solution negotiated, and the team's work allowed to progress. Occasionally, no agreement can be reached. If one person outranks the other, the superior would likely direct the appropriate change. If the individuals are of equal rank, it may be that all that can be accomplished is a respectful disagreement, some open-mindedness regarding a reevaluation in the near future, and the maintenance of enough good will to permit the team to continue on its way. But all of these situations are better than ignoring legitimate feedback, and all promote mutual respect and further communication.

Checklist for Success

A successful mission is more about putting the right pieces together than having the right process formula. As we conclude part 3, I would like to proffer the following checklist as both a summary and a call to best practice:

- ☑ Have team members been carefully selected and matched to their roles on the team?
- ☑ Do the team members have, or can they acquire, the appropriate knowledge and skills for the task?
- ☑ Do they have the right mix of experience and potential for growth?
- ☑ Are the team members diverse in their backgrounds and thinking styles?
- ☑ Do they have the courage to take on a demanding challenge in uncertain circumstances?
- ☑ Do they, as individuals and as a team, have the character to respond to the challenge and to deal with potential adversity?
- ☑ Have they formed themselves into a true team?
- ☑ Does the task have significant value and are the team members motivated to accomplish it?
- ☑ Do the team members have a sense of urgency?
- ☑ Does the team leader's style match the task and the team?
- ☑ Has the team developed constructive norms with regard to problem solving, decision making, personal interactions, and so forth?
- ☑ Do all members share a core of ethical and social values?
- ☑ If high-performance levels are required, have team members developed a positive synergy of their abilities and traits?
- ☑ Is the team's mandate clear especially with regard to the purpose of the mission?
- ☑ Is the team aimed at the right goal at the right time?
- ☑ Is the team adequately supported logistically?

☑ Does the team have the moral support of its supervisors?

☑ If the team is involved in a creativity and innovation effort, will it have at least one senior-level champion to protect its efforts and advocate for it?

☑ Has the team been given operational decision-making and planning authority?

☑ Will this team be able to learn on the run?

That is the checklist, and it seems like a tall order. But here is what makes it really demanding: if the challenge that the team faces is for high stakes and must be accomplished in a high-intensity environment, the only passing score is 100 percent! A no answer to any of the above questions undercuts the potential for team success. For lesser tasks, maybe a 90 percent rating would do, but for the challenges that represent the context of this book, a team has to max out on the checklist.

Part IV

THE LEADER

9 Be, Know, Do

Leadership is a combination of spirit and skill. It derives from a powerful fusion of character, vision, commitment, knowledge, and interpersonal ability. That synthesis actualizes and activates a dynamic relationship between leaders and followers. This leader-follower dynamic is mutualistic; it sustains and benefits both sides of the equation. The leader empowers, enables, enhances, and directs the efforts of the followers. The followers respond to and energize the leader, as all join efforts to achieve the vision that they share. In effect saying, "Follow me," the leader challenges followers by setting high standards and calling for great commitment—and then providing the best example of both. Followers inspire leaders by their dedication and hard work—in effect saying back to leaders, "Keep up with me." This is an intriguing relationship, because everyone benefits, not primarily by what they receive, but by what they give.

Leadership in high-stakes situations is not easy; much is demanded of special action team leaders. They are expected to be visionary, knowledgeable, courageous, creative, encouraging, and steadfast. They must be dedicated to the team and organizational mission, and they must offer an example of the highest values. They must bring a deep understanding of human nature, prudence in decision making and wisdom regarding ultimate values.

The Army Leadership Framework

Just as a diamond requires three properties for its formation— carbon, heat, and pressure—successful leaders require the interaction of three properties—character, knowledge and application.[1]

—Gen. Edward C. Meyer

The U.S. Army Leadership Framework is captured in three small words: *Be, Know, Do.* Living up to those words represents great personal challenge, yet one that applies to, and must be met by, each Ranger. And if they are to be successful, it is a challenge that also applies to leaders of high-stakes civilian teams.

In fact, these words represent three intertwined strands or dimensions to the challenge of leadership. Be: the leader must be a person of good character. Know: the leader must be technically and tactically competent. Do: the leader must move and direct others to accomplish the mission and to improve the organization. Like three strong cords that are braided to fashion an even stronger rope, the aspects of character, competence, and application must each be addressed and then intertwined to produce the outstanding leader. The strength of the rope of leadership depends on the strength of each of its three strands. A weakness in any one of them makes for a weak rope overall; strength in all three produces greatness.

Goal

Be

The contemporary world cries out for leadership with character. Heroes and role models who are persons of honor and virtue seem hard to find. Rocked by corporate greed, anxious for safety and security, discouraged by the petulance and cunning displayed on reality TV, we seek someone to look up to, someone to give us hope and strength. It could be that we have just been looking in the wrong places. There have been and are heroic leaders among us. Some enjoy fame, others are known only to their families and communities. What they all share, what they all start with, is character.

We noted earlier that character is really a cluster of traits. A person of good character has courage, integrity, honor, honesty, persistence, self-discipline, and more—all rolled up within them. To be a Ranger or to lead a high-stakes team on an impossible challenge, a person needs all these attributes—and they need to display them consistently. Why? Because good character lies at the heart of good leadership. Ranger and now corporate CEO Alex Gorsky says, "Leadership is predicated on character." He notes that the character of a leader is "preeminent . . . the whole essence of [one's] being." Conversely, a person lacking in honesty, fairness, integrity, and the other attributes of character can only lead brigands or fools—although they may deceive good people for a while. People will not willingly, nor confidently, follow someone who lacks character. They surely will not take on great challenges that may demand self-sacrifice if they feel they are being led by someone who cannot be trusted, someone who is likely to falter, or someone who might sell them down the river if it suits their personal agenda. People are, on the other hand, willing to fight battles, to fight fires, or to fight for social justice if they believe that the people they follow are people who stand for and are willing to do what is right.

The challenge of character in leadership is not, however, reserved for presidents, generals, or the leaders of great social movements. Good character in those who lead teams, corporations, or institutions is just as essential.

■ **CASE STUDY**

A TEAM IS AS STRONG AS ITS STRONGEST LEADER

The leader's character is fundamental to team and organizational success. People need to know that they are dealing with someone who is honest, fair, and honorable. The gauge of such character has been called *referent power*, which denotes the consistency of a person's beliefs, values, and behavior. The great leaders of history had referent power. Even as they faced difficult circumstances, their values and the behavior that flowed from those values remained consistent. Whether people agreed with them or not, they knew where an Abraham Lincoln, Elizabeth Katy Stanton, Winston Churchill, Mahatma Gandhi, or Eleanor Roosevelt stood.

Sid Salomon has referent power. At age eighty-nine, he is tall and strong and is the oldest competitive rower in the country. He has a roomful of national and international championship medals and trophies—many earned in his eighties—that attest to his physical strength and mental discipline. Also in that room are two Silver Stars, two Purple Hearts, and the French Legion of Honor medal. They attest to his leadership and courage.

As 1940 approached, Sid was training hard and had become a member of the U.S. Olympic Rowing Team, but the onset of World War II caused the cancellation of the 1940 Olympics. Friends tease that Sid was so mad at Hitler over the Olympic cancellation that he joined the Rangers, but Sid is and always has been a patriot. On June 6, 1944, while others hunkered down, Ranger Lt. Sidney Salomon stood in the bow of Landing Craft 1038 as it approached the Normandy coast at Pointe de la Percée. He was the first in his boat to step ashore into intense enemy fire. Sid once told me, "When I lead my men, I *lead* my men."

Wounded by a mortar round as he ran across the beach and thinking that his end was near, he sought to give his maps to his platoon sergeant. An enemy machine gun zeroed in on him and the sergeant, and, despite his wound, Sid led the sergeant in a dash for the base of the cliffs. The "easy part" was over. Now the Rangers faced the climb of 90-foot cliffs while the enemy fired and dropped grenades down onto them. Sid and his Rangers climbed the cliffs using their bayonets to gain handholds. They pulled each other along and fought against devastating enemy fire. Of the thirty-seven Rangers assigned to the mission, nine lived to reach the top and complete their task of capturing the fortified point that controlled so much of the beach. Of the nine survivors, seven were wounded. Sid Salomon earned his first Silver Star that day, and his exploits provided part of the basis for Tom Hanks's character in *Saving Private Ryan*. Sid is often invited to speak at large formal ceremonies and in school classrooms, and President Clinton personally selected Sid to be his official greeter and guide during the fiftieth anniversary of D-Day. Sid continues to represent his country well. A leader's character counts for something.[2]

Lee Iacocca came from a poor immigrant family. After years of struggle and success with greater and greater challenges, he became president of Ford Motor Company. In 1979, he became president of Chrysler Corporation, but things were not looking rosy. The world economy was in great trouble; auto fuel prices were increasing sharply, and fuel-efficient imports were shouldering domestic vehicles off to the side. On the day that Iacocca's hiring by Chrysler was announced, the company also announced the largest deficit in its corporate history.

Chrysler was about to collapse as a company. But Iacocca was a good strategist, and he developed a strong two-pronged approach. He went to the U.S. Congress asking for a bailout in the form of loan guarantees. Facing great skepticism and reluctance on the part of Congress, Iacocca reframed the problem in terms other than

Chrysler's survival. He had researched the economic impact of Chrysler's demise, and he projected it so that each member of Congress could see the potential damage to the economy in each of their congressional districts. Rather than risk a total of $2.75 billion in unemployment payouts and a deepening of national and local economic woes, Congress agreed to the loans.

But that left Iacocca to face an autoworkers' union seeking higher wages. His stance was strong and his words straightforward. He made it clear that Chrysler was about to collapse and told union members, "I've got thousands of jobs at seventeen bucks an hour. I've got no jobs open at twenty." But beyond his hard-bargaining approach, Iacocca took another gigantic leadership step. He announced that until the crisis was over he would take only one dollar a year in salary. He wasn't going to ask sacrifices from others while he enjoyed the perks of his position; he was going to lead Chrysler forward. Galvanizing the company from within, supporting it externally with loans, developing new types of vehicles, and promoting them with a new marketing theme, Iacocca epitomized and led the greatest corporate turnaround in American history. A leader's character counts for something.

Which brings us to the greatest corporate collapse in American history. Enron Corporation grew from a regional energy provider to one of the world's largest companies. It did so by shifting its emphasis from energy production to the development and brokering of energy-related financial products. It managed to keep investment momentum going by encouraging investments from its employees and advertising its financial strength to stockholders and outside investors. But the company had certain fiscal weaknesses and rather than admit to and correct them, corporate management hid those weaknesses through creative accounting in collusion with its supposedly objective accounting firm, Arthur Anderson. When the house of cards began to tremble, top managers sold their stocks reaping many millions of dollars. Executives managed to keep employees in the dark and even prohibited sales of employee-owned stocks. In December 2001, with Enron about to drive off a cliff, CEO Kenneth Lay was publicly proclaiming how strong the company was.

Unlike Sid Salomon's self-sacrifice, the Enron managers were greedy and self-centered. Unlike Lee Iacocca's tough honesty, Kenneth Lay's remarks were dishonest and dishonorable. Enron's collapse caused many thousands of people to suffer great financial loss while Enron executives managed great financial gain. The corporation's crash into bankruptcy sent powerful shock waves against American and world economies that were already seriously afflicted. Good or bad, a leader's character greatly affects an organization. ∎

VALUES

Ranger leadership is leadership by example, the highest form of leadership. Ranger Instructors are the first to demonstrate what they ask others to do. Ranger commanders like Sid Salomon lead into combat. Such leadership motivates and encourages followers. It sets standards and moves people to be more than they think they can be. Leadership by example makes values come alive.

The U.S. Army offers a very clear set of values that it expects its leaders to exemplify.[3] Those values are as follows:

> **LOYALTY:** Bear faith and allegiance to the U.S. Constitution, the Army, your unit and other soldiers.
> **DUTY:** Fulfill your obligations.
> **RESPECT:** Treat people as they should be treated.
> **SELFLESS SERVICE:** Put the welfare of the nation, the Army, and subordinates before your own.
> **INTEGRITY:** Do what's right—legally and morally.
> **PERSONAL COURAGE:** Face fear, danger, or adversity.
> **HONOR:** Live up to all the Army values.

Values are important to people, and when we speak of leading by example, one of the most important aspects is leading by values. We primarily gauge a person's character by the values she exemplifies. We do not go by the values that people may espouse; we attend to the ones they actually live by and manifest through their behavior. This perspective applies to teams as well. It was noted earlier that it is very important for a team to establish its values and norms early in its life cycle. But establishing those values must mean more than composing a high-sounding statement. Such a statement is worthless unless the values it proclaims are lived day by day. And the best way a leader can get team members to live by their espoused values is to be the best personal example of those values. Whatever the team's values set—honesty, fairness, loyalty, shared responsibility—the team leader must provide the clearest, most consistent example of those values.

Consider the converse: a team espouses fairness, honesty, and loyalty only to find that the team leader plays favorites, lies, and is out for self over others. It would be bad enough if a team member came up short on those values, but what could we expect if the team leader is the chief culprit? How likely is it that team members will be inspired to live those values? Not very. It is far more likely that the betrayal of those values by the team leader will prompt a downward spiral of self-centered, paranoid behaviors among team members. Clearly, a team leader must be a stellar example of team or organizational values.

Values refer to more than personal qualities such as integrity or honesty, and there are other ways in which a person may lead by example. A strong commitment to the mission also demonstrates what a person values, and the work of the team offers other opportunities for leaders to provide model behavior. We see important values exemplified in a leader who works hard and long without complaining, who personally produces high quality work, who maintains a sense of humor, or is the first to pitch in to help another. Importantly, we are willing to follow leaders who take responsibility and never shirk accountability. Such behavior is a key aspect of referent power. It is easy for people to accept praise for what is successful, but it takes strength of character to take responsibility for *all* that happens—good and bad. It is especially gratifying to see a leader take personal responsibility for what went wrong, but be quick to praise others for what went well. In contemporary times, working with civilian leaders who practice what Rangers refer to as no-excuse leadership is a refreshing and uplifting experience.

The point here is that whatever the character traits required for a team to excel, the team leader should be the best example of those traits. That is the essence of *Be* in the Army Leadership Framework.

Know

> Good leaders are always striving to become better leaders.
>
> —U.S. Army Field Manual 22–100

KNOW YOUR STUFF

The U.S. Army challenges its leaders to be knowledgeable, versatile, and proficient. The *Know* or competence dimension of the Army Leadership Framework requires that leaders continuously develop in four skill sets: technical and tactical skills (which we have combined under the designation of domain skills), conceptual skills (which we have referred to as process skills), and interpersonal skills.

For military leaders, technical skills comprise basic soldiering ability, including knowledge and facility with military weapons and equipment. Tactical skills relate to the accomplishment of military missions. They involve knowledge of military doctrine and proficiency in employing and maneuvering resources in order to accomplish the mission. Across the different branches of the Army, these skills will vary in their specific composition. We have combined the two skill sets into the generic cluster called domain skills, a term from cognitive psychology.

The second set of abilities is made up of conceptual skills. These skills focus on a person's ability to reason carefully and well. Included in this set are sound judgment, creative thinking, analytical reasoning, critical thinking, and ethical reasoning. These are what we have referred to as process or cognitive skills, and we will continue our investigation of them in coming chapters.

The framework also encourages the acquisition and development of strong interpersonal skills. Included in this cluster are the specific skills of coaching, teaching, counseling, motivating, and empowering. We, too, have labeled these interpersonal skills, and we will continue to explore their development.

Character is at the heart of leadership but, in addition to character, leaders must have well-developed skills if they hope to accomplish their missions. As has already been noted, this is a case of the more the better. Continual development of any and all of the skill clusters will enhance a leader's ability to get the job done and move a team to successful accomplishment of the mission.

KNOW YOURSELF

Beyond knowledge of their field, good thinking skills, and a facility with people, leaders need to know themselves. Leaders have to have a sense of their personal capabilities. They need to know their strengths and weak spots. They need to be aware of their leadership styles and how those styles may come out in different circumstances. Leaders especially need to be honest with themselves about their values and their personal goals. It could be that in certain circumstances a person may choose not to take a leadership role because her values or personal agenda would be at odds with the team or organizational mission. Bowing out gracefully under such circumstances may be both courageous and wise.

Self-knowledge is important to a leader. One of the greatest personal benefits that Rangers derive from successfully completing Ranger School is a deep sense of themselves—in their cases, knowledge of the extent of their courage, strength, leadership skill, and ability to perform under impossible conditions. They know that most challenges will dwarf in comparison to what they have endured, and they have confidence in their ability to act and lead others. High-stakes team leaders should do what they can to approach that level of self-knowledge. Through honest reflection, 360° evaluations, the counseling of a mentor—or whatever else it takes—leaders will benefit themselves, their teams, and their organizations by gaining a true sense of how they handle leadership challenges.

■ **Case Study**

A Tale of Two Teams

Every team member influences every other team member directly or indirectly. The team leader of a high-stakes team, however, cannot help but influence everyone on an ongoing basis. The Army has found, for example, that the personality and even the appearance of a squad leader often becomes characteristic of the squad as a whole. Over time, I have witnessed how subtle, yet definite, the influence of the team leader can be. Consider the following examples:

Team One: This was a high-intensity I/D team. It was given one of those impossible mandates to develop outstanding new products in a hurry. The team leader was rather new to the organization but came with both a background of several years as a military officer and a high PWF (Personal Weirdness Factor[4]—eccentricity that involves a different way of looking at the world and potentially leads to high creativity). He was enthusiastic about team building at the start of the team's time together and led the team in developing a unique identity and motto. When he addressed the team the first day, his message was, in effect: "I don't have the answers to what we have to accomplish. I bring certain knowledge and skill to this task, but you have a lot more knowledge. I want each of us to learn from each other. In terms of support, you tell me what you need, and I'll get it for you. We are the future of this company. We are going to do our job, and we are going to have fun doing it."

Throughout the time the team was together, he exemplified a combination of gung-ho military enthusiasm and servant leadership. He worked to get the job done and, at the same time, to take care of the troops. The team as a whole took on that persona. They worked extremely hard—well beyond what they were expected to do. They really gelled as a group and learned to support one other. Their PWFs came to the fore, and they did have lots of fun—at work, over lunch and over beers at the end of the day. And they delivered big time on the mandate given to them.

Team Two: This was also a new-product development team that was expected to produce a lot in a relatively short period of time. Again, the team members were chosen well; some were team leaders in their own right. This team's designated leader was considered one of the organization's outstanding thinkers—bright, willing to take on frontier challenges, and with several successes already in the bag. And that was part of the problem.

This team leader had such a reputation for professional accomplishment that the other team members looked to him for direction in all matters. And he gave it, but so subtly that I don't think he was aware of how his style was affecting the team. It was an interesting phenomenon to observe. Although he permitted some team-building activities early on, his countenance was one of tolerance rather than enthusiasm. The result was that the team did not take on a clear identity other than its task orientation. Although they worked well together, they did not socialize except at breaks. They complained to one another about how difficult it was to get team tasks done because of how busy they were with other work. If on a given day, the team leader would announce his interest in a particular alternative, the team would work enthusiastically on that idea. If on another day, he would indicate that he had doubts about the same idea, even though others saw potential in it, the concept would be shelved.

Often his feedback on ideas was nonverbal, and it was clear that all team members were watching to see how long he hesitated, how he framed his response, or how his countenance subtly altered. His personality was low key, and he did not take a heavy-handed approach at any time. Yet ideas came and went on the basis of his favor as team members heard his responses and read his nonverbals.

The leader of Team Two was a *creative leader*. By himself, he had great capability of generating and developing strong ideas. The team, to a large extent, became a pool of resources that supported his efforts. The leader of Team One was a *leader of creativity*. His style encouraged and brought out ideas from all team members. Both teams were successful; both produced good ideas. But Team One was a higher-performing *team* that investigated challenging new approaches, while Team Two, by its leader's own admission, produced new versions of ideas that had been around for a while. There is an interesting follow-up to this anecdote. At the end of our assignment together, the Team Two leader asked me for feedback to help improve his leadership. He seemed very open to the feedback, including the observation of how his style subtly affected team processes. He deserves credit for his desire to grow as a leader and for his efforts at greater self-awareness. ■

Lessons learned: there are a couple of lessons here. The first is that there is a difference between a creative leader and a leader for creativity. If a task requires expediency, choose the former to head the group. In that way, you can leverage that person's brainpower and more directive style. If the challenge demands higher levels of creativity and risk taking from all members of the task force, choose a leader with the latter style, someone who can bring out the best from all team members. The second lesson is that self-awareness is an important aspect of good leadership. Leader One came into the process with greater self-knowledge and did a good job of positioning himself within his team from the beginning. Leader Two seemed relatively unaware of how his style affected the team, and the team probably moved more slowly and tentatively because of it.

The two teams above had very similar situations, and so they offer a good comparison of their leadership. In addition to them, let us consider other high-stakes team leaders who knew how to play to their strengths.

The first was J.C., the leader of a higher education task force that took on the mandate to redesign the academic experience at a liberal arts college. J.C. was unassuming and low key. During team meetings, he tended to stay in the background contributing both serious professional inputs and occasional jokes, as appropriate. Outside of team meetings, J.C. worked long and hard at planning, data collection, and liaison with the administration. He also provided a willing ear to the various constituencies in the larger community, and all felt confident in dealing with him. As team members started working much longer and harder than expected, he provided for their needs and did what he could to make their work easier. He carefully put together an approach for gaining approval that was patient and inclusive of all key groups on campus. The result was that the team's recommendations included some very innovative programming ideas, and the greater (usually skeptical) community was accepting and even enthusiastic about the team's concepts. The steward leadership of this task-force leader did not put him in the spotlight, but had the effect of lubricating the team's processes and gaining broad-based support for new ideas.

Another leader was the team's "parent" and a very good example of how to take care of the troops. A seasoned professional, N.P. was affable and generous. This leader's attitude was that the team was a family. Taking good care of family members, N.P. argued on their behalf when necessary and made sure they were well fed—to include providing them with unexpected afternoon "treats." When squabbles occurred, N.P. patiently smoothed the feathers of each individual, while at the same time ensuring that team integrity was maintained and the mission went forward. Given the task of generating high-quality product concepts, the team produced an abundance of strong ideas and invested extra energy in the details of their work. And when their work was coming to a conclusion, they celebrated with a "family dinner."

L.M. was a community builder. This leader took on the daunting task of developing and implementing a major new kindergarten-through-senior-high curriculum component in a wealthy suburban school district. It was an uphill march to begin with, and it was made more difficult by the weight of the variety of political agendas supplied by teachers, administrators, and very active parents. Yet L.M. personified the paradoxical qualities of the contemporary leader. Maintaining a clear sense of strategic purpose, L.M. also kept an open mind to the final form that the program would take. Single-minded about accomplishing the mission, L.M. remained patient and trusted the unfolding of the creative process. Convinced of the appropriateness of the goal, L.M. patiently listened to and addressed the myriad concerns of several constituencies. Although capable of personally wielding significant power, L.M. resisted doing so and instead empowered many others to take ownership and move the process forward. The result was a model curriculum that was broadly supported and carefully implemented.

It was my good fortune to work with these leaders as they tackled the above challenges. It seemed that if these individuals had weak spots, they were well overshadowed by their strengths. Knowing themselves and leveraging their capabilities, they matched their leadership styles to the tasks they faced.

The above examples also emphasize that there is no one or best leadership style. These leaders succeeded because they had the right style for their mission and the people with whom they worked. That is a key point: leadership style should match the team and the situation. We can think of style as a mode of operation. If a person has only one style, they will be limited in terms of where they can best serve. On the other hand, if a person can flex her mode of operation and adjust her behavior to fit the demands of a variety of situations and teams, she will probably be more successful as a leader. Ranger Lt. Col. Mark Meadows makes the point well: "The guy that is most successful . . . is the guy that spans that whole spectrum [of styles] . . . [yet] the guys are seeing the same leader." Referent power combined with flexibility of leadership style is a winning combination.

KNOW YOUR TEAM

In addition to knowing themselves, the leaders in the above examples succeeded also because they knew their team members and the capabilities that those individuals brought to the challenges at hand. Having a fairly accurate perception of the strengths (and weaknesses) of individuals aids leaders in selecting members for a team, matching them to specific tasks, and guiding their efforts once work is under way. Leaders who know their team members and who have a sense of the team as a whole will likely find it a lot easier to organize and direct efforts, deal with interpersonal and process issues, and keep motivation high.

Knowing the team does not mean knowing each individual in depth or conducting a psychological assessment or background check on each one. Nor is it a matter of knowing team members as close friends. Ideally, it is having a sense of everyone's skills, talents, and level of expertise; professional background and experience; thinking style; and values and motivations. Sometimes, it is helpful to have a feel for what is going on in their lives in general, for "where their head is." This would especially be the case if they appeared to be under unusual levels of stress.

As indicated, such is the ideal and without prying into personal or confidential matters, the more a leader knows and understands how individual team members tick, the better. Matching individuals to tasks can provide great benefit, but another important reason is that sometimes leadership is a one-to-one dynamic. Military leaders can order troops as individuals or as units to perform their duties. Civilian team leaders, on the other hand, often find it necessary or appropriate to deal with team members on a more personal basis. This is not just a matter of making assignments well, but in providing them with the leadership to which they can best respond. This may mean offering strong direction to one while merely nudging another, or continually encouraging one while leaving another alone. Meshing leadership style to the peculiar styles of individual team members takes energy, but it is often the approach of strong leaders. Each person on their teams has a sense that the leader knows, respects, and cares about him as an individual.

In addition to awareness of the competencies and styles of team members, it is also good for a team leader to have a sense of the psychological state of members and the morale of the team as a whole. It may be quite helpful to know how individuals are handling the stress of a high-stakes challenge, whether the team is blocked or going at full speed, whether internal or external dynamics are affecting an individual or the team in general. Even given the authority of military leaders to order troops to their duties, it is important for small-unit leaders to have a sense of the competence and condition of individual soldiers. Providing guidance or support to an individual who may be struggling or allowing someone a little extra time off to deal with a personal matter is often not only a benefit to that individual, but also to the team and its overall efforts.

Having a sense of each individual's style and abilities and matching them to appropriate tasks can greatly add to the effectiveness of a high-stakes team. Staying aware of a team's dynamics and morale and being able to adjust to changes is a crucial aspect of leadership. And the practice of relating to and leading each person as an individual moves leadership to an art form.

KNOW THE MISSION

As we will see in more detail in the next chapter, it is crucially important for the leader to have a strong sense of the overall mission. This includes being able to visualize several aspects of the situation: the current state, the general conditions (and how they may change), the goal, and the means of moving a team toward the goal. It would actually be a mistake to attempt to capture all these things in detail or to presume that once envisioned, they will not change; the conditions in which high-stakes teams usually work are too complex and fluid. But a strong sense of the mission provides the axis around which the leader's thought processes will revolve.

Having a strong sense of the mission illuminates the process aspects of leadership. The better one can visualize a goal and the means for achieving it, the easier the decision and planning processes will be. Further, being able to describe the vision and direction to others has powerful process and affective impact on them. A clear vision sparks motivation in the team. A core direction enables team members to supply the details and modifications, thus enhancing team planning and operational processes. And, especially in those cases in which the challenge is great, the leader's depiction of the goal, how it will be accomplished and that it *can be* accomplished, greatly enhances team confidence.

Know your stuff, know yourself, know your team, know the mission—all significant individual challenges, yet all must come together in the mind of the leader. The following case study points to what can be accomplished, even in the face of considerable difficulty, when they do:

■ CASE STUDY

SOMETHING FROM NOTHING

Growing up as a farm girl, Dr. Joyce Juntune's sense of how work got done was through what we now call self-organizing systems. Everybody pitched in, and when the work on your farm was completed, you went down the road to help your neighbor. There was no formal organization; there were no designated leaders. Good-intentioned people got together and made things happen.

Operating in that mode, Joyce has twice taken on and succeeded at very difficult challenges. They were especially difficult because in taking them on Joyce had no authority, no funds, and no resources.

She began in each case as a leader without a team. In the first case, her mind caught fire with a concept that she and some colleagues were almost jokingly discussing. Wouldn't it be great to have a professional community that would investigate creativity and its innovative applications? Two years later, on the strength of Joyce's vision and the tremendous energy she invested in developing an action network of colleagues, the American Creativity Association (ACA) came into being. Joyce then worked for several years as the (unpaid) first executive director of the association, effectively expanding its membership and programs. ACA has since become the national academy of creativity professionals with hundreds of members from business, industry, science, communication, academia, and the arts, and with several international affiliates.

Her second major success is the new Institute for Applied Creativity at Texas A&M University. Again starting without much more than a vision and a lot of determination, Joyce worked for three years to enlist colleagues and sponsors. Proceeding patiently, she led the formation of a nucleus of dedicated colleagues. Working together and sharing ideas, they developed a compelling concept for a new educational enterprise that would contribute importantly to the university's graduate and undergraduate programming. With millions of dollars in pledged sponsorships, the new institute was approved in the summer of 2002. In addition to her duties as a faculty member in Educational Psychology, Joyce serves as the institute's director of educational initiatives and outreach.

When asked how she accomplishes so much starting from scratch, Joyce says, "I don't take on something unless I am passionate about it, and part of the passion about something is because I can clearly visualize its possibilities. After that, everything is kind of easy."

Of course, it is not so easy, and there is more to her leadership. As an educational psychologist, Joyce is very familiar with the concept of intrinsic motivation, which she refers to as "passion." After forming a vision that fires her, Joyce looks for others who might share that passion and offer important contributions. As clearly and as authentically as possible, she explains the possibilities and opportunities surrounding the vision. Rather than giving a sales job, she shares her strong personal belief and makes the vision come alive in the minds of her listeners. Living by the principle that she would rather have people join her than follow her, she indicates how she feels others could play an important role, but then enters into a dialogue with them to determine where and when they might fit. In doing so, she learns about their talents and skills, and they begin to see how they might contribute to something bigger than themselves.

In garnering the support of others, Joyce shares the power of her vision, but does not impose it, claim ownership, or protect it from change. Just the opposite is the case. Never feeling that she owns the idea, she shares the vision and how she sees it unfolding, while remaining open to input from her new colleagues. Her early vision changes and grows as it fuses with the visions of others. A new core vision takes shape—one that is clearer and more compelling, one that is shared and owned by all members of the new action team.

In taking on her impossible challenges, Joyce initially seeks to form and develop a dedicated core group. For this core, she seeks variety in backgrounds, skills, talents, and expertise; she keeps her "antenna" out to locate people with the interests and abilities that could make a significant difference. Then, working together, the early members move into outer concentric circles to enroll more people who can contribute to the effort. She notes that she has never taken on something without having the sense that there were other core people who would join quickly.

Joyce feels that once the process is under way, her chief role is to keep her team's thoughts and energies focused on the common goal. She looks to form a critical mass of support and is quite willing to move slowly in order to gain greater commitment and more shared owner-ship of the project. The result is that the pace picks up in the long run.

Twice starting from nothing and succeeding in giving life to two important institutions, Joyce Juntune is someone who knows her stuff, knows herself, knows her team and knows her mission. ∎

Do

Developing the right values, attributes, and skills is only prepa-ration to lead. Leadership doesn't begin until you act.[5]

—U.S. Army Field Manual 22–100

The application dimension of the Army Leadership Framework, *Do*, sets out three tasks for the troop leader: influencing, operating, and improving. As will be seen, these are tasks for the high-stakes team leader as well. Leadership operations and the challenge of continual improvement will be the subjects of the next four chapters. Because of its close connection to operations, that aspect of influencing that focuses on providing a strong sense of purpose and giving clear direction will be also be discussed. Here, we will explore other aspects of *influencing*, specifically those that relate to leadership communication skills and motivation.

INFLUENCING THROUGH COMMUNICATION

In order to accomplish the task at hand, leaders must exert a continual, constructive influence on their subordinates—and sometimes on their superiors as well. A key means of bringing that influence to bear is good communication. To be a highly effective leader, a person must have strong oral and written communication skills and must continually seek to enhance those abilities.

> "Remember . . . an order that can be misunderstood will be misunderstood."[6]
>
> —Field Marshall Helmuth von Moltke

The reality is that the leader's ability to get a message across may be crucial to the success of the mission. Therefore, a leader capable of speaking and writing clearly and effectively brings important competencies to the task and the team's efforts. Whether it is a matter of setting out the challenge, clarifying the purpose, or providing specific directions for team operations, leaders must be able to communicate well both verbally and through the written word.

Yet, as important as oral and writing skills are, being a good listener may surpass even those abilities in value. Lee Iacocca has said that listening skills are the most important a manager can have, and many of the Ranger leaders interviewed for this book repeated that perspective, especially as it applied to listening to subordinates. Why this is the case has to do with two things: the complexity of human communication and the importance of achieving understanding.

While most people seem to believe that communication is easy and just speaking or writing something is all that is necessary to achieve understanding, the reality is much different. Human communication is tremendously complex. Transmitting even a simple message equates to negotiating an obstacle course littered with the sender's and receiver's intentions, expectations, and sensory abilities; their communication skills; their psychological filters and experiences; the medium selected; the words chosen; physical distractions and interference; and the context in which all of the above takes place. Given the complexity of communication, it borders on miraculous that we can achieve any understanding at all. Leaders, therefore, require good listening skills just to increase their chances of comprehending the message at all.

Further, it should be noted that sending and receiving a message are the means, not the goal of communication; the goal is achieving understanding. This goal provides a second underscoring of the importance of listening skills. We often focus on the need to get information to team members in order to facilitate their understanding of the situation; the need for the leader to take in information and gain understanding is at least as important. This makes an aptitude for listening immensely valuable. And going beyond data gathering, good listening allows leaders to check for understanding and to *hear behind the words*. Through good listening, leaders gain an enhanced picture of the reality of the situation and the status of the team.

One can extend this last concept to include the value to be derived from team dialogue. By convening and facilitating team dialogue sessions, leaders not only enhance the prospect of gaining greater understanding personally, they encourage all team members to do so as well. Dialogue is a group process that involves honest talk and active listening, and dialogue sessions can be tremendously fruitful. Good dialogue sessions may serve to surface assumptions, reveal deeper issues, explore the future, and help in the construction of new meaning. Because they prompt risk taking, authentic speech, and deeper listening, they can have a positive effect on a team. They can contribute to greater shared understanding, to enhanced commitment, and to the heightening of esprit. Especially for leaders of teams that are expected to stay in operation for an extended period, the acquisition of skills for conducting dialogue may be a very worthwhile objective.

Returning to listening per se, there is another aspect of good listening that can have a powerful influencing effect. When people feel they are truly being heard, they are affected in a very positive manner. Especially when times are tough or conflict has arisen, knowing they are being listened to gives people hope and a sense of dignity or worth. The fact that a leader will take the time and put in the effort to listen well—and good listening takes effort—manifests how the leader values the team member and what that team member has to say. In such instances, listening in itself *transmits* a message about the worth of the individual and about team values.

INFLUENCING MOTIVATION

Rangers are among the most motivated people in the world. They are proud that they are three-time volunteers: they volunteer for the Army, for Airborne (paratroopers), and for Rangers. Motivation is not a problem among Rangers. And for those individuals who have volunteered or who have been carefully selected for high-challenge civilian teams, motivation is usually not a problem; they need only be pointed toward a goal. But motivation can be a concern on occasion, and even on good teams sustaining motivation and focus when stress is high and things start to go really bad can be a challenge. This prompts us to take a look at another area of leader influencing, motivation.

I think "influence" is an appropriate verb to use when it comes to motivation. My belief is that the wellspring of motivation is to be found in the value system of each individual. As noted earlier, a person is more or less motivated to pursue a goal depending on how much or little they value that goal and the degree of confidence they have that it can be achieved. (We can complicate things a little bit by adding that since people generally have an array of goals they can pursue, a particular goal will be chosen if it competes well against other potential goals.) In any case, a person will not be highly motivated to pursue goals that are of little value or that will not likely be achieved. Conversely, the more a person values a goal and/or believes it is attainable, the more motivation potential that goal will have.

It was also noted earlier that a person may be motivated intrinsically or extrinsically: they may be motivated by the goal itself or by the external benefits that would come their way if they accomplished the goal. In actuality, people generally hold some mix of both kinds of motivation simultaneously with regard to work projects. I, for example, love the work I do, *and* I am grateful for the pay that accompanies it. But whether a goal involves intrinsic and/or extrinsic motivation, a person will be induced to pursue it only if it has enough of a "positive charge" for the person, and that charge or pull comes from what the person already values.

People, then, are motivated by what they rate highly in conjunction with their personal values. They will tend to value a goal or the incentives that attend that goal, or they will not. A leader's potential success at influencing a person's motivation will depend on that person's values and perceptions. Accordingly, it does not make sense to talk about *motivating people*, if by that we mean dangling something in front of them to *cause* them to be motivated. What does make sense is considering how we might activate or enhance the motivation potential that people already have within them.

In attempting to spark others' motivation, there are a number of alternative approaches that the leader may take in order to bring about constructive change. If a leader believes that a person or team would be motivated by a particular goal, but observes that they are not active in pursuing that goal, three possibilities (or their combinations) exist. The person/team may not be aware of the reality of the current situation, not realizing perhaps that there are problems to be addressed or that there is a need for change. Addressing this *lack of awareness* requires that the leader demonstrate clearly that the current situation is untenable or undesirable. Occasionally, this requires painting a big picture; at other times it is a matter of providing specific data that may not be obvious or available to those concerned.

Sometimes, a person or group may realize that change is necessary or a goal is worthy, but may not know how to proceed to bring about that change or accomplish that goal. This situation represents a *lack of means/ability*. Here the leader's role is to fill in the gap. There are two possible approaches here. Either the leader needs to point the way to acquiring the necessary resources or abilities and/or she needs to provide a plan for accomplishing the goal. In taking either of these avenues, the person/team is provided with the means and direction to accomplish the goal, and with that heightened sense of capability, their confidence will grow.

The third major possibility is that people do not see the need to change or accomplish a goal because they do not perceive the goal state as substantially better than the current state. While all of these circumstances are motivational challenges, this case can be referred to specifically as a *lack of motivation*. People do not see the need to put in effort on a particular goal because they do not see why it would be worth accomplishing. Here the leader's challenge is to paint a vivid and compelling picture of the goal state; the people need to "taste" what it will be like. Further, they need to feel that leaving the comfort of the status quo and putting in substantial effort will be well worth it. In this case, the leader must authentically and convincingly depict the goal as clearly better than the present situation and very much worth the effort required to accomplish it.

Depending on the circumstances and the perceptions of the individuals involved, a leader may need to take one or a combination of these approaches to spark motivation and stiffen resolve. To do so will generally require that the leader bring her critical and creative thinking ability as well as strong communication skills to bear. To be part psychologist, part researcher, part artist, and part orator may be required. Fanning the flames of people's motivation often requires strong thinking matched to eloquent and persuasive rhetoric. Additionally, and perhaps most important, it requires personal credibility on the part of the leader. The leader must be seen as consistently and vividly living the vision. Not only the leader's words, but also her daily behavior must proclaim that the goal is worth the effort.

In the best of circumstances, the goal is not just "the leader's idea" or "the leader's vision." Rather, perhaps through the leader's efforts, it is something that all members of the team or the organization see as both desirable and viable. (Recall the case study, Something from Nothing, above.) People need to come to the same understanding about the challenge and their need to respond to it. Even if individuals have differing personal values, the leader can often help to align and fuse those values into an effort to which all can commit. All of this is, of course, very challenging, but nobody said that leading teams or organizations in difficult situations would be easy.

The Leading Attitude

> You can take the twelve best guys and bring them together and fail on a mission. You can take the twelve worst guys and bring them together and succeed on the same mission. To me, the difference between the two is the leader.
>
> —Lt. Col. Mark Meadows, U.S. Army Ranger

Be, Know, Do. These words provide the crucial dimensions for leaders of Rangers and other high-stakes teams. They provide the essence of leadership and greatly shape the leader's attitude toward the mission, the team, and life in general. And attitude, in turn, is critical.

It is not enough to fight. It is the spirit which we bring to the
fight that decides the issue. It is morale that wins the victory.[7]

—General of the Army George C. Marshall

Attitude is so important that maintaining a confident attitude should
almost be a principle of war. But beyond its relevance to the outcomes of
battles, attitude has been shown throughout history to be essential for success. Whether it was Edison's perseverance at invention or Gandhi's and
Martin Luther King's steady courage in the face of great odds, attitude made
the difference. The reason is that attitude translates into behavior, and both
are contagious. World War II Ranger Sid Salomon says that in combat he
could never manifest anything but confidence in front of his men, and
Ranger/CEO Alex Gorsky lists the leader's confidence as the prime element
in asking teams to take on the impossible. Whether in combat or in the
meeting room, leaders with confidence and vision inspire their teams and
organizations. And when attitude is conveyed through strong, consistent
behavior, leaders' actions resonate and affect others like the vibrations of a
dominant tuning fork.

Attitude is not easy to fake, and it is not easy to change. It would be naïve
to think that a person's attitude could be substantially changed simply by
talking or reading about it. Attitude is a function of a person's worldview,
values, experiences, desires, and beliefs. This probably means that not everyone is suited for leadership of a high-stakes team. But for those who have a
can-do attitude, it is important that it clearly show forth and be manifested
in their demeanor, communication, and behavior.

There are other points that can be offered with regard to attitude. The
first reflects the Ranger expression, "Don't rest on your Tab." Even if a leader
has a great track record, the future still lies to the front. Rather than be complacent, outstanding leaders move on to more demanding missions. Rather
than getting comfortable with what they know, they move farther out to the
frontier of their field where they can build new expertise. Rather than bask
in the glow of previous success, they take on new and different challenges.
They are not foolhardy or overconfident; they just do not stop growing and
testing themselves.

Great leaders have a *bias for action*. Their approach may be prudent, and
it can be patient. But in general, their inclination is to be aggressive and to
take action. They tend to believe that a proactive stance is best. They want

to participate in the vision process and in strategic thinking. They would rather make decisions or contribute to the decision process rather than let others, especially an enemy or a competitor, make decisions for them. They heed the principle of Offensive described earlier: *Seize, retain, and exploit the initiative.* This axiom dictates that offensive action is the key to achievement and success. Even though they may not control events, leaders with a bias for action are likely to have more effect on the dynamics of situations. They will substantially affect, perhaps even establish, the nature, scale, and pace of operations. Up-tempo leaders seek to maintain momentum. They observe the operational definition of audacity as a "simple plan of action, boldly executed."[8] They heed Napoleon's warning: "Hesitation and half measures lose all in war."[9] They do not act impulsively, nor are they rash, but their preference is for action. A bias for action is a belief that bold, creative, well-executed plans will win the day.

What further contributes to a winning attitude is the belief that as a leader you and your team can accomplish anything. We have seen numerous examples of teams and units that were asked to do more than most would dare attempt, and yet the job got done. But the goals would not have been achieved unless the leaders and the team members first believed that they could be. *Self-confidence* is a key aspect of the leader's attitude; and when a leader demonstrates conclusively that he believes in the team's ability to accomplish the mission, the stage is set for success. Not swagger, not arrogance, but a leader's deep belief in his personal ability and the capabilities of the team inspires teams to take on the impossible.

Building upon that thought are the concepts of *high expectations* and *high standards.* When a leader believes in the potential of a team, it is appropriate to set high expectations for the team's performance. Accompanying high expectations should be appropriately high standards—standards that leaders set for themselves and their teams. Both high expectations and high standards are what make for great military units and high-performance teams. The great accomplishments reflected in Ranger tradition, as well as in the anecdotes and case studies offered here, largely resulted from leaders asking more of their teams—asking them to fight harder, go farther, go faster, do more. When a leader sets legitimately high expectations, even if those expectations challenge a team beyond normal, it is a positive reflection of the leader's belief in the team. When challengingly high standards are set and met, a team positions itself for greatness.

Yet great self-confidence and high expectations do not necessitate bravado or loud leadership. Great leaders are usually not braggarts, nor are they martinets with their teams. Often, the opposite is the true. Great leaders are often humble and they treat their teams with great respect. Whether jovial and extraverted or quiet and low key, they are strong and solid in their self-confidence and belief in their team. And when the going gets tough or chaotic, they offer the team a *calm center* and a *source of strength*. They keep their minds under control, and their demeanors reflect that inner self-discipline.

> I cannot trust a man to control others who cannot control himself.[10]
>
> —Gen. Robert E. Lee

Combat leaders know how devastating it would be to unit morale if the commander were to be seen as unsettled or uncertain. The execution of military actions would suffer greatly from the confusion that would follow if the leader appeared to lose focus or control, and will proceed better when the opposite is true. (See In a Calm Voice below.) As Ranger/FBI Agent Nick Panagakos notes, "If you're calm, you're going to convey that and calm your subordinates; if you're totally out of control, that's going to be conveyed to your subordinates." D-Day Ranger Sid Salomon agrees, noting that when you are faced with chaos, you have to overcome it within yourself. These combat leaders enjoin other leaders to deal with chaos and confusion by maintaining a presence of mind and staying focused on the mission.

One way to do so is to ask yourself, "What do I need to do right now?" By maintaining an offensive posture and focusing on taking action, leaders work on priorities and what can be affected, rather than throwing up their hands or wastefully scattering effort into things that cannot be controlled. This is a helpful approach for action team leaders. Some high-stakes teams such as firefighters or emergency rescue or law enforcement teams often operate under near-combat conditions. Other teams operate under less dangerous circumstances, but may have to deal with great stress, complexity, and confusion. In all cases, the leader must provide the core of strength and calm direction. Although turbulent inside, the leader's outer attitude and demeanor must be solid, and her inner focus steady. Remember, attitude affects behavior and both transmit strong messages to the team.

■ CASE STUDY

IN A CALM VOICE

Whether on the battlefield or during an organizational crisis, the leader must provide the calm center in the vortex of chaos. The leader must be a person through whom strength flows in a steady and uninterrupted stream, unbroken even in the face of confusion or the emotions of others. I have learned a simple technique for staying calm and for allowing calmness to become contagious. In Vietnam, in between command and executive officer assignments on small teams, I spent a good amount of time as an assistant operations officer for the province advisory team. Assigned to the Tactical Operations Center (TOC), I often was the officer who coordinated province military operations during the night. Additionally, I was generally the officer in charge of the Forward Command Post (FCP), the coordinating group that moved with the troops on combat missions.

I suppose that in an early episode I had gotten a little excited in communicating with troops. It is not difficult. When bullets start to fly—even if they are not flying at you personally—the voices of those involved in radio communications tend to go up in both decibel level and tone, and exchanges occur at a very rapid pace. Coherence and understanding are quickly lost. The operations officer, an experienced major, provided me with some coaching about how to handle myself in such situations. His advice, which I readily accepted, was very simple: keep your voice calm. When you are talking to people under fire, when you are their leader or their lifeline, it is crucial that they have the sense that you are in control of yourself and the situation. There is perhaps no better way to project that sense than through a calm voice and a poised demeanor. Functionally, speaking distinctly and coherently provides others with clearer direction and support; psychologically, it helps to settle and encourage them, as they come to feel that control has not been lost.

Speaking calmly on the radio became normal for me, and my voice control did have its affect on others, as two incidents in particular demonstrated. The first, with me on night TOC duty, was during an extended attack on our most distant advisory team camp.

The fighting was intense, and there were many friendly casualties. I helped to bring supporting forces to bear, while at the same time coordinating numerous medevac missions. The camp held, and later the American commander thanked me for the steady assurance he felt from the way I supported him through the night.

The second incident found me in the Command and Control (C&C) helicopter on an airmobile operation. Captain Thanh, the District Chief and my counterpart, commanded the South Vietnamese assault forces, while I commanded the advisors with them and the American resources such as the helicopter gunships and troop transports. Shortly after the assault on the objective began, one of our gunships was shot down, halting the further transport of troops. Fortunately, two other gunships were in the area asking to join in. Coordinating with the air commander, we brought in the new firepower and a large Chinook helicopter to rescue the downed crew and lift off our disabled bird. Meanwhile, from the air, we spotted what the ground troops could not: the objective was protected by five concentric rings of booby traps. I warned my advisors what to expect and guided them as they proceeded forward. After a day-long battle, we took the objective with only one friendly wounded. This was my first time commanding an air assault, and I simply did what I was trained to do. But when I returned to base, I found out that people listening in on the radio net wanted to know who was directing the action and staying in charge with such a calm voice. ∎

Take Care of the Troops

Military missions are primarily undertaken for purposes of national defense; in recent years, more of them have been as part of peacekeeping and humanitarian initiatives. Given the grave importance of such work, the first mandate for the military leader is to accomplish the mission. The second mandate, however, is to take care of the troops. Clearly, the second mandate serves the first, but there are basic humanistic motives involved in its fulfillment as well.

A question arises: What should be the order of priority of these mandates with regard to civilian teams and task forces? This is a question that cannot be answered comprehensively here. It may be that for some missions of some special teams, for example, those involved in protecting the community, the mission may come first. But, it would seem that for most civilian teams, even those in high-stakes situations, it may be appropriate to value the people more than the mission. It would be pretty coldhearted to prefer human loss or suffering to a business setback. In any case, whether out of benevolence or to get the job done, it makes good sense for leaders to be concerned about the welfare of their team members.

The U.S. Army believes that one of the best ways that leaders can take care of their troops is to create a disciplined environment in which soldiers can learn and grow. It calls on leaders to treat soldiers fairly, to hold them to high standards, and to prepare them to do their jobs well. The Army also encourages empathy—challenging leaders to understand and share the hardships their troops are enduring and to do whatever is appropriate to mitigate or eliminate problems. Leader actions may range from ensuring that a soldier's basic needs are taken care of to counseling him through tough times. In fact, besides its internal resources, the Army has established relationships with a multitude of human-service providers in order to care effectively for soldiers and their families. It would seem that meeting these obligations and responsibilities is clearly appropriate for civilian leaders as well.[11]

■ **CASE STUDY**

THE "LEGEND" OF THE SWINGING GATE

Troop commanders are responsible for everything. They are responsible for accomplishing their missions, and they are responsible for taking care of the soldiers in their unit. A true leader feels both sets of responsibility; after a while, shouldering them becomes second nature.

One of my first assignments as a troop leader was as a platoon leader in the 82nd Airborne Division. Being in "America's Guard of Honor," meant keeping my self and my troops on the sharp edge of readiness. In between periods of serving as a rapid deployment force, we trained hard and took exceptional care of our equipment. During all these times, it was leadership's responsibility—especially for small-unit leaders such as myself—to take care of the soldiers.

One day, my platoon sergeant took me through the details of a problem he had been having in getting one of our paratroopers paid properly. My sergeant was frustrated, and it seemed to me that it was a situation that had gone on too long. I told my sergeant that I would take care of it. Accompanied by the trooper who was having the pay problems, I proceeded to the finance office of Division Headquarters. Greeted by a finance clerk, I explained, perhaps a little assertively, that there was a problem that needed to be rectified now. The trooper and I were invited into an inner office to take care of the matter. We had to pass through a swinging wooden gate between the reception counters. Walking through first, I pushed on the gate with what I thought was normal pressure. But the gate may have been a little loose; it swung very easily and smacked loudly back into the wooden counter to which it was attached. I did not say anything, and we proceeded to quickly deal with the pay problem to everyone's satisfaction.

We returned to our troop area, and feeling the matter had been resolved, I put my attention to other things. A short while later, my platoon sergeant came to see me wearing a Cheshire grin on his face. With obvious pride, he said, "I heard about how my airborne lieutenant nearly tore the door off the hinges at Division Headquarters." Although I had already forgotten about the matter, the word was apparently spreading that I was an officer who would aggressively take care of his men. As I recall in the conversation that followed I didn't mention the gate being loose. ∎

If necessary, leaders should be prepared to fight for their team or for an individual team member. Even civilian special teams need to feel that their leader is protecting them and/or offering a buffer against outside interference and distracting circumstances. Given the two overarching mandates of leadership—accomplishing the mission and taking care of the troops—respect, from team members and from outside of the team, will flow to leaders who manage to achieve both.

Respect the Troops

Respect must also emanate from the leader. Taking care of team members is not a matter of coddling or showering them with luxuries. As in the military, beyond fair treatment and caring for their basic needs, team members may be best served by being challenged to grow and achieve. What is crucially important is that leaders show respect for their team members. They should do this face-to-face with the individuals, treating them with tact, civility, and professional appreciation. They should similarly display the respect they have for their team to outsiders, evincing pride in their team and being careful to not disparage or denigrate team members.

Lt. Col. Mark Meadows, quoted above, is resolute in his belief that at the heart of true leadership is a deep respect for subordinates. A Ranger veteran with considerable time in special operations, Mark can speak from experience. But it can also be said that Mark learned from the best. His father, Maj. Richard "Dick" Meadows, is, without exaggeration, an Army legend—as the statue of him at Fort Bragg attests.[12] A Ranger, Green Beret, and early member of the super-secret Delta Force, Dick Meadows led many special ops missions. Most notably, he commanded the assault element on the Son Tay raid into North Vietnam and, disguised, secretly operated within Tehran in preparation for Delta's attempt to rescue the U.S. Embassy hostages. Dick and Mark had many conversations about leadership over the years, and the Meadows household became a major forum for leadership studies, as special operations luminaries such as Arthur "Bull" Simons, Wayne Downing, and others would gather there for nighttime dialogues. Mark reports that in all those conversations the conclusion was the same: leadership comes down to the respectful treatment of people.

One of the best ways a leader can show respect is by ensuring that team members have opportunities to significantly contribute, not just to the work of the mission, but to its design and direction. A conviction shared by all the Ranger leaders that I interviewed for this book was that it is crucial to listen to subordinates. This is not simply a matter of being available to subordinates; it is a matter of actively seeking their advice and counsel. To the extent that time and circumstances permit, a leader should discuss visions, missions, concepts, decisions, and plans with team members in order to tap their experience and wisdom. Leadership is a dynamic relationship with followers. Talking respectfully with subordinates deepens and enhances that relationship. Authentically seeking their input and feedback is one of the best ways of demonstrating respect—and it has the effect of sparking the motivation of team members and reinforcing their loyalty.

Leadership means organizing and directing, but another aspect of respect is letting people do their work. Micromanagement is not leadership, and it tends to snuff out any spark of motivation and responsibility that a team member may have. Leaders may be involved in encouraging, nudging, and giving feedback to subordinates, but, otherwise, they should generally stay out of their way.

In fact, I am generally in favor of *transparent leadership*. This is leadership that is effective, but inconspicuous. It is leadership that gently suggests and guides, rather than exhorts and demands. Its basis is the leader's respect for team members. Recognizing and appreciating the abilities and motivations of good people, transparent leaders prepare and train their teams well; they help steer the course, while providing resources, support, and encouragement. But, otherwise, they trust and avoid heavy-handed control. These leaders allow their teams to feel responsible and enable them to answer challenges in their own way. This kind of leadership could also be labeled Taoist leadership, as it and its effect were described over two thousand years ago in the ancient *Tao Te Ching*:

> The very highest (leadership) is barely known by men.
> Then comes that which they know and love,
> Then that which is feared, then that which is despised.
> He who does not trust enough will not be trusted.
> When actions are performed without unnecessary speech
> People say, "We did it!"[13]

First Among Equals

Leadership is, or should really be, about others. It should not be about self-promotion or self-aggrandizement. When it is, leaders and their organizations tend to falter. A leader's charisma can serve a team internally and externally, but as soon as the focus on the leader becomes too great, the team suffers. Therefore, even allowing for difference in rank, a leader must always be one of the team; that is, she should not position herself above the team in the sense of being separate from it. Teams and military units value their leadership and, in fact, will often place their leaders on pedestals. But the leadership role is really one of helping and guiding others to *their* accomplishments. The leader can rightly take pride in the result, but that feeling of accomplishment must be felt among all team members as well. In some recent research that led to the book *Good to Great,* Jim Collins studied several average companies that became outstanding and sustained a high level of achievement. One of the characteristics that these companies shared was Collins described as "Level Five Leadership." Level Five leaders are humble and unassuming in their personal manner, yet hardworking and dedicated to their companies' visions. While personally shouldering the blame for problems, these leaders pointed to their workers when it came time for praise.[14] This kind of leadership, whether we call it transparent, Taoist, or Level Five, is leadership to which effective followers readily and eagerly respond. People want guidance, they want support. But they also want to achieve the goal, and when they do, they want to be able to say with pride, "We did it!"

10

Visualize, Describe, Direct

The art of command lies in conscious and skillful exercise of command authority through visualization, decision making, and leadership.[1]

—U.S. Army Field Manual 3–0

Alex Gorsky graduated from Ranger School while still a cadet at West Point. After leaving military service, he signed on with Janssen Pharmaceutica, a Johnson & Johnson company. Taking on one tough assignment after another, he rose through the ranks to become Janssen's president. Meanwhile, Janssen was growing from $100 million to $3 billion in annual revenue and gaining a reputation for its forward-leaning stance in pharmaceutical development. When asked about leadership, Alex said that the first essential aspect is having a vision, being able to "see through the fog and clearly articulate what is the mission." One must "distill from the complex . . . simple clarifying thoughts that rally people. Secondly, it is the ability to put one and one together to get three with people—that ability to motivate, to challenge, to inspire others to do more than they think they can do on their own."

This response mirrors the U.S. Army's formula for battle commanders: *Visualize, Describe, Direct.*[2] This approach provides good guidance for leaders of high-stakes teams and for leaders in general. It succinctly captures the key elements of leadership, and it applies to both long-term, relatively smooth change initiatives and intense, stressful high-stakes challenges.

This formula demands that leaders bring all their experience and skills together. It requires strong analytical ability, as well as creative thinking. It requires skillful conceptualization and the ability to effectively communicate both visions and plans. And it requires maintaining a steady direction while steering and encouraging the team over and around obstacles. It generates the outputs of leadership: clear understanding and sense of direction; thoughtful decisions; focused, yet flexible planning; continual guidance and supportive supervision; and inspiration and encouragement.

We begin here with a broad-strokes description of the decision-making and planning processes. The remainder of this chapter and the next two chapters will provide specific details and important guidelines and techniques that help drive those processes.

Visualize

> Vision is the ability to take what is and determine what could be.
>
> —Fred Walker, U.S. Army Ranger

Similar to a combat leader, high-stakes team leaders must first visualize. They must make sense of the complex totality of the challenge before them. They must, often quickly, analyze data and intelligence to conceptualize the current situation. Using their experience, they must determine the true nature and type of challenge they face; they must form an understanding of underlying principles and interacting forces.

Then they must envision the desired end state. Depending on circumstances, they will work alone or closely with others to crystallize the vision. To be effective, they must establish a definite direction and create a clear picture of the future. Then they must devise the means of getting from where they are to where they want to be. Informed by their experience and employing (versions of) the Principles of War and tenets of operation, they will produce decisions and plans for achieving the goal.

Describe

Once leaders perceive the vision and the means of achieving it clearly in their mind, they must then describe their concepts and plans to their team or subordinates. They must, in clear and direct language, translate their vision into a mission statement. Importantly, they must establish the intent or purpose of the work ahead and the value it has.

The leader must stimulate motivation by providing the team or organization with an understanding of the challenge they face and the benefits to be derived by achieving the vision. They must help everyone to understand what must be done and how each person can contribute to the effort. In those cases in which a complex plan must be broken down, the leader must ensure that everyone has an understanding of how the pieces will fit together. Specifically, they must paint a clear and, when necessary, detailed picture of how actions must be coordinated and synchronized. They must also ensure continuing information flow and cooperation. Through the leader's description, the goal and the process of the project must come alive in the minds of everyone involved.

Direct

Both in the formation of plans and in their execution, the leader must direct activity. In fluid situations, circumstances may change even as decisions are being made and plans are being composed; they will almost surely change as plans are implemented. The leader, utilizing the most appropriate style and mode of operation, must continually steer processes and guide the team to the goal.

Primarily, the leader must keep all members of the team or organization focused on the vision; no one should lose sight of the goal or its value. He must also ensure that the general direction is followed. Recognizing that winds of change can blow a team off its original course and adaptations may be required, the leader must help team members to continually adjust to accomplish the intent of the mission.

Leaders must remain aware of the impact of their presence and personal direction. As in the examples of Ranger leaders from Rogers to the present day, the leader's sharing of the work and the hardships can provide both inspiration and encouragement. Sometimes it is the leader's drive and determination that energize and reinforce others. On this point, Army doctrine declares: "The commander's will is the constant element that propels the force through the shock and friction of battle." Sometimes, as noted earlier, it is the leader's calmness at the center of activity, his confidence in the team and his personal dedication to the mission that may prove to be the difference between success and failure. In any case, the team or organization will look to the leader for direction, and the leader, through example and supervision, must provide it.

Decision Making and Planning

We have already described civilian versions of the Principles of War and tenets of operation, and those guidelines will apply as we move forward. In this chapter and the next, we will concentrate on optimizing decision making and planning. We will examine helpful tools including the situation analysis and the leader's statement of intent. We will discuss in detail the functions of planning, development of intelligence, risk mitigation, preparation in the face of uncertainty, and other important aspects of operational leadership that apply to high-stakes teams and organizations. We begin our look at decision making and planning with a rather remarkable statement from a great military leader.

> Plans are nothing; planning is everything.
>
> —Dwight D. Eisenhower

General of the Army, and later president, Dwight D. Eisenhower clearly knew something about planning. As Supreme Allied Commander of the European theater during World War II, he shouldered responsibility for some of the most significant strategic planning in world history, and he succeeded. Yet Eisenhower asserted, almost paradoxically, "Plans are nothing; planning is everything."

Why would a top general, whose job in life was to make decisions and oversee the planning of their implementation, think so little of plans, yet, at the same time, think so highly of the planning process? Is there an inherent contradiction here?

No, there is no contradiction. Eisenhower, as a student of military history and a seasoned officer, had learned through experience that specific plans, while perhaps more valuable than nothing, were remarkably fragile in the face of real-life events. He was echoing the observation of Field Marshal Helmuth von Moltke, the victor in the Franco-Prussian War, that "no plan . . . extends with any degree of certainty beyond the first encounter with the main enemy force."[3] In the planning tent, it is nice, if only hopeful, to talk about executing action A, at time T, at place P. The reality, as any combat veteran can attest, is that when the first bullet is fired, all plans go out the window.

But one should not go to an extreme here. Plans clearly are not worthless. Often, people do implement plans successfully; things do proceed according, or almost according, to plan. Sometimes, they even exceed expectations. On the battlefield and in important civilian endeavors, success is often the product of great preparation, discipline, leadership, and planning.

■ **CASE STUDY**

AND THE TOWER CAME TUMBLING DOWN

Carefully planned and well coordinated, the destruction of H3 could serve as a textbook example of a special operations raid. H3 was the designation of a fortified compound in the western desert of Iraq during the first Gulf War. The centerpiece of the compound was a huge International Radio Relay (IRR) microwave tower that was capable of communicating over very long distances. But in addition to the tower, intelligence reported a substantial amount of coaxial fiber optic cable connected to the site and an underground vault containing a large communications junction box. A chain-link fence encompassed large cinder-block walls with a massive steel entrance. Nine 57-mm antiaircraft guns protected the compound, and it seemed likely that antipersonnel mines were embedded in the ground outside the fence. With two different systems of high-speed communication and that much of a defensive emplacement, the indications were that this facility was an important command and control site. In fact, it was believed that H3 was a strategic communication node used to control Iraq's Scud missiles and western air defense system. The Scuds were already a major problem, as they had been launched into Israel and against allied forces in Kuwait. The dangerous air defense system presented a major obstacle to allied control of the skies.

On the night that the ground campaign of Desert Storm began, a joint operation was staged against H3. The attack began with a flight of F-15 Strike Eagles hitting and knocking out the antiaircraft guns just minutes before the arrival of helicopters carrying troops from B Company of the 1st Ranger Battalion commanded by Capt. Kurt Fuller. The first Rangers on the ground were a support and security element that took up positions to set conditions for the main assault force. By means of suppressive fire, this element was to keep defenders' heads down as the assault force, following five minutes behind, attacked. It was also to block any counterattack from Iraqi forces that might come up the nearby highway.

Intelligence had noticed vehicles leaving and entering the gates and using the access road. Because of the possibility of land mines on the sides of the road, the primary operations plan called for the assault force to land on the road and, using explosives, breach the gate on the fence and the steel entrance through the wall. But an alternative was activated on the chance that it might improve the situation in the five minutes between the insertion of the first Rangers and the arrival of the assault force. Armed with an 84-mm Carl Gustav recoilless rifle, a member of the security element fired an antitank round and blew the gate of the heavy chain-link fence off its hinges. Supporting AH6 helicopter gunships then fired rockets at the steel gate and blew it down. When the assault force landed moments later, the soldiers did not have to use explosives to breach their way through the gates; they could proceed immediately to their objectives.

Using ninety-six pounds of explosives the complex demolition required, the Rangers brought the tower down. They seized the vault and destroyed the cable junction box there. The site was so deep into Iraq that it took two hours of flight time to get to it, but it only took the Rangers a total of twenty-six minutes on the ground to complete their mission, and they did so without casualties.[4] ∎

As this example shows, even complex and dangerous operations can proceed according to plan, and we will investigate in depth the kind of planning that yields such success. But we must still attend to Eisenhower's caution, which, while he may not have known it, also presaged new sciences and a new worldview that were coming into being as the wars of the twentieth century were being fought. These new models of reality, quantum mechanics and general systems theory, dictate that with regard to complex systems, the future is inherently uncertain and unpredictable. That means that not only is the battlefield an unpredictable place, so also are business, politics, health care, international relations, and life in general.

Such uncertainty calls for a shift in emphasis. It is not the *plan* that is important, it is the *thought processes of planning* that are crucial to success on the battlefield, in the boardroom, or in the Oval Office. Accordingly, our focus here will not be on the specific mechanics of decision making and planning; those procedures are relatively well known or easily available. We will, instead, put the spotlight on the functions of decision making and planning, the quality of thought required, and the leadership aspects that promote success in those processes.

Decision Thinking

Thoughtful decision making and planning combine experience, imagination, rigor, and discipline. Decision making establishes goals and sets direction. Planning is an extension of decision making and a transition process that turns a decision into action—and a vision into reality. Both decisions and plans are the products that result when one combines goals, the situation, resources, obstacles, and time. Often, it is difficult to clearly demark where decision making ends and planning begins. In reality, they represent two aspects or modes of the same process. We can apply the term *decision thinking* to capture their affinity and interrelationship, and in this book, we will keep the focus on how they affect each other.

It should be noted that good decision thinking is generally not a linear process. Rather, it is usually a recursive or iterative process that moves back and forth between the two aspects of decision making and planning. What is clear, however, is that for any major initiative, for any short-term or long-term goal of significance, thoughtful decision making and careful planning will be crucial for success.

Decision Making

Visualize, Describe, Direct, the imperatives of what the U.S. Army calls the Art of Command, apply to both decision making and planning, as well as to the implementation work that follows them. Accordingly, decision making is a multifaceted thinking process. It incorporates the visualization aspects: information gathering, analysis, meaning making, judgment, and choice. The leader and team members must, in their minds, move from what may be an ill-defined or even confusing mess to a clear and viable sense of direction. A great aid to making that transition is a good process plan.

THE PROCESS PLAN

Process plans are overarching cognitive strategies or models. They outline a thinking process for the leader and the team. For military commanders and their subordinates, the Military Decision Making Process (MDMP)[5] provides a model of how they should proceed with decision making and planning. The foundational process plan at the heart of the MDMP is the *Estimate of the Situation*, and it outlines a good basic decision-making approach. Its elements include:

1. Detailed Mission Analysis
2. Situation and Courses of Action
3. Analysis of Courses of Action
4. Comparison of Courses of Action
5. Decision

The Detailed Mission Analysis involves gaining a firm understanding of the mission and the nature of the challenge. It includes understanding the intent or purpose of the mission, the essential tasks to be accomplished, the time available, limitations, and any guidance that may come from senior leaders. The Situation and Courses of Action phase requires the leader and team to study the crucial elements and factors that make up the current situation. (See more on this in the section on METT-T below.) At this point, initial alternatives or courses of action (COA) are generated. Each COA should be feasible, reasonable, and distinguishable (i.e., substantially different from other COAs). Then the leader and team will conduct an Analysis of Courses of Action. This involves playing out each course of action. It also involves the process of wargaming, which tests each course of action in light of responses from an enemy or a competitor. (Wargaming is described below.) Comparison of Courses of Action follows. This is an assessment process that has, as its objective, the determination of the best COA. Each alternative is analyzed for its strengths and weaknesses. Finally a Decision is made. A course of action or combination of COAs is selected for implementation, and the process moves to action planning.

METACOGNITIVE STRATEGIES

In civilian organizations, problem-solving and decision-making models represent process plans. Such process plans are really *strategies for thinking*. They are an aspect of *metacognition*, our ability to think about and direct our own thinking. They are valuable because they keep people from re-inventing the thinking wheel. For example, rather than developing a new thinking strategy for solving each problem as it occurs, it is more expeditious to have a general problem-solving model that can be applied to all sorts of problems.

Thus, the function of process plans is to guide and expedite team processes. This is especially important for special projects teams with short timelines. With newly formed teams whose members lack a common background and understanding, confusion can ensue and time can be lost as individual members assert what should be done first. For example, having received a mandate to develop new-product concepts, some team members are likely to immediately start generating alternatives, others might call for research and data collection, and still others may jump to conclusions by putting forth pet ideas that they think should be presented. A process plan provides a scheme of action and gets all team members on the same page. Often, the responsibility for process planning falls to process leaders or facilitators. One of their key roles is to provide the process plan for special teams, another is to exercise enough control over team members to ensure that the plan is followed.

It is important to note that while most process plans are often portrayed as linear schemes, decision making and problem solving in complex situations are rarely straight-line processes. In reality, they are iterative and recursive; they require repetition of mental operations as the situation unfolds and more data become available. A team, for example, may define a problem a certain way, begin to generate alternatives, and as new data arrives, find it necessary to go back and redefine the problem. In fact, in real-life problem solving, just about every phase of a model may be repeated more than once. A team (and its process leader) should always be ready to return to a previous phase of the process plan as circumstances dictate.

Planning

PLANNING FUNCTION 1: FORMING AND TURNING DECISIONS INTO ACTION

> Planning is the means by which the commander envisions a
> desired outcome, lays out effective ways of achieving it, and
> communicates to subordinates his vision, intent, and decisions,
> focusing on the results he expects to achieve.[6]
>
> —U.S. Army Field Manual 3–0

THE ACTION PLAN

When people think about this first function of planning, they often think of it as *action planning* or *operational planning*. That is, of course, appropriate. To the What supplied by decision making, action planning adds the How, Who, Where and When. And since it is generally the case that the higher the level at which a decision is made, the more conceptual it is likely to be, action planning is required to translate concepts into constructive and effective activities.

Take, for example, a case in which the vice president of the R&D function of a major company decides that it would be good strategy to focus some R&D resources on discovering and addressing the unmet needs of consumers. The decision, then, which may be transmitted to a special projects team as a mandate, would be to "develop highly profitable new products that meet currently unmet consumer needs." This decision/initiative is meaningful and motivating, but it will require substantial action planning to turn it into an operational reality.

As noted, action plans describe the activities and/or events that must occur for successful completion of the project. They also provide direction as to how processes will be performed, who will be responsible, where actions will take place, and when or by when actions should be completed. They vary from simple matrices and linear timelines to complex project management charts that show parallel processes and interconnections.

A note of advice: planners should not presume that all will go according to plan. It is usually best to presume that something will go wrong, even if it represents only a slight delay in the process. I recommend that, if possible, time buffers ranging from 30 percent to 50 percent additional time should be built into action plans.

THE APPROVAL PLAN

While action plans usually get appropriate attention, there is another important type of plan that is often overlooked or is left until late—sometimes too late—in the special project process. This is the *approval* or *acceptance plan*. It is true that some special teams, for example, different types of emergency response teams, are generally not concerned about their ideas or actions being approved. These teams are called upon in crisis situations to do the best work they can, and their credibility and qualifications are generally such that they have the trust of those around them and proceed according to their own discretion.

Other special projects teams, usually those working in less demanding circumstances, are often confronted with the need to gain the approval or acceptance of others. An invention/discovery team, for example, may be tasked with the challenge of developing or uncovering important new product concepts. But for its work to come to fruition, the team will have to gain the approval of several other individuals or groups. These others, who often control the funds for further research and development, may include immediate supervisors, a new-products review committee, brand managers, a management board, regulatory agencies, and senior management. After all of which, the hope is that the team's idea will receive the approval of the buying public in the form of purchases.

Therefore, it is very important for those special teams that require the approval of others to begin acceptance planning at the very beginning of the process. When I lead a special projects team, I ensure that all members know at the first meeting whom they will have to face for a Go or No-Go decision. We then keep such information in mind as we proceed with our work. As we prepare for our presentations to these judges, we try to learn as much as we can relative to their concerns and criteria, their styles of thinking, and their preferred channels of communication. My philosophy is that it is generally easier to come up with creative ideas than it is to get those ideas approved. Acceptance planning, begun early and carried out carefully, is necessary for most special projects teams.

To summarize, the first function of planning is to turn goals into reality by devising the means or action pathways to those goals. But this is not the only role of planning. The planning process has other functions and provides the opportunity for other significant benefits.

PLANNING FUNCTION 2: UNDERSTANDING THE SITUATION

> Any plan is a framework from which to adapt, not a script to be
> followed to the letter. The measure of a good plan is not whether
> execution transpires as planned but whether the plan facilitates
> effective action in the face of unforeseen events. Good plans
> foster initiative.[7]
>
> —U.S. Army Field Manual 3–0

The second major function of planning, and one that extends the decision process, is the development of a deep understanding of the total situation. Creating such understanding enhances the probability of mission success for two reasons, one obvious, one less so. The obvious reason is that gaining knowledge of the situation and developing a more comprehensive picture of reality promotes more thoughtful and thorough planning. For a patrol leader, gaining intelligence regarding the enemy's strength and emplacement is better than knowing that the enemy is "out there somewhere." Likewise, for an innovation team tasked with the development of new products, *competitive intelligence* is very valuable. It is important to know what products are currently on the market, what their market shares are, what consumer trends seem to be taking shape, what competitors are likely to do, and who is doing new research.

The second, less obvious, reason for developing a deep understanding of the situation is that such understanding promotes agility. Rangers are taught to memorize the key terrain features of their area of operation, in effect, to form a map in their heads. In fact, in some Ranger training, the use of printed maps is not allowed. Everyone must develop a clear sense of the area's topography before leaving for patrol. Should things not go according to plan, knowledge of the area, the location of an alternative landing zone or objective, where to regroup, and so on, is already internalized. Such preparation allows for rapid and relatively simple transitions when time is short and chaos abounds. Developing a deep understanding of the situation enhances a team's ability to move to an alternative plan and/or creatively improvise should circumstances change dramatically.

SITUATION ANALYSIS

One of the first crucial steps in military decision making, as called for by the Estimate of the Situation above, is to develop a clear understanding of the situation. To provide common direction and vocabulary, the Army uses the METT-T Analysis. This acronym/template requires that leaders study and understand the Mission (the purpose and intent of operations); the Enemy (size, type, and disposition of enemy forces; enemy strengths, weaknesses, intentions, and probable courses of action); Terrain and weather; friendly Troops and supporting resources available; and Time available (including time for planning). (Given the nature of recent military operations, a modified template, METT-TC, which includes Civil considerations has been developed.) For the business planner, there are analogous elements to be considered: short-term and long-term initiatives; competitors (strengths, weaknesses, probable courses of action); the market, the economy, and the changeability of each; resources to include personnel, equipment, technology, and capital; and, again, time available. There would be similar analogs for the health care planner, law enforcement officer, and so forth.

Such analysis protocols are very helpful. They quickly add structure and offer a sense of direction to a team's efforts. When I facilitate a special projects team, the first activity completed is an intelligence briefing in the form of the IDEATECTS *Situation Analysis*. The elements of this template are:

> **ESSENCE OF THE TASK:** a very concise statement of the chief purpose or goal of the work to be performed.
>
> **PERSONS AND ROLES INVOLVED:** those individuals and groups who have a significant stake in the problem situation and what their roles are.
>
> **VALUES/MOTIVATIONS:** the rationale or reasons for taking on the task.
>
> **SITUATION SUMMARY:** a brief history or description of the situation to date.
>
> **IDEAS AND OUTCOMES PREVIOUSLY GENERATED:** any ideas that have already been generated or considered; any outcomes or results thus far.
>
> **SUCCESS CRITERIA:** the attributes of a successful solution; the characteristics or properties we hope for in our outcome.
>
> **ACCEPTANCE/APPROVAL NEEDED:** people whose consent or acceptance will be required for the project's success.

Several clients have reported that this is a very effective technique, and that developing the sense of clarity about their situation that comes from completing a Situation Analysis greatly aids their efforts. This technique is especially good for organizing the thinking of new teams and for briefing new members of existing teams.

INTELLIGENCE

> Intelligence: the product resulting from the collection,
> processing, integration, analysis, evaluation, and interpretation
> of available information concerning foreign countries or areas;
> information and knowledge about an adversary obtained
> through observation, investigation, analysis, or understanding.[8]
>
> —U.S. Army Field Manual 101–5–1

Gaining a clear understanding of the situation requires good intelligence, which in turn requires a good intelligence collection process. To gather intelligence, military commanders may rely on reconnaissance patrols, area photography, or satellite data. Business intelligence, on the other hand, is generally less costly and less dangerous. Great amounts of information are to be found through database searches over the Internet. Many businesses have information centers or libraries staffed by specialists who have the capability to turn out reams of data on the marketplace, competitors, and so on.

But intelligence, even about the marketplace, must be gathered carefully and well. Decision makers must avoid looking for, and seeing, only what they want to see. To conduct this activity well, researchers and decision makers should probably put in as much effort at *disconfirming* their plans and ideas as they do in confirming them. In gathering and processing data, they need to be as objective and open-minded as possible. Consider the following:

■ **CASE STUDY**

GATHERING INTELLIGENCE—THE WRONG WAY

Success depends on innovation and creative thinking. It also depends on solid strategy and critical decision making. All of these things in turn depend on a broad and clear awareness of reality, what the military calls the "intelligence preparation of the battlefield." Military intelligence is about finding out how things really are. The business equivalent is the cluster of fact-finding initiatives that are designed to paint a picture of the market or how the market might take shape if a new product were to be introduced. These initiatives go by such designations as market research, consumer science, and most recently, in an allusion to its military cousin, competitive intelligence.

Intelligence and market research should paint as comprehensive a picture as possible—not of how we wish a situation to be, but how it actually is. They should be conducted to get at reality, not wishes. Ranger/FBI Special Agent Nick Panagakos provides a commonsensical warning: "If you ask a biased question, you get a biased answer."

Coca-Cola did conduct a large number of taste tests, 190,000 in fact, when it was considering the introduction of what would be called New Coke. But one of the major criticisms of those tests was that the subjects, who remarked favorably on the potential new product, did so not knowing it was designed to replace classic Coke. When you are asked to assess a product, it is one thing to say you like it; it is another to say you would want it to replace a product that you have known about and have perhaps been buying for years. The introduction of New Coke was a major blunder that had to be rectified almost immediately as consumers clamored for the return of the original formula.

Cynthia Crossen in *Tainted Truth*, provides an exposé of how statistics, surveys, and consumer research can be used to tell the story one wants to express or hear. In dealing with taste tests, and especially cola taste tests, she itemized how such research may give questionable answers even to people who are seeking the facts. Among the things she reported is that most people's taste buds are not sophisticated enough to distinguish among colas. Not only can they not tell Coke from Pepsi, if the caramel coloring is removed, they can't tell colas from 7 UP or Sprite! Additionally, the first product tasted will apparently garner some votes just because it came first. Products labeled A or 1 will tend to be liked more than products labeled B or 2. And temperature affects response. In a test in which drinks were first tested at thirty-two degrees and then at thirty-eight degrees Fahrenheit, twenty-two of twenty-five subjects changed their preference at the higher temperature.[9]

Where one gathers research is important. Sample testing at a shopping center or mall, for example, may not give one access to a truly representative population. Geography may also play a role shaping results. Going head-to-head over their diet lines, Coke and Pepsi both chose sites that garnered desired results rather than intelligence. Coke chose "non-random" cities and largely ignored the western United States; Pepsi conducted all of its research within 100 miles of four of its processing plants.

Military intelligence is designed to find where the enemy is, what its strength is, and what it is doing. Tragedy follows when intelligence is faulty or misinterpreted. Likewise, if you are going to conduct market research, make sure it is designed to provide a true and full sense of the market, not a self-serving picture. ∎

MAKING INFORMATION MEANINGFUL

Note that the gathering of intelligence, even if done well, must yield more than a pile of data. It must produce meaning. As noted in the Army operations definition offered above, intelligence involves more than collection; it involves integration, analysis, interpretation, and evaluation.

∎ CASE STUDY

DATA FOR DISASTER

The problem with O-rings, the protective bands of insulation material on the space shuttle's engines, did not suddenly occur. Amazingly, for nine years prior to the launch of *Challenger* on January 28, 1986, the NASA space shuttle program had had problems with O-rings. The data on temperatures and O-ring damage were available to the decision makers. The story told by that data was that whenever the temperature was low, there had been problems with "blow-by," the escape of hot gases through O-rings made brittle by the weather. But internal political pressures within one of the shuttle's contractors blinded very intelligent decision makers. "Groupthink" set in, and *Challenger* was tragically lost.

Having data is useless unless the data are made meaningful, yet the expectations and hopes of the decision maker can keep data from taking a helpful form. ∎

INFORMATION SUPERIORITY

> The side possessing better information and using that infor-
> mation more effectively to gain understanding has a major
> advantage over its opponent. . . . At its essence, information
> superiority is about Army forces being able to see first,
> understand first, and act first.[10]
>
> —U.S. Army Field Manual 3–0

Good intelligence and gaining what the Army calls *information superiority* comes about through the development and application of a good
information-gathering plan. For high-stakes teams, information should be
gathered and processed, not once at the beginning of the work, but on an
ongoing basis. The reality of complex situations is that they are subject to
rapid and continual change. Gathering and processing information must
therefore also be rapid and continual.

If a special projects team is lucky enough to have an information specialist as either a dedicated or adjunct team member, it is important that the
specialist not only perform data searches and share the information with
other team members, but also that they advise all team members on expe-
dient and fruitful ways of accessing information. Even with a dedicated
specialist as a team member, it is the responsibility of all team members to
look for and communicate important pieces of data to the team.

In any case, it is crucial that both global and specific data searches be
continually conducted. The global searches would have as their objective the
development of the big picture, that is, constantly defining and updating the
general situation the team is facing. Just as on the battlefield, situations in
civilian arenas can change surprisingly quickly. One I/D team, for example,
had worked on new product ideas for about thirteen weeks. Team members
had already presented their new concepts to their supervisors and were
about to present to the vice president for R&D. The day before that second
presentation, a patent for one of their key ideas was granted to another
company. Another I/D team had spotted a very attractive opportunity to
license or acquire a new product from a smaller company. The team was
scheduled to present its findings just after the winter holidays. Shortly
before Christmas, however, a major rival swooped in and bought up the
smaller company and its products. The opportunity evaporated.

CRITICAL INFORMATION REQUIREMENTS

General searches must therefore be ongoing. Special projects teams need the latest information available in order to maintain a good and comprehensive sense of the situation they are facing. Specific data searches, on the other hand, may be even more important. These tightly focused searches should key on *critical information requirements* (CIR). Within Army operations, the Commander's Critical Information Requirements (CCIR) are those pieces of information that confirm or disconfirm the commander's current vision of the battlefield.[11] Accordingly, CCIR directly and significantly affects command decisions and dictates the execution of operations.

Critical information requirements for civilian special team leaders would be those data elements that would crucially affect team decisions. For example, if a team has an idea for a new product, it is immensely important for team members to know if someone else, especially a competitor, holds a patent for such products. Team leaders should think of crucial information requirements as data points that prompt Go or No-Go decisions. Since they are so significant to decision making, the team leader should inform all team members of the critical information requirements and task them to constantly seek and update knowledge of those elements.

INTELLIGENCE PREPARATION

> *Intelligence Preparation of the Battlefield*
> A systematic and continuous process used to reduce uncertainties
> about the weather, enemy, and terrain in a specific battlefield area.
> . . . This provides (the commander) with means to influence
> rather than just react to enemy actions.[12]
>
> —U.S. Army Field Manual 7–20

Army doctrine dictates that every soldier at every level is involved in intelligence preparation.[13] As indicated above, it should be the case that members of a special projects team, and any adjunct or support staff, be constantly on the lookout for information pertinent to the team's work. Once the critical information requirements have been set and/or specific problems have been defined, all members of the task force should be on the lookout for relevant data or potential solutions.

It is not unusual, because of the incubation and mental preparation phenomena, for even passive searches to yield results. *Incubation* is that process by which the mind subconsciously continues to work on a problem even when the person is attending to other matters. We experience incubation when the answer to a problem that we had been working on suddenly and unexpectedly pops into our mind even though we were not thinking about the problem at the time. Numerous inventions and discoveries have arrived in people's minds by way of incubation. Incubation works best, however, when the mind is prepared. Alexander Fleming's famous saying that "fortune favors the prepared mind" is relevant to this point. Strong motivation and substantial efforts at solving a problem prepare the mind to notice things and make connections that would ordinarily be overlooked. After having been immersed in a problem for some time, a person may, for example, be gardening or out toy shopping when she sees something and makes a connection that helps to solve the problem.

But, of course, passive searches are generally only a very small part of information gathering. Active and in-depth review of technical material, Internet databases, archives, special resources, and the like must be conducted. Networks, even informal communities of practice, should be lit up. And, especially in those cases in which creative solutions are needed, searches should extend beyond the traditional domain or area of interest. Team members should cross the boundary lines of disciplines and investigate how people in other fields solve similar problems. Such analogical problem solving has yielded many great inventions and discoveries.

But what are we looking for? First efforts are generally aimed at compiling what we know or can easily find. It is often the second effort, looking for gaps, that is crucially important. Once initial information is gathered, the team leader or the whole team should study it for what it does not contain. What are the (crucial) unknowns in this situation? What don't we know that we wish we did? Where have we not looked for information? Whom have we not asked who might know something helpful? The gaps, especially those that can now be identified as critical information requirements, need to be filled quickly.

WEAK SIGNALS

But there are other pieces of data that must be attended to, and it will be difficult to do so because such data comes under the heading of *weak signals*.

These are pieces of data that generally go unnoticed. They may take the form of a slightly uncommon occurrence, an unusual request, an uncharacteristic delay, or a slight blip in a data stream. In his writings on the history of science, Thomas Kuhn[14] has pointed out that little anomalies sometimes portend great changes. It is not the great amount of normal data that signals change; it is the small bit of data that doesn't fit that may be most important. On the macro scale, such anomalies often herald what Kuhn labeled "paradigm shifts." On a smaller scale, they may foreshadow a significant problem or opportunity. The problem with such anomalies or weak signals is that people generally do one of three things: they fail to notice them, they try to justify them and force them into the mold of normal data, or they ignore them.

I think something similar happens with organizational and individual decision making. We look for the big pieces of what we expect to see, and we ignore the little oddity that doesn't seem to fit. But when we pay attention to weak signals, if it isn't too late, we may see something both surprising and important. Consider the case studies below.

■ CASE STUDY

WEAK SIGNALS—VIETNAM VISITS

It was our custom as advisors to visit the villages in our district. We would meet with village officials, check on military defenses and operations, and discuss local needs. One day, a team sergeant, our translator, and I traveled by Jeep to a small village that had not been visited in some time. As we drove down the dirt road in the heart of the village, my senses perked up. It was not that something extraordinary was happening; it was that something ordinary was not happening. There were no smiling children running alongside the Jeep asking for chocolate. A quick scan of the village showed that the adults were going about their work, but with heads down and generally ignoring us. I ordered the sergeant, who was driving, to "Get us out of here quick!" Perhaps it was my training at the JFK Special Warfare Center, but I remembered being advised that such atypical behavior often meant that the enemy was in a village, perhaps even hiding in the huts we were passing. We left that village quickly, but without incident.

Another visit took place by helicopter, and the location was much more remote. At the time, I was the District Senior Advisor of Hong Ngu, the district on the east bank of the Mekong River at the southern border with Cambodia. This visit was a big deal: John Paul Vann, the American civilian in charge of all pacification efforts in IV Corps, wanted to visit one of the two Special Forces A-teams in my district. With my boss, the Province Senior Advisor, onboard, the command chopper picked me up at our remote district headquarters and then flew out to the even more remote Green Beret camp. After landing and the exchange of greetings, someone determined that it would be a good idea to go look at the Cambodian fort a very short distance to the north. Our party traveled by small boat up the vertical base of a Y-shaped canal network. The two top branches of the Y represented the Cambodian border, and the fort was tucked between them. Not counting the Green Beret officer and myself, the small craft contained two noteworthy VIPs, and here we were in an unprotected boat a few feet from the fort and Cambodia. Official guidelines dictated that we were not to cross the border. (Actually, on the trip into the camp, the helicopter had accidentally crossed over the border causing my boss to aggressively jump up and get the pilot's immediate attention.) But now, things were remarkably quiet. In fact, there was exactly zero activity to be seen at the fort—even with foreign visitors at the doorstep, not even a lookout was to be seen. We turned around, went back to the A-team camp and completed our visit.

I'll never know about any danger that might have lurked in the village in the first example. Acting on the weak signal of the lack of smiling children, we made our quick exodus, and that may have precluded any trouble from occurring. It is noteworthy, however, that in a similar incident in Operation Iraqi Freedom in 2003, U.S. troops did ignore the feeling that some of the civilians they were encountering were behaving funny. Shortly thereafter, those "civilians" reached under their robes and fired rocket-propelled grenades at the U.S. troops, inflicting casualties. As to the Cambodian fort—two days after our visit, the Green Beret camp came under fire from this "friendly" installation. It had been quietly taken over by Viet Cong and/or North Vietnamese troops. Maybe if they knew about Vann and the PSA being in that little boat, the enemy would have moved up their attack timetable. But as it was, the unusual quiet and lack of activity that we witnessed probably signaled that the enemy was present, but not yet ready to tip his hand.

WEAK SIGNALS—THE TOO-HOT FIRE[15]

Gary Klein in *Sources of Power* reports an incident of a fire ground commander who led his crew to what seemed to be a simple fire in a standard one-story residence. The firefighters entered the kitchen at the back of the building where the fire seemed to be located. Attempts to kill the fire with water were surprisingly ineffective. While not clear why, the lieutenant sensed that something extraordinary was happening. The fire was not reacting as expected, and the living room was hotter than it should have been from a small kitchen fire. And for such a hot fire, it was surprisingly quiet. These symptoms prompted the lieutenant to pull his firefighters out of the building—just moments before the floor they were standing on collapsed. The fire only appeared to be in the kitchen; a much larger blaze was raging in the basement, but had not yet manifested itself.

Here we have an example of a leader of a high-stakes team making a spontaneous judgment on the basis of his experience and expertise. It is important to note that the decision was made *against* the bulk of obvious data and in line with the weak signals felt by the experienced lieutenant. Here paying attention to weak signals saved lives.

WEAK SIGNALS—TRACKS IN THE MUD

During one of its intensive training exercises at the Joint Readiness Training Center at Fort Polk, Louisiana, the Ranger Regiment was given the mission of securing a realistically constructed European-style city. The mission promised some tough urban fighting, but there was another factor that caused the Rangers much concern. The "enemy" was known to have a powerful mechanized force that could be used against the lightly armed Rangers and could potentially inflict significant "casualties." The problem was that this force, which would likely be used in a counterattack, was nowhere to be found. Multiple intelligence sources yielded nothing of its whereabouts.

As the time for attack drew near, a soldier from the Ranger support platoon was making an ammunition run when he noticed some tracks in the mud. Thinking that it did not fit the kind of vehicles the Rangers had, he reported it to his superior. This little piece of data was quickly relayed to Ranger headquarters, and a reconnaissance team was dispatched to follow the tracks. The team spotted the elusive counterattack force well-hidden in a creek bottom. A preemptive strike was ordered. The strike was successful, and the enemy mechanized force was "destroyed" before it could be put into action.

WEAK SIGNALS—GRAFFITI IN KOSOVO

Peacekeeping does not equate to peaceful. When U.S. peacekeeping forces were sent to Kosovo, armed and dangerous adversaries from the Kosovo Liberation Army (KLA) still operated in the region. U.S. soldiers had to remain vigilant and ready to respond to that threat. Their operations often involved patrols through the towns and villages of the region. One day, soldiers of the U.S. 2nd Battalion, 14th Infantry, were on such a patrol when a soldier from that unit spotted some graffiti written in Albanian on the side of a building. He did not remember the graffiti being there during patrol the day before and he was curious about it. Summoning an interpreter, he asked about the meaning. The interpreter quickly identified it as a significant signal among the KLA. It indicated a meeting was to take place in that location on the following night.

The next night, American troops surreptitiously put the site under surveillance and moved a ready force into position. At the appropriate time, they sprung their trap and seized a "most wanted" KLA leader who had been evading capture for several months.

In both these episodes, the portending signals were indeed weak; they could easily have been overlooked. Given that the soldiers' minds could rightfully have been focused on the tasks at hand, it is almost amazing that they spotted the signs. But while maintaining their primary focus, these individuals also *widened* their perception. They exemplified the Army doctrine that every soldier is involved in intelligence gathering, and their curiosity and prompt action paid dividends for their units.[16]

WEAK SIGNALS—2001

Weak signals come in a variety of forms. In December 2001, as noted earlier, Enron, a major energy broker and one of the world's largest companies, went bankrupt. It imploded due to the actions of several of its top managers, some of whom were later shown to have engaged in a variety of fraudulent fiscal transactions, and, in some cases, outright theft from their own company. Enron's collapse also brought down the accounting giant Arthur Anderson, which was found to have colluded in some of the nefarious practices.

The weak signals? For several months prior to its collapse, Enron's price-to-earnings ratio seemed unusually high. There was a serious discrepancy between its profits and its cash flow. Some of its financial statements seemed incomprehensible even to knowledgeable professionals. Top executives started selling large quantities of company stock, and in the eighteen months prior to Enron's nosedive, sixty-eight high-level managers left the company.

These symptoms were noted by some, but largely ignored. We must guard here against a *hindsight bias* that would allow us to believe that people should have known in the past what we clearly know now looking back. But take, for example, the exodus of the managers from a supposedly high-flying company. What those departures did signal was that a sizable number of managers thought that it was better to be someplace other than at Enron. Combined with the mismatched numbers and confusing financial reports, that should have at least prompted the curiosity of investment firm managers and Wall Street watchdogs.

Also in the summer of 2001, instructors at some civilian flight schools in Florida reported that a group of Middle Eastern men were undergoing training on flight simulators for large commercial jets. That by itself was not noteworthy; a person can get good flight training in American flight schools. What puzzled the instructors was that these students wanted to focus their efforts on controlling planes in the air. They did not seem interested in landing procedures, something that even experienced pilots find to be one of the most exacting and dangerous aspects of flying.

On September 11, 2001, the world learned why these students did not need to know about landing commercial jets. It was never their intention to land the aircraft, and they did not want to take time to learn how. ∎

Again we want to avoid a hindsight bias, and the odd approach to learning to fly did not in itself clearly signal what would happen on September 11. In fact, weak signals generally do not clearly paint a picture of what is to come. If they did, they would not be considered weak. Rather, weak signals call for curiosity and imagination. First someone has to notice that something unusual is occurring. Then she has to wonder about its significance. That should lead to some brainstorming: what *could* this data mean?

For example, one might have asked in the Florida flight school incident, why do these would-be pilots, who are spending thousands of dollars for this training, not feel the need to know how to land? The potential answers may have been enough to at least prompt an investigation—especially if they were tied to some of the other signals that had been noticed by the intelligence community, for example, a 1999 National Intelligence Council report that "al Qaeda suicide bombers could fly an aircraft filled with explosives into the Pentagon, CIA Headquarters, or the White House." The tragedy of September 11 was not a failure of intelligence, it was a failure of imagination.[17]

It is especially important to pay attention to weak signals when they repeat themselves. An anomaly that appears again and again is no longer an anomaly. It may be appropriate to heed the Army's dictum on such circumstances: when something happens once, it is an event; when it happens twice, it is a coincidence; if it happens three times, it's enemy action. In the world of business, repeated random events need not represent enemy (competitor) action, but they could signal an important coming together of factors or the beginning of a new trend. In any case, they should be attended to and evaluated.

Anomalies and bits of odd data are not always significant, and, when they are significant, they do not always signal disaster. They may be the harbingers of opportunity. The point here is that in high-stakes situations, weak signals should not be ignored. People need to ask, what could this mean? And, if one or more of the answers offers significant opportunity or the potential for disaster, warning lights should start flashing, and someone should probe a little deeper.

MULTIPLE MINDS

One point about weak signals and intelligence development in general is that it is a challenge to taken up by many minds, rather than by a person acting alone. Something insignificant to one person could be a warning flag to someone else. People bring different skill sets, experiences, and educational backgrounds to problem solving and decision making. One of the expected values of teams in general and high-stakes teams in particular is that the knowledge, skills, and experiences of *all* team members will be melded to produce the highest level of positive synergy. The military may be viewed by many as a top-down type of organization, but many sharp commanders, particularly those involved in special operations, provide as much time and opportunity as possible for their staffs and subordinate leaders to consider the challenge ahead and to contribute to, even to challenge, the commander's thinking on how best to achieve success.

The U.S. Army describes its operations process as a cycle of planning, preparation, and execution that is directed by command authority and constantly upgraded on the basis of continuous assessment. What may be surprising to some is the degree of input from multiple minds that informs this process. Clearly, the military has authority structures that exceed those in most civilian operations (although there are many businesses in which the CEO's slightest whim becomes law and employee fear of authority runs high). But among the best military units such as the Rangers and other special forces, the operations process is an alternating current of ideas and energy that runs up and down the chain of command.

The force commander, having received a mission, will inform staff officers and subordinate commanders of that mission, suggest an initial operational concept, and offer planning guidelines to staff members. They, in turn, conduct a mission analysis and then generate and test alternative means to accomplish the mission. Meanwhile, subordinate commanders are replicating this basic process at their respective levels. At each level, as time permits, discussion is conducted with the intention that the best ideas and plans will emerge.

The Ranger leaders interviewed for this book especially underscored the importance of talking to their subordinates in order to get their perspectives and advice, and recent modifications to the decision thinking process within the Ranger Regiment call for getting that input as early as possible.

Thus, as mission analysis continues and ideas are tested, information flows back up the chain of command so that each higher level can incorporate the best information and insights from those below. Intense combat may, of course, cause this process to be abbreviated, but it is noteworthy that Ranger leaders view consultation with subordinates as very important.

At the heart of intelligence preparation, decision making, and planning is thinking. Each of these complementary leadership processes involves bringing experience, knowledge, and judgment to bear on current data in order to turn it into a meaningful picture of the present and likely future circumstances. Since that is the objective, it makes sense to tap as much experience, knowledge, and judgment as possible. Where circumstances permit, all relevant data should be accessible to all team members, and it should be assembled and analyzed collaboratively. Even when the final decision falls to the team leader, the cognitive resources of all team members should be tapped.

Since 9/11, this is the approach being taken by the FBI in its intelligence analysis. Ranger/FBI Special Agent Nick Panagakos describes intelligence work and information processing as putting together a bunch of puzzle pieces without benefit of the picture on the box. Recognizing that we never get the whole picture, he suggests that we can still derive important information, and the best way to handle such a process is to engage many minds. In all information development efforts, especially regarding what may be weak signals, data must be disseminated up, down, and around. In the FBI's case, it now goes to superiors, subordinates, and other special agents. In an effort to prevent terrorist attacks, even classified information is now pushed down as far as permissible with the hope of triggering connections. The objective is to connect as many different perspectives as possible. What may be meaningless to one person, may be significant to another; what may be random to someone, may make an important connection for someone else.

This approach of involving multiple minds helps to neutralize one of the natural effects of education and experience. We all see the world the way we have been trained to see it. Fortunately, because of the individual nature of our experiences, we all see the world slightly differently. It is helpful, whether in information processing or decision making, to fight against our normal schemas and mental models in order to consider how data might be meaningful from a different perspective. Since people are still limited by their individual imaginations, having others look at and interpret the same data can produce important new insights.

THE LEADER'S RECON

The leader's reconnaissance is crucial to every operation.

Your responsibility as a Ranger leader is to confirm what you think you know, and to find out what you don't.[18]

—Ranger Handbook

Intelligence preparation, market research, consumer science, diagnosis—whatever designation is used—these activities are integral to decision making and planning. They are crucial because they enable visualization. It is through them that a mental, sometimes physical, picture of the situation is formed. We make decisions and conduct planning on the basis of the pictures available to our minds, and one of the best things special projects team leaders can do is to conduct a personal reconnaissance of the situation they face.

In infantry offensive operations, and especially in Ranger offensive operations, the troop leader makes a personal recon of the objective. Technology has altered how this patrol leader's recon is conducted. Now aerial maps and satellite photos may be part of the recon, but traditionally it was a matter of the troop leader stealthily approaching the objective in order to see the situation for himself. The leader would attempt to study enemy emplacements and activities, but also access routes, potential cover and concealment, and so on. This recon provided the leader with a personal, vivid mental picture of the objective and the surrounding terrain. It enabled the leader to confirm the tentative plan that had already been drawn up, or it caused that plan to be modified or replaced.

Following reconnaissance, the leader can transmit his mental picture to the entire patrol. The purpose is to form a *common operational picture* in the minds of all involved. By gaining and sharing firsthand knowledge of the mission and the objective, the leader sets an example and provides all team members with a clear sense of what will be required.

Conducting a leader's recon can be of significant value to high-stakes civilian teams. Studying spreadsheets in an office has value, but it is immensely important that a special team leader go where the action is or will be. Consider the following case study:

■ **CASE STUDY**

PHARMACY RECONNAISSANCE

Fred Walker, former Airborne Ranger and now executive director of new markets for McNeil Consumer and Specialty Pharmaceuticals, believes that the essence of leadership is leading by example. He was tasked by McNeil, a subsidiary of Johnson & Johnson, to move to Japan and lead the product launch of its flagship brand, Tylenol, in that country. It was a mission replete with unknowns. McNeil had no office or current sales in Japan and no experience with Japanese customs and business practices. The Japanese had no awareness of the Tylenol product line.

The team could have been satisfied studying annual reports, demographic information, and market research and could have planned the launch accordingly. Fred's approach as team leader was to set an example that would move people out of their comfort zones, and one of the ways he did so was to conduct his own version of the leader's recon. Gaining fluency in Japanese, he would personally visit three to five pharmacies each week, asking questions of pharmacists, clerks, and customers. His efforts yielded big information dividends that could not be gained by way of traditional market research. He shared that information with the rest of his team, and soon, because of his example, all members of the team were out doing their own reconnaissance. They found themselves listening to potential clients and consumers on their home turf, and they began formulating their plans around this "real live up-close data."

Many ideas came from these leader recons, including the need to change Tylenol's traditional red coloration to a more soothing blue for the Japanese consumer. The pharmacists and customers assured the McNeil team that the Japanese would never buy a red product for pain relief. Although a challenge to Johnson & Johnson's approach to brand identity, senior management listened open-mindedly and incorporated this and other findings of the recons, which represented the most current and available data, into launch plans. The introduction of Tylenol in Japan was a success, and two independent Japanese industry groups recognized the effort as the product launch of the year—the first time an American company had been awarded that honor. ■

Here personal reconnaissance had the effect of gathering important information, including information not available or obvious in the dry spreadsheets and reports. But it had an unexpected benefit as well. Through their personal contact and willingness to truly listen, the team members directly involved the potential outlets in the product launch process. When Tylenol launched, those who had contributed information were among the first and biggest buyers. They became the biggest proponents and the biggest accounts, and they developed the largest share of the market.

Fred Walker's advice to high-stakes team leaders carries over from his experiences in Ranger School: "Look with your own eyes; listen with your own ears. Go out and see it yourself, especially if it is the objective."

CONSTANT RECONNAISSANCE

> See the enemy first.
>
> —Rogers' Rangers Standing Order Number 3, excerpt

> You can never do too much reconnaissance.[19]
>
> —Gen. George S. Patton Jr.

Information superiority does not happen on its own. The gathering and processing of data and intelligence cannot be an occasional activity. The organizational library or information center must run at high speed every day and must quickly push new information to whoever needs it. Sometimes, circumstances may require that special action teams be formed and tasked with a reconnaissance mission to acquire and develop specific intelligence that will inform organizational strategy. Additionally, all members of the organization must constantly have their eyes and ears open and must quickly get any relevant data where it can best be incorporated into organizational awareness. I learned the value of the two tenets quoted above on a dark night in the Mekong Delta.

■ CASE STUDY

EYES IN THE DARK

It was quiet and almost peaceful sitting in our wooden-slated, sandbagged team house in the village of Hong Ngu just south of the Cambodian border. As advisors, we were living among our

Vietnamese military counterparts, but there were relatively few troops in our particular camp. And at this time, there were no other Americans nearby. In fact, the only other American troops on the ground in the district were two Special Forces A-Teams. Composed of twelve men each, one team was several kilometers to the west of our five-man team; the other was a similar distance to the east. All three teams had missions to advise and provide American support to the South Vietnamese troops in their specific locations. Unfortunately, there were other troops in the area, including two North Vietnamese Regiments parked safely on the Cambodian side of the border—safely, because our rules of engagement did not permit us to fire into Cambodia.

On this night, the radio in our communication bunker crackled, and someone whose call sign I did not recognize was asking to talk to me. A U.S. aircraft, Dark Delta 13,[20] told me something that quickly changed my sense of how the evening would go. There were 200 darkened sampans quietly crossing the border and heading south. It was the rainy season in the Plain of Reeds, which meant that most of the region was flooded with water that could range up to ten feet in depth. This meant that boat travel was not restricted to canals, and this invading force was not using canals. Rather it was currently pointed midway between the Special Forces team to our west and our district team. If this was a supply convoy, they could be trying to slip between us with a couple hundred men and lots of materiel. If this was an attack force, it could consist of a battalion with as many as 800 men. A right turn would aim them at the Green Berets; a left turn would point them toward us.

My decision, which I transmitted to Dark Delta 13, was easy and quick: engage and destroy. Within minutes, the fireworks began. Friendly artillery began to pound the invaders, and then friendly aircraft, including a C-47 gun platform sometimes known as Puff the Magic Dragon, began to pour fire from the sky. Even though we were a few kilometers away, the spectacle was dramatic.

As things began to unfold, I had the opportunity to ask Dark Delta 13 who or what they were. It turned out they were an aircrew in an old World War II aircraft flying a quiet and dark night reconnaissance over our region. They had equipment that allowed them to spot the shadowy convoy, and they had the capability to call for and direct fire onto the enemy. The one-sided battle continued into the morning, when all that could be seen floating on the flooded plain were the wooden fragments of the sampans. The invasion had been repulsed and destroyed because of our eyes in the dark. ■

Good and vigilant reconnaissance in combat can mean the difference between life and death. Businesses and other institutions, likewise, must remain both watchful and forward looking. Through the great variety of means currently available, they must be heedful of what is transpiring in the present. They also need to see where the trends and signs are pointing with regard to the future. They must especially learn to be attuned to weak signals and to connect the dots to get a sense of what those signals may portend. Above all, they need expert leaders and teams who can bring both analytical and imaginative skills to bear in order to turn the abundance of complex information into successful strategies.

11

Be Prepared for Anything

Don't never take a chance you don't have to.[1]

—Rogers' Rangers Standing Order Number 5

Offensive and Defensive Thinking

Decision making and planning should not take place in a vacuum. It would be naïve to think that decisions will be perfect and plans will be implemented flawlessly and without difficulty. Generally speaking, competitors don't stand still, all desired resources are not available, and circumstances are less than ideal. Situations will likely be dynamic, fluid, and uncertain. Such is almost always the case in Ranger operations; it is also the case in contests between martial artists. We can learn from both.

As we noted in the section on individual process skills, a good martial artist must stay poised to be on both offense and defense simultaneously. Likewise, a good military tactician, even while focusing on an offensive operation, must remain ready to protect against enemy attack. As in these practices, special team decision making and planning must have both an offensive and defensive aspect to them. The proactive decision making and planning of the previous chapter represent offensive thinking, they are oriented to making something good happen. In this chapter, we will look at ways of thinking and planning that are defensive in nature; that is, they are oriented to keeping something bad from happening. Here we take special heed of Rogers' Standing Order Number 5, which exhorts Rangers to never take an unnecessary risk.

211

Risk, Uncertainty, and the Unexpected

People sometimes use "risk" and "uncertainty" as synonyms, but they actually denote different things.[2] Risk, generally speaking, is our exposure to something undesirable. It can be viewed as the product of the probability of something negative happening and the size or measure of that danger. Thus, the spectrum of risk runs from a low probability of something minor going wrong to a high probability of a catastrophe. How people approach risk is a function of their personalities and thinking styles. Some individuals are more risk seeking, while others are more risk averse. The same can be said for teams and organizations.

Risk on the battlefield comes primarily from the enemy and the enemy's weapons systems, which can be many and varied. Although Rangers are trained to fight in any kind of weather and terrain, in daytime or at night, those conditions may heighten risk. Additionally, in some recent conflicts, concerns about the civilian population have amplified risk. For a business or organizational special task force, the major sources of potential risk can be categorized as personnel, facilities and equipment, procedures and external sources. There is, however, a laundry list of the subcategories that contain potential problems: personnel (lack of qualifications, poor or insufficient training, poor decision making and planning, communication breakdowns, mental lapses, inadequate supervision, incompetent management, and poor morale), facilities and equipment (hazardous conditions, dangerous substances, poor or inadequate facility design, improper installation, lack of appropriate maintenance, inadequate safety measures and testing, the human-machine interface, and inadequate security), procedures (deficient or dangerous work practices, incompetent procurement, inappropriate resource allocation, incomplete documentation, the lack of learning, and unethical or illegal practices), and external (competitor action, changes in governmental or industry regulation, disruptive technologies, vendor breakdowns or shortages, poor economic conditions, shifts in client or consumer trends, social unrest, weather, terrorism, war, and sabotage).

Sometimes the probability of risk is known. A certain medical procedure may have a success rate of 90 percent. The odds of winning a lottery may be forty million to one. The chance of flipping a fair coin and having it come up heads is one out of two. Often, however, we do not know what the odds are.

There are, then, three problems when it comes to risk and risk management. The first is that even in cases where risk statistics are well established, we still can't predict the future for any specific occurrence. Another is that often the degree of risk is not clearly known. And the third, and perhaps biggest problem of all, is that almost all important efforts have risk attached to them. They come with the potential for failure, unexpected occurrences, or unintended consequences. And we just cannot know what will happen in advance. That brings us to uncertainty.

While risk has to do with probability, uncertainty has to do with doubt. Uncertainty is a lack of absolute knowledge about a situation; it is vagueness as to what is really the case or what the risks may be. The roots of uncertainty are in complexity. Because we live in a dynamic and complex world with many changing variables, we generally find ourselves in uncertain circumstances. Uncertainty should be viewed as a given. In reality, most things, even those things that we take for granted, are actually uncertain. That is why, even if only on rare occasions something out of the ordinary occurs we are surprised because it was completely unexpected.

There are two meanings for the word "unexpected." The first has to do with the unusual nature of an occurrence. Something happens that is rare, perhaps unique. It was unexpected because it was so extraordinary. The nuclear accident at Chernobyl and the terrorist attacks of September 11 were unexpected in this sense of the word. The second meaning focuses more on the timing of an event. The event may not be so unusual in nature, but it presents itself suddenly or at a surprising time. People win the lottery every day, but today it happened for you.

We may put out considerable effort to reduce risk and uncertainty and to gain control of our circumstances. The reality, however, is that risk, uncertainty, and the unexpected, these *unknowables*, are part of the human condition. We can be confident that whether we face them as individuals or teams, the most important challenges and initiatives that we take on come with a substantial dose of these elements. As leaders and members of high-stakes teams, we can and should develop the foresight and the competencies to deal with these concerns. Strong risk assessment must be a part of any decision making, and the more important the decision, the better the risk assessment must be.

In this chapter, we will look at those aspects and elements of decision making and planning that focus on the unknown and unknowable. Our objective will be to mitigate risk. That is, we will examine the situation to determine as best we can what could go wrong, then we will develop plans to avert and/or reduce risk.

Planning Function 3: Developing the Decision Process

> One makes plans to fit circumstances and does not try to create circumstances to fit plans. That way danger lies.[3]
>
> —Gen. George S. Patton, Jr.

In the last chapter, we examined the first two functions of planning: turning decisions into actions and, in doing so, gaining a greater understanding of the situation. The third function of planning is to develop and extend the decision process, especially in terms of facing risk, potential failure, and unexpected events.

There are three points to keep in mind in pursuit of this objective. The first was introduced earlier: decision making and planning are so interconnected that they are really two aspects of the same cognitive process. More like two sides of a coin, decision making and planning should support and reinforce one another. Good thinkers interweave these two processes in order to design, select, and implement the best courses of action. Even when these functions seem somewhat distinct or are handled by different individuals, thoughtful leaders and planners double-check themselves and each other in order to produce the best results.

The second point is decision making should be viewed as a process, not an event, and it is the decision *process*, not a particular decision, that should be developed and enhanced. Good planning is often intellectually rigorous and demanding. In combat or in business, the greater the importance of the undertaking, the greater the effort invested in planning must be. In military special operations, for example, a mission designed to last only an hour may be planned and rehearsed for days or even weeks; a mission of a few days may be planned over a period of many months. Two missions involving Rangers demonstrate this point. Operation Just Cause in Panama, which involved only a little more than a week of fighting, had been planned for two years; the lightning-fast rescue of Pfc. Jessica Lynch during Operation Iraqi Freedom had been planned for two days.

The energy and effort invested in planning often yield important insights. An initial decision may show itself to be a good one, and polishing through planning makes it better. Sometimes, however, planning reveals weak spots or fault lines in the initial decision that demand corrections or modifications. And in some cases, planning may reveal that a completely different course of action would provide clearly better results. Because it requires meticulousness and extended effort, good planning often provides the benefit of higher quality decisions and schemes of action.

The third point is related to the second: planning may best improve decision making by challenging it. The role of planning here is to purposefully *test* the decision. This is especially important in initiatives that involve substantial risk and uncertainty. In order for improvement to be derived from challenge, however, the leader must allow and encourage team members to openly question the original decision. The leader must be open to the new developments, new insights, new dangers, and new opportunities that may be discovered by a good planning process. Planning for Ranger and other special operations is often iterative and developmental; that is, plans will be worked and reworked not only at the commander's level, but also at each operational level below. If the process is successful, the best ideas and insights at each level will be incorporated into the final plan. In fact, we should not be surprised to find that often more creativity and better ideas develop *after* the initial judgment and decision have been made.

Testing Decisions

REHEARSAL

> Combat rehearsals are conducted to help a unit gain agility, to ensure synchronization, to increase initiative, and to improve the depth of a force through practice.
>
> Combat rehearsals identify problem areas and contingency actions, determine movement reaction times, enhance coordination and enable the commander to refine his plan.[4]
>
> —U.S. Army Field Manual 7–20

There are a number of ways of testing, verifying, and developing decisions and plans. The first is rehearsal. By adding rehearsals (of different sorts), a team enhances the probability of overall mission success. Although not unheard of, rehearsal is a relatively uncommon business procedure, and this is especially so at the highest levels, where some of the most influential planning is done. It may be more likely that lower-level staffs will put more rehearsal time into an award ceremony than upper management will put into implementing a major corporate strategy. The rationale offered is that business people are just too busy doing things to rehearse doing things. Yet Rangers and other special operations troops have long known of the benefits of rehearsal. Lt. Col. Dave Anders commanded the III Corps Long Range Surveillance (LRS) Company and the Long Range Surveillance Leaders Course at the Ranger Training Brigade. He fought with the Ranger Regiment in Panama and Desert Storm, and he served as the brigade operations officer—the chief planner—for Task Force Falcon, a near-division-sized unit on peacekeeping duty in Kosovo. Of rehearsal, Dave says, "It is absolutely, positively the most important thing you can do." His reason: "Planning and rehearsal diminish risk."

Whether for a specific mission or a certain type of mission, Rangers train and rehearse repeatedly. If a mission involves scaling a cliff, then cliff-climbing skills will be sharpened. If a mission requires storming a building, it is quite possible that a duplicate of the building would be erected so that the mission rehearsals will be as realistic as possible and the lessons learned as meaningful as possible.

Learning is always the goal, yet with learning comes the welcome byproduct of competency and confidence building. The main objective of rehearsals is *getting it right*, moving toward flawless execution. But rehearsals also show what can go wrong and where improvements can be made. Rehearsing often produces enhanced plans—plans that take more possibilities and more variables into account. The special ops team is more ready, more capable, and more confident when team members know not only what should happen, but what *could* happen—and what to do about it if it occurs.

While rehearsals are not a regular part of much business planning, there are good examples or versions of rehearsals in the business world. The test marketing and pilot studies conducted by many businesses provide important advance data about how successful a product or project is likely to be. The multiphased clinical trials conducted by pharmaceutical companies are important tests that yield results on the safety and efficacy of new drugs. The development of models or full-scale prototypes in the automotive and aeronautical industries allows for safe testing of new concepts (usually on a computer or in a wind tunnel).

In areas that are less science and more art, a relatively new technology in the form of computer simulations is providing new possibilities for rehearsal and testing of decisions and strategies. These simulations can be designed to incorporate a great number of real-life variables and to see projections many months or years in advance. Because the simulations are run in the microworld created by the computer, managers can run and rerun them, altering their decisions and changing variables to map different results. Management teams can thus use these microworld simulations to test ideas, to learn (hard) lessons while avoiding real-life disasters, and to develop optimal strategies. For many years, scientists, technological organizations, and the military have used such programs to conduct tests. Recently this software has been developed for businesses and other organizations. While current drawbacks include initial cost and the need for someone with considerable competency to design simulations with multiple variables, their value in testing scenarios is significant. It is likely that we will see their utilization increase in the near future.

WARGAMING

> The enemy gets a vote.
>
> —Military Aphorism

When time is short, it is not feasible to conduct either full-blown rehearsals or computer simulations. Even though military special operations troops value rehearsal, combat circumstances sometimes do not permit that luxury. To compensate, military decision making incorporates an activity known as *wargaming*.

Military leaders know that planning should not occur in a vacuum, nor should it be carried out with naïve optimism. Their expression is, "The enemy gets a vote." Military operations are conducted against a foe that will actively seek to thwart friendly actions, but they also occur in changeable circumstances that are beyond anyone's control. Experienced leaders know that the battlespace is a highly dynamic, unpredictable arena. Its danger flows not just from enemy action, but also from the variety of forces at play. Ranger Lt. Col. Mark Meadows captures this in his version of the above aphorism: "The enemy gets a vote, the weather gets a vote, the terrain gets a vote, civilians on the battlefield get a vote—everybody's got a vote into your plan." Success or failure will be a function of how well a unit can cope with and manage these complex dynamics. In order to consider the vagaries of the battlefield, military planners use wargaming, a method of directly testing potential courses of action by confronting them with probable enemy responses and various battlefield circumstances.

Wargaming is different from war games, which are elaborate training maneuvers. Wargaming is a thought process conducted by an individual leader as part of the Estimate of the Situation. It is also conducted by staffs at battalion or higher levels as part of the Military Decision-Making Process. Small-unit leaders wargame in their own minds. All look at the potential courses of action open to them and imagine what the enemy would or could do in response to each. At higher command levels, wargaming is usually conducted between the operations officer and the intelligence officer. The operations officer develops friendly courses of action and plays them out. The intelligence officer, whose competencies include having in-depth knowledge of enemy forces and tactics, plays the role of the enemy and attempts to counter/defeat friendly actions. In this manner, alternative courses of action can be tested and evaluated fairly quickly.

Wargaming helps to test and develop courses of action. It is a means of assessing the viability and completeness of plans. In a sense, it also provides leaders with a chance to "fail upfront," to see what could go wrong and where danger may lie. In addition to the military, the FBI uses wargaming and rehearsals in planning arrests and searches. Agents, formally or informally, go through the plans looking for obstacles, what could go wrong, where there will exposure to danger, and how the mission could be compromised. Where appropriate, they build in contingencies and then ensure that everyone is aware of them. All of this is an effort to protect the plan, mitigate risk, and build agility.

The concept and methods of wargaming, however, are useful beyond military tactics or law enforcement operations. Wargaming does not require an enemy or a suspected criminal, and it can easily be adopted as a business decision and planning tool. An individual leader can challenge her own thinking, but it would be even better if another person or several other people offer counters to proposed courses of action. These challenges could include potential competitor responses, changes in governmental regulations, fluctuations in the marketplace—whatever is appropriate to a specific situation. An attorney, for example, may choose to test tactics in a mock court with colleagues playing the roles of opposing counsel and judge. A negotiator may ask a friend or colleague to take on the other side's perspective in a practice negotiation. (In these examples, it is sometimes even better if the colleague takes on your role so that you are forced to see the world from your opponent's point of view.) In any case, the challenges must be authentic and offered in true devil's advocate form. The results of this wargaming should be assessed as objectively as possible so that the team or organization goes into action with a clear sense of the strengths, and potential weaknesses, of their plan.

SCENARIOS

Planning is about possibility—what could happen, what could go well, what could go badly. Wargaming provides a good tool in tactical situations, those circumstances that are more immediate and relatively circumscribed. For strategic planning situations in which several factors and variables will play out over a longer time frame, scenario thinking provides a more sophisticated approach.

LOOKING INTO THE FUTURE

"Scenario" is a term that originated in medieval times and derives from the Latin for stage. Its present meaning comes out of its use during World War II and in the years following in which military and civilian planners began writing descriptions of how tomorrow could take shape. Scenarios are stories of *possible futures*; they paint pictures of life or conditions in the future and how such circumstances could come about. They are not predictions, rather, they depict the future if certain forces or elements came together.

Scenario thinking is a big part of military planning. Strategically, the military does not wait for a hot spot to develop and then start planning from scratch. Rather, on the basis of the national security strategy, military planners work at anticipating either where a trouble spot might develop and/or what kind of event might require a military response. They may, for example, develop operations plans should an insurrection occur specifically in Country A, or they may develop more general plans about how to respond if an American ship is taken in international waters. One can bet that on the shelf right now there are sets of operations and contingency plans for every major threat situation that can be anticipated.

As in the tactical situations discussed previously, such strategic plans are wargamed using opposing minds and technology to determine strengths, weaknesses, and alternatives, and they are improved and updated as necessary. They are not, however, just plans on a shelf. These scenarios and their corresponding strategies provide the specific *mission-essential tasks* of major Army line units. In effect, these strategies inform and direct those units in what they must be prepared to do so that the units can train, equip, and otherwise prepare themselves to quickly execute the plans.

It is important to note that military strategists do not develop just one plan in light of one scenario for a particular situation. For any specific threat, they design a cluster of plans, with each plan based on a different set of assumptions or circumstances. Likewise, scenario planning in business should not focus on just one scenario. Because it would limit thinking, that approach would actually be more troublesome than helpful. Rather, good scenario thinkers develop a few, usually about four, scenarios. They provide these multiple pictures of the future for a couple of reasons. First, they want to make the point to decision makers that there is not one definite and predictable future for which they should prepare. Second, multiple futures represent multiple tests for alternatives. The best course of action will be robust, that is, it will likely produce good results regardless of which future comes to be.

ASSUMPTIONS

To be optimally effective, military strategists and their civilian counterparts must remain aware that they have assumptions, and they must guard against a too-facile acceptance of those assumptions—including those that have proven true in the past. This attitude applies in wargaming, scenario thinking, and decision making in general. Change must be considered likely, and the most up-to-date intelligence must be gathered in order to continually adjust the picture of reality.

Col. Kurt Fuller is a graduate of the Army War College. He has served with the Rangers and other units on many successful missions. He took part in combat operations in Grenada and Panama, led the Ranger force in Iraq during Desert Storm, and conducted peacekeeping duties in Kosovo. Because of his background, he maintains a guarded perspective relative to assumptions. His review of the failed military campaigns of history shows that "almost in every case it was an issue of a faulty assumption being made before the operation began." He sees the role of assumptions as allowing a commander to continue planning. Where there are gaps in the intelligence picture, assumptions are made so that thinking can continue. But once assumptions are made, they should not be forgotten or accepted as true; they must be challenged, verified, or discarded. The more integral an assumption is to a commander's vision of the battlespace, the greater the effort should be in confirming or disconfirming it.

Unfortunately, many businesses and organizations take pretty much the opposite approach. They do not surface their assumptions for discussion and review, and therefore forget that their thinking is shaped and constrained by those unconscious mental models. They often presume that the future will largely be like the present or that change will come slowly and in manageable increments. They tend not to challenge current assumptions and mental models, and they almost never consider disruption, that is, that their industry or market could be restructured or turned turbulent in a very short period of time. This attitude allows them to comfortably proceed day to day with status quo thinking while the world changes around them.

Assumptions do structure and constrain our thinking. Good military planners make a conscious attempt to recognize or generate the assumptions that form the basis for their plans. Further, they gather intelligence to assess those assumptions with the objective of either validating them or throwing them out. Leaders in high-stakes situations should do likewise. Wargaming prompts this approach at the tactical level, while scenario development, with its longer time frame, requires an even more critical assessment of assumptions.

■ **CASE STUDY**

ASSUMPTIONS AND SCENARIOS

In the 1960s, General Motors operated under the assumptions that gasoline was cheap and plentiful and that consumers were more concerned about design than quality of performance. Given those assumptions, it is not hard to believe that GM continued to build large gas-guzzlers with more emphasis on exterior styling than quality of construction or fuel efficiency. Unwittingly, the management at GM positioned the company for a downfall, which came when the first oil embargo hit and Japanese manufacturers were waiting in the wings with smaller, fuel-efficient, well-constructed alternatives. The combination of not challenging current assumptions and not considering the potential for disruption allowed

GM managers to stay comfortably lethargic in their thinking until reality hit.

Contrast that example with the strong scenario thinking that was going on at Royal Dutch/Shell. At the time, the oil company ranked a lowly seventh among oil producers. But management's approach to strategic thinking was very keen and quite different from that of General Motors. At Royal Dutch/Shell, scenario thinking had become an important part of long-term planning. Rather than presuming that there was one future and that it would look a lot like the present, their strategic thinkers challenged current assumptions and seriously considered multiple ways the future could take shape. They purposely generated a variety of conditions and events that resulted in substantially different outcomes, including the possibility of the oil shortages. Thinking in advance about how to handle such difficulties, the company was prepared when those shortages actually occurred in the 1970s. Using the same techniques, Royal Dutch/Shell has outpaced its competitors in such areas as anticipating price drops and shipping overcapacity, and the result is that it has become the number one oil producer.[5] ■

We can see that done well, scenario planning helps to neutralize status quo thinking that often goes unquestioned. Scenarios serve to surface and challenge assumptions, and, because they paint vivid pictures of potential futures, they help to evoke imaginative and reflective responses regarding those situations. Scenarios can, and should, grab decision makers by the throat. This forcing open of minds is one of their chief benefits.

Scenario development can be a real art form, and fortunately there are some good resources available to guide scenario thinking (see endnotes).[6] There are, however, some basic steps that one could follow to develop these challenging pictures of the future.

1. Identify the main focus or area of study.
2. Determine the time frame (distance into the future).
3. Gather information on relevant forces, trends, players, and so on.
4. Develop an understanding of the impacts and interrelationships of these elements.

5. Construct imaginative descriptions of potential futures that are rich in detail.

6. Give each scenario an evocative title that encapsulates its substance.

7. Study the scenarios for insights, problems, and opportunities.

8. Conduct strategic dialogues based on the provocations posed by the scenarios.

These strategic dialogues can be initiated and structured around some or all of the following questions. (Note: These questions or versions of them could also be used during wargaming and in the decision process in general.)

- What are the special challenges that present themselves in each of the possible futures?
- What are the particular challenges and/or problems that each scenario presents?
- What are the opportunities?
- What could cause a disaster that would not allow accomplishment of our goals?
- How might we minimize the risk of such a disaster?
- How might we insure readiness and success, or as much success as possible, in each potential future?
- Where are the key decision points?
- How will we know when we are approaching such points? What are the triggers for decisions?
- What should our choice be at each of these junctures?
- What aspects will require creativity (that we should begin to think about now)?

Importantly, ask:

- What are our core competencies as we approach each of these futures?
- What are our potential weaknesses in light of these futures?
- What competencies will we have to build in order to be successful?

- What values and attitudes must we develop/preserve as we move to the future?
- Which of our current attitudes will have to change?

Extended Decision Making

Expect nothing, be prepared for anything.

—Zen Swordsman Motto

PRECAUTION/OPPORTUNITY PROTOCOLS

Wargaming and scenario development represent *what-if* thinking. Our purpose in conducting those activities is to consider a range of possibilities and to develop plans that would serve to nicely position us to deal with those potential events and circumstances. Whether it be a Ranger operation or an important business initiative, it is natural to be concerned first with what could go wrong, with those potentialities that could spell failure. On the other hand, some potential events may be quite positive; things may go better than expected. We will need to consider both eventualities.

Precaution/Opportunity Protocols are key questions that can prompt our thinking and enhance our planning. These protocols help to focus us on what could go badly, what could go exceptionally well, and what should we be prepared to do in either case. Some (small or large) event or confluence of events could have the effect of destroying or diminishing our efforts. On the other hand, it is prudent to also consider the possibility that our actions will achieve results that exceed expectations and/or that certain opportunities may open up. Good planning processes will devise the means to deal with and react to either situation. The following protocols are designed to evoke such thinking:

1. What could happen that would jeopardize our plan?
2A. Which of those hazards are preventable?
2B. For those that are preventable, in which ways might we keep them from occurring?
3A. Which of those dangers are beyond our control?
3B. For those circumstances beyond control, what alternative plans should we have ready to activate if necessary?

3c. When would we put those alternative plans into effect?

4a. What opportunities may arise?

4b. What alternative plans should we have ready in order to leverage those opportunities?

4c. When would we put those alternative plans into effect? (What are our trigger points?)

Prevention Planning

The answers to protocols 1 and 2(a, b) lead to the first form of extended decision making and planning, the *prevention plan*. A prevention plan is a design or program that is devised to avert undesirable occurrences that could threaten a situation or a chosen course of action. As its name suggests, this type of plan deals with preventable occurrences. Prevention planning is sometimes known as *barrier analysis*, which seeks to safeguard a situation or plan by blocking potential threats. Sometimes the barriers it constructs are literal, for example, physical structures like walls or fences around a nuclear facility. Sometimes the safeguards take other forms: safety programs, inspection teams, operational checklists, or warning systems. In either case, the objective is the same: protect people, resources, or planned courses of action.[7]

The basic reasoning behind prevention planning is that unwanted events have causes, and the way to forestall those events is to keep their causes from occurring. To develop a prevention plan:

1. Consider what (preventable) potential problems could arise that would undermine your success.

2. Identify the causes of those problems.

3. Then generate the safeguards or actions that could be taken to preclude the causes of the potential problems.

A prevention plan is not an alternate to the main action plan; it is an extension of that plan. Once a course of action has been decided upon and its means established, a prevention plan should be developed to avert trouble where possible. The prevention plan should then be incorporated into the principal action plan.

Branches and Sequels

> A plan is a continuous, evolving framework of anticipated
> actions that maximizes opportunities.[8]
>
> —U.S. Army Field Manual 3–0

Decision making and planning are processes, they are not events. One of the critical mistakes a leader or a team could make is to fail to recognize that decisions and plans have both short-term and long-term consequences. In making a decision and committing ourselves to a course of action, we do two things simultaneously: we open the door to a multitude of potential futures, and we collapse all other current possibilities.

With regard to the latter, we noted in an earlier chapter that it may be best to keep all options open as long as possible. This promotes flexibility and maneuverability. It allows a team to continue to gather intelligence and read the circumstances until a final commitment is a must. The agile, opportunistic special team will want to have as many options as possible at any one time.

But we also must make decisions. Procrastination, indecisiveness, and inactivity are clearly not the marks of a high-performance team. We just need to remember that when we make a decision, we select a fork in the road. We should, therefore, peer as far down each fork as we are able in order to see what awaits us in terms of next challenges and next decision points.

Sometimes people get overwhelmed, and they make a decision just to get through the discomfort and confusion. They recognize there may be problems ahead and they adopt an attitude of "I'll cross that bridge when I come to it." The problem is that some roads do not come with bridges; they end on the banks of raging rivers. We need, as best we can, to make decisions that open up positive possibilities and that avoid dead ends. But we also need, as much as time and resources will permit, to anticipate the next decision, and the one after that and the one after that and so forth.

It is said that the chiefs of the Iroquois Nation made important decisions very slowly because they were concerned about the consequences for seven generations into the future. Considering that that would be about 140 years, the chiefs deserve great credit as strategic thinkers! But that may be longer than most people can manage, and, as we noted earlier, the future is beyond real prediction. We are capable of foresight, however, and we need to use it.

Ranger commanders on the tactical battlefield do not have the luxury of great amounts of time or resources. The situation is fluid and the intelligence picture keeps changing. But they do anticipate as best they can by using a military decision approach known as *branches* and *sequels*.[9]

> The art of tactical planning lies in anticipating and developing sound branches and sequels.[10]
> —U.S. Army Field Manual 3–0

Branches are contingency plans—options that augment the primary action plan. Because contingencies may call for a change in mission or direction, developing branches prepares a team to deal with probable circumstances that would call for a purposeful response. While prevention planning deals with circumstances that can be kept from occurring, contingency planning addresses those potential threats or opportunities that are beyond the action team's control.

Protocols 1 and 3(a, b, c) above prompt our thinking about things that would jeopardize our success. Such obstacles may be events or conditions; they could take the form of a stock market downturn, bad weather for an outdoor ceremony, or a competitor getting an important patent. The fourth series of protocols (4a, b, c) challenge us to consider events going better than expected—situations that might also call for a significant change in our original thinking.

In either case, we will need to develop three-point contingency plans. The first thing we must do is to identify all likely contingencies, either advantageous or detrimental. Then for each we must design a reaction. For those occurrences that would jeopardize our success, we will need to devise responses that would neutralize them or minimize their potential damage. For opportunities that might extend our success, we will need to be prepared to exploit and leverage them. The third part of a contingency plan is important and should be clear to all involved: we must decide on *action points* or *decision points*, those events or circumstances that would signal the need to activate our planned responses.

When they served in the 10th Mountain Division as Battalion Commander Battalion Operations Officer, Kurt Fuller and Dave Anders, who had served in combat together in the 1st Ranger Battalion, used a *decision tree* approach to planning. They would develop a *playbook* of branches and their decision points. Anticipating likely occurrences that would either extend or endanger their operations, they would develop alternative courses of action and the events or circumstances that would trigger them. These contingency plans would then be assessed in terms of their ramifications. For example, if they planned the insertion of a reconnaissance and surveillance team, it could be anticipated that the team could conduct its mission without compromise or it could be spotted by local civilians or enemy forces. In the first case, the original plan would stay in effect. If spotted by locals, a decision would have to be made to reposition or extract the team. If spotted by the enemy and fired upon, the team may have to break contact and move to another location to conduct its reconnaissance or, again, it may have to be extracted. In those branches in which the team is extracted, there would be no eyes on the objective. New branches involving other assets may have to be activated. One such branch may involve the launching of an Unmanned Aerial Vehicle (UAV) to cover the gap in intelligence. These and other branches, their ramifications and decision points would all be plotted on the decision tree. They would then be shared and discussed with subordinate leaders in advance of the operation so that the transition from one branch to another would be as seamless as possible.

Consider how an I/D team could develop branches in its initial planning. The team may have as its primary task the invention of new consumer products in a particular market. What could be anticipated, however, is that ideas that may manifest themselves could already be patented by a major competitor, could already be patented by a smaller competitor, or could be undergoing initial research by a third party. The branches for each of these contingencies might be: forget the idea and put effort elsewhere, consider licensing or acquiring the product, or investigate the potential of sponsoring the promising research with the option to purchase down the line. In each of these cases, the action point may be the time that the new situation is discovered.

Sequels are follow-up phases. They involve tasks or operations that can be anticipated to succeed the current operation. The military thinks in terms of sequels that would follow upon success, failure, or stalemate. Business teams should plan sequels that would best position themselves for the future.

When it comes to branches and sequels, Just Cause and Desert Storm veteran Dave Anders thinks in terms of four decision points: one that confirms the primary plan, one that disconfirms it, one in response to catastrophic failure, and one in response to what he calls "catastrophic success." In the first case, his unit would continue to execute the primary plan. In the second case, he would switch to a branch, a contingency plan that would adjust his unit's efforts to changes on the battlefield. Catastrophic failure would mean that the mission could no longer be successful and the unit would be in extreme danger. It would call for all-out efforts to save the force and would require activating an emergency branch, for example, shifting from an offensive to a defensive posture. Something like what Dave facetiously calls catastrophic success characterized the Persian Gulf War. Coalition efforts against Iraqi forces went so well that commanders had to drastically modify their decisions and plans because their forces were overrunning the enemy at an unexpected rate. In fact, the ground war that liberated Kuwait and forced an Iraqi surrender took only 100 hours.

We call plans for catastrophic success *opportunity plans*. They can be as important as emergency plans that deal with catastrophic failure. Consider the following case study in which the inability to deal with great success actually led to great failure:

■ CASE STUDY

DESTROYED BY SUCCESS

People Express Airlines was founded in 1980. It offered innovative, remarkably low-cost air travel while providing great customer service. It also became known for its exemplary human resource policies. It did a lot right.

People Express soon became one of the most profitable airlines, and by 1985 it had grown to be the fifth largest air carrier. But its explosive success led to dramatic failure, and in 1986 it was purchased by another corporation after experiencing dramatic financial losses.

Because of its low fares and great treatment of customers, People Express began drawing customers in very large numbers. But it did not handle its growth very well. Larger numbers of customers prompted the need for more airplanes and a much larger staff. Substantial investments were made to increase capacity. New employees were hired, but to meet demand, they were not given the same quality training as earlier employees. Supervision, customer relations, and quality of service quickly declined. Meanwhile, the airline was feeling growing pressures to keep its fares low. It could not handle all the growth pains and soon was bleeding money. By the time it folded, it was derisively known as "People Distress."[11] ∎

People Express represents a significant failure to do opportunity planning; the Persian Gulf War serves as a great example of how to leverage success. Both represent very large enterprises, but even small special action teams need to think in terms of branches and sequels. They must engage in what-if thinking for both their current operation and any that might follow.

SUMMARY

A good planning process incorporates and addresses all three functions of planning: turning decisions into action, gaining greater understanding of the situation, and improving decision thinking. These activities are often conducted and achieved concurrently, and, of course, they support one another. Executed carefully, these forms of sophisticated planning enhance decision making and provide our best means of preparing for all that may occur. They are immensely important, and they substantiate Eisenhower's dictum that "planning is everything."

Additionally, there is an interesting paradox related to the application of such a comprehensive approach to planning. The more we consider the what-ifs and the more we build branches and sequels into a plan, the less our plan is likely to change! Plans that are well integrated in terms of having as many team or staff members as possible participate in their development will be better wargamed. They will be better tested in advance by multiple minds. Plans that take in as many what-ifs as possible and that extend as far into the future as possible will be more comprehensive in scope, in terms of both breadth and depth. Plans that incorporate many and various branches and sequels will provide greater flexibility and ease of transition even in the face of chaos. And plans that are well rehearsed and tested will not only be more vivid and refined, but also will promote greater confidence in teams. They come to realize that they can take on the impossible because they have figured out how to make the impossible happen. In returning to Eisenhower's quotation, the rigor and discipline of such a full and deep planning process underscores that planning is everything. In a funny twist, however, such a process tends to produce plans that are worth considerably more than nothing.

12 Accomplish the Mission

Sua Sponte

"Of their own accord"

—Ranger Heraldic Motto[1]

Sua Sponte says it all. Once a Ranger understands what the purpose of his mission is, then, by God, he will accomplish that no matter what he has to do.

—Lt. Col. David Anders, U.S. Army Ranger

Meticulous and comprehensive planning is extremely valuable, yet, in itself, it will never be enough. In fact, leaders and team members must be careful to avoid both overconfidence and the planning quagmire. In the first case, planners may come to feel that their exhaustive efforts have taken everything into account, and there will be no surprises. This is how boats named *Titanic* get built. The planning quagmire is at the other end of the spectrum. Extensive planning uncovers increasing complexity and numerous possibilities for failure. These promote insecurity, which prompts even more planning. The cycle repeats indefinitely with no action taken, but with planners' neuroses reaching new heights.

Successful planning should result in a clear understanding of key goals and the nature of the challenge. It should contribute to a strong sense of the situation in general, including what can go wrong. We saw that good planning should result in a multifaceted scheme of action—a well-designed primary course of action, as well as alternative, preventive, and contingency plans that will buttress a team against failure.

231

Everything starts before combat.
—World War II Capt. Sid Salomon, U.S. Army Ranger

Thus, careful planning is essential, but it is best to regard it as a very valuable prologue for what will likely become a highly improvisational implementation. We cannot know the future. Our decision making and planning must be carried out in a manner that takes that uncertainty into account and that prepares us to do as well as we can despite what the future may bring. We can, by asking challenging questions, by incorporating broad resources in developing our information, and by thinking systemically, develop decisions and plans that give us the best probability of success in an uncertain future. But as noted earlier, we best prepare ourselves, as individuals and as organizations, for unpredictability and potential chaos by developing those operational competencies that will allow us to be responsive, agile, and versatile with regard to the unfolding of events.

Special teams and task forces come in too many forms and varieties to provide one-size-fits-all operational directions. The differences in challenges and circumstances faced by, for example, firefighters, new-product development teams, law enforcement agencies, and educational task forces make it very difficult to provide advice regarding specific actions. There are, however, some overarching guidelines and concepts that would help us to transition from planning to implementation and that would provide guidance as we adjust to complexity and even chaos. These include mission clarity and alignment, the commander's intent, decentralized decision making, information flow, and team values.

Mission Clarity

Accomplishing the mission is the first priority of military units. High-stakes civilian teams should likewise define their success in terms of completing their mandate. Given that both military and civilian special teams face dynamic and challenging circumstances, one of the first steps in accomplishing the mission is to gain a clear sense of its essence.

As noted earlier, special teams need to be crystal clear about their mission and where their mission fits into larger plans. It is necessary that these teams stay up-to-date on the organization's mission and, where appropriate, its strategic initiatives. They should plan to put considerable effort and energy into any initiative that is aligned with those strategic goals. On the other hand, for any initiative that is not so aligned or is in some way questionable, the team leader should quickly connect with whoever has set the mandate to discuss any possible inconsistency. Any special initiative that is not consistent with the organizational mission and current strategic initiatives is pretty much doomed to fail.

■ CASE STUDY

IDEAS GOOD FOR NOTHING

One I/D team that I facilitated as a process leader was a high-performing team that was terrifically productive in generating top-quality new product ideas. When their ideas were presented to leadership, their vice president was very pleased. There was, however, a problem. Some of the ideas had crossed over some corporate boundary lines that had been established by the parent corporation. Although the ideas were worthwhile, the company would not be able to implement them. For them to come to fruition, they would have to be transferred to another subsidiary of the parent corporation— an uncomfortable and tricky political process. The vice president felt that perhaps patent applications should be initiated for some of the ideas so that the team could get some credit. But in reality, any ideas that the company was not prepared to implement pretty much withered, and nothing came of them. ■

When the organizational mission and current strategy are clear and well understood by all team members, courses of action are easily set and decisions are easily made. If something is not justifiable in terms of the ongoing mission or the current strategy, it probably should be abandoned. Minimally, it should be brought to a higher level for review and assessment. Nothing, or nearly nothing, is more frustrating than to put considerable time and effort into an idea or project only to find out, after it has been presented, that it will go nowhere because it wasn't aligned with the company's strategy.

There is, however, a little tension here that has to be carefully resolved by the special team. Sometimes, a team working on the frontier develops an invention or uncovers a discovery that is unaligned with current strategy and expectations. The team feels, however, that the new idea could be very important. It may be so noteworthy that it could prompt higher management to revise priorities and, perhaps, reevaluate current company strategy. How should the team proceed?

The key criterion to be addressed in dealing with this issue will probably be the fit with the organizational mission. There is a key difference between a) an idea that falls outside current organizational strategy but has the potential of furthering the organizational mission, and b) an idea that falls outside both current strategy and organizational mission. While ideas in the latter category are, generally speaking, dead on arrival, ideas in the former category have not only the potential for life, but could come to represent important dimensions of an organization's future. That still does not mean gaining acceptance for them will be easy. It will still likely be an uphill battle. The more radical the idea, the more difficulty it will have in gaining acceptance, and one should not expect that top management will always be attuned to possibility. Let us consider two case studies in which new, but unexpected, concepts were developed and see how they were handled by the companies' groups.

■ CASE STUDY

THE WATCH THAT DIDN'T LOOK LIKE A WATCH

One of the biggest failures to realize the value of a truly exceptional idea occurred in the watch industry in the 1960s. At that time, Swiss watches dominated the market. They were the gold standard of the industry and had a market share of about 65 percent. By the 1980s, that share had dropped to about 10 percent because the Swiss had missed the boat on quartz crystal technology. American and Japanese firms such as Texas Instrument and Seiko had turned the watch industry around with this new technology that provided greater accuracy with fewer moving parts.

The remarkable part of this story is that electronic quartz technology was invented by the Swiss! But they had a mind-set of what a watch looked like, and that turned out to be a set of gears and springs. When R&D inventors showed management a new kind of watch that operated on the vibrations of quartz crystals, they simply thought of it as a strange, although interesting, curiosity. They thought it noteworthy enough to put on display at an international exposition, but not significant enough to patent and protect it. When Seiko and Texas Instruments got a look at the new technology, they recognized its tremendous potential and were astonished to find that it was not protected. They simply took up the technology and rewrote the book on how watches could be made.[2] ■

■ **CASE STUDY**

"ACCIDENTAL" SUCCESS

3M is one of the most innovative companies in the world. It sells its 50,000 products in more than two hundred countries and reaps over $13 billion in annual revenues. Traditionally, it has encouraged, demanded, and supported innovative efforts and has a history of taking a second, third, or fourth look at ideas that go awry or that have strange properties.

One of its better-known innovation stories is the explosive success that came to Post-it Notes when new product researcher Art Fry came up with a sticky bookmark idea built on a "poor" adhesive developed by research scientist Spence Silver. Lesser known is the story of how Patsy Sherman, a young chemical researcher, turned her fascination with a small accident into a major product line.

Working at 3M for only about a year, Sherman was involved with a project to develop material that would resist deterioration from contact with jet fuel. One day a lab assistant accidentally spilled a few drops of a test compound, and they landed on the assistant's new tennis shoes. Although numerous substances were tried, nothing could remove the compound from the shoes. Sherman translated her curiosity about the resistant spots into an effort to purposely develop the properties of the compound. Working with chemist Stan Smith, Sherman invented a fluorochemical polymer that could repel oil and water from fabrics. 3M launched the product as Scotchgard Protector, and it has led the market from its inception. Sherman did not succeed at her original task, but her efforts were amazingly successful in terms of 3M's purpose to bring profitable innovative products to market. Contrasted with the Swiss reaction, 3M's culture was open to curiosities and accidents that could be translated into market winners.[3] ■

Serendipitous mistakes are often the sources of inventions or discoveries that can reshape organizational strategy. Penicillin was an accidental discovery, and Ivory Soap's floating characteristic came about through a manufacturing error. There are many other examples. Such "mistakes" have a chance to succeed, however, only when a team and its parent organization are open to unexpected possibilities that are aligned with the organizational mission—even if they are off target in terms of a specific task.

Commander's (CEO's) Intent[4]

Operations never proceed exactly as planned.[5]

—U.S. Army Field Manual 3–0

Never tell people how to do things. Tell them what to do and they will surprise you with their ingenuity.[5]

—Gen. George S. Patton Jr.

We noted earlier that it is immensely important for a team to know both its Task and its Purpose, and that should the two somehow become opposed, the team should execute in favor of Purpose. Now at the leadership level, we need to reaffirm that principle and discuss how leaders can make clear to teams what is crucial for success. The concept that helps us here is that of *Commander's Intent*.

■ **CASE STUDY**

INITIATIVE AT NORMANDY

U.S. Army Field Manual 22–100, Army Leadership: Be, Know, Do, notes: "As an Army leader, you can't just give orders: you must make clear the intent of those orders, the final goal of the mission. In combat, it's critically important for subordinates to understand their commander's intent. When they are cut off or enemy actions derail the original plan, well-trained soldiers who understand the commander's intent will apply disciplined initiative to accomplish the mission."

As an example the manual incorporates the actions of a small group of soldiers who were part of the D-Day invasion at Normandy.

The amphibious landings on the morning of June 6, 1944, were preceded by a large night airborne assault of American and British paratroopers. Jumping from thousands of aircraft, the intent of their mission was to cut off roads leading to the beaches, thus stopping German counterattacks that could push the invasion forces back into the sea.

But due to enemy fire and darkness many of the aircraft transporting the paratroopers went off course. The result was that the airborne units were scattered across the countryside often far from their drop zones and designated targets. Lost and under fire, individual paratroopers from the 82nd and 101st Airborne Divisions formed ad hoc fighting units often made up of soldiers from different commands. One such unit was formed and led by Capt. Sam Gibbons of the 505th Parachute Infantry Regiment. His group of twelve paratroopers first liberated a small village and then proceeded, without demolition equipment, to destroy the Douve River bridges nine miles away.

Their success was one example of what was happening throughout the Cotentin Peninsula of France. Such actions were characterized as follows: "Because they knew their units were well-trained and their leaders would do everything in their power to support them, small unit leaders were able to focus on the force's overall mission. They knew and understood the commander's intent. They believed that if they exercised disciplined initiative within that intent, things would turn out right. Events proved them correct."[6] ■

Especially in fluid situations in which either crises or opportunities may arise, it is imperative that high-stakes teams have great mission clarity. In the case study above and in Army operations in general, the Commander's Intent provides that clarity. The Commander's Intent is a clear, concise statement of the commanding officer's vision. It specifies the purpose, general method, and desired end state of an operation, and in doing so describes what will count as success. Because it is given in the context of combat and with the presumption that things may not go according to plan, it does not dictate specific tasks to accomplish; rather, it says how things must be at the end of the mission. In effect, it says that even if circumstances get chaotic and even if communications break down, *this* must be accomplished *somehow*. It spotlights the essential goal of the mission, and it provides strong direction; yet, at the same time, it empowers subordinates to improvise as necessary to get the job done.

The Commander's Intent by its nature focuses motivation. It establishes the value of, and a rationale for, a mission, and it highlights the role that a unit will play in the overall endeavor. In doing so, it establishes a single-mindedness and sense of purpose among all soldiers involved.

Contrast this with how often in the business world one hears someone moan, "Why are we doing this?" Too often people do not know the purpose of their work or where it fits in the larger organizational scheme. Their moans reflect their low motivation and frustration. But it is difficult to fault individuals in such circumstances. Remember, motivation is largely a function of the value of the effort. If people do not have a sense of how valuable their work is or that it is part of a worthy enterprise, one should expect their motivation to be low and their frustration level high. Meanwhile in Ranger operations, each successive commander's intent is clearly understood *two levels down*. Rangers not only understand their boss's intent, but their boss's boss's intent. In that manner, individual Rangers get a well-defined sense of the big picture and the role their unit will play.

It would be beneficial, especially for high-stakes civilian teams, to borrow this concept. The CEO's intent (or the vice president's intent, etc.) should provide the touchstone of special teams. This, of course, requires that leaders take the time to clearly formulate their intent and ensure that it is transmitted to special teams. Just as with military commanders, the CEO's intent for high-stakes teams should be a concise written statement. It should describe the essential mission while authorizing teams to do what is required to accomplish that mission.

■ CASE STUDY

INTENT FOR A CAR

The Taurus had been called the "car that saved Ford" and the "hottest car in years." When this midsized line was introduced in 1986, it quickly became the flagship of the Ford fleet and soon was the best-selling car in America. It also pulled Ford sales out of their nosedive. In 1992, plans called for the second generation of Taurus and its Mercury cousin, the Sable, with the redesigned models to be introduced in 1996. Given the car's popularity at the time, the redesign was seen as a challenging task akin to "reformulating Coca-Cola."

But while Taurus was selling well, it was losing market share to the Honda Accord, which had recently surpassed it as the best-selling car (import or domestic). Dick Landgraff was appointed leader of the Ford team assembled to redesign Taurus. For comparison purposes, his team had purchased a newly introduced car, the Toyota Camry, and team members took turns driving it. When Landgraff took his turn, he was taken aback by the car's quality and performance. He ordered the purchase of another Camry and had it completely disassembled down to its individual screws. He then had the parts mounted on display boards and ordered part-to-part cost comparisons with Taurus.

Landgraff did not have a military background but believed that military principles applied to corporate planning efforts. His personal experience with the Camry reshaped his vision of what his team must accomplish. His planners had previously provided several pages worth of vision statement material, but all their words didn't get it as far as Landgraff was concerned. So he personally composed a new and concise mission statement that read, "Deliver a Product Competitive with the Japanese on Quality and Function and Better in Styling, Features and Value." Below this statement he added a two-word team leader's intent that clarified to all concerned what really had to happen. He wrote: "Beat Camry."[7] ■

It is important to note that in this case study, we see the value of both the Leader's Recon and the Commander's Intent and how the former established the latter. Landgraff's recon, his personal driving experience with the Camry, gave him a clear sense of the real challenge facing his team. Despite present market share figures, the Taurus wasn't going to be facing the Accord; it was going to be in a head-to-head duel with the new Camry. He then captured that challenge in his pithy "Beat Camry" commander's intent. This had the effect of making clear to his team members where their efforts had to be directed and, by setting a new standard, provided them with clear motivation.

■ **CASE STUDY**

BOTTOM-LINE UNDERSTANDING

Ranger Nick Panagakos served as a rifle platoon leader in the 82nd Airborne Division in Operation Desert Storm. He went on to duties as a Rifle Company Commander and Brigade Assistant Operations Officer with the 25th Infantry Division. He now is a Special Agent for the FBI assigned to the Counter-Terrorism Task Force. He was one block away from Ground Zero when the first of the World Trade Towers fell.

Nick says that one of the most powerful carryovers from Ranger School to his work with the FBI is his ability to initiate positive action even without direct or current orders from above. Adjusting for titles within the FBI, he credits this source of responsibility and latitude to the supervisor's intent. He contrasts the tight focus provided by intent statements in the Army and in the FBI with the daze and confusion he witnessed among Iraqi forces during Desert Storm. Nick estimates that 90 percent of the Iraqis that were captured did not know their mission or what to expect in terms of allied operations. Betrayed and abandoned by their leaders, they had no sense of which actions to take or how to take them. Surrender and defeat became the rational choices. (This scenario seems to have repeated itself in Operation Iraqi Freedom.)

In the U.S. military and in the FBI, everyone in the unit must know what the mission is, understand its purpose, and be prepared for all contingencies. Nick refers to this as "bottom-line understanding," meaning that what must be accomplished must be understood down to the lowest ranking person. He also extends the timeline of what counts as a mission, observing that within the FBI, the supervisor's intent may apply for six months or a year.

Nick provides a flip side to the concept of an intent statement. When the mission is understood down to the lowest rank, everyone is charged with, and must take on, responsibility for its completion. He recounts an incident in which a helicopter crashed killing Ranger commanders on a reconnaissance mission. Their executive officers and subordinates immediately assumed leadership roles and completed the mission. No confusion, no excuses. A clear sense of duty plus empowerment equals responsibility to get the job done. ■

FIRST WHY, THEN WHAT AND HOW

The CEO's or team leader's intent can take a number of forms; it need not follow the Army's format. It may be a team mission statement or a vivid vision. It may be couched as an analogy or promulgated as a slogan. The concept of clearly understood intent is what is important.

Betsy Scarcelli, a vice president and chief information officer of a major insurance company, has led many successful high-challenge projects in her career. Her approach to developing mission clarity has been to make sure that all her teams start with a clear understanding of what she refers to as the Why of their mandate. By analyzing and discussing the situation analysis and incorporating project parameters, she then pushes her teams to develop a strong picture of their core goal, their What. Then, armed with that deeper understanding and provided with operational freedom, the teams more easily proceed to How, the specific processes they will use to accomplish their goals. In this example, Why, What, and How equate to the Commander's Intent elements of Purpose, End State, and Method. ■

Providing high-stakes teams with a definitive statement of the core function to be fulfilled gives them a clear orientation, while at the same time empowering them to get the job done as creatively as necessary. Such statements have great value, especially when adversities arise or team decision situations become unusually difficult. As in Ranger operations, the mission clarity provided by the leader's intent, combined with operational freedom, enables special action teams to maintain focus on the essential goal and to improvise appropriately in order to accomplish the mission.

Decentralized Decision Making

Special action teams work in situations with relatively short time frames and under conditions that run from highly intense to chaotic. In such circumstances, opportunities may open for only a moment, and crises may come on quickly. Both types of situations require quick response. Fortunately, special teams often comprise highly qualified people who are in a position to do the most good.

Such teams must be allowed a high level of decision-making authority. If the action and learning are happening out on the frontier, then that is where the appropriate level of decision making must occur. In situations that are changeable and require quick response, it is critical that decision making be timely and effective. Decision making should take place where the action is.

When a Ranger unit comes under fire, that is no time to call head-quarters to find out if it should return fire or take cover or maneuver or whatever. Reactions must be those of skilled and well-practiced profession-als who have a clear sense of their mission and of the situation. Ranger leaders have the responsibility and must, therefore, have the authority to make the best decision possible on the spot. And, of course, they do have such authority. There are many kinds of civilian special action teams that should have such operational authority.

As the new science of General Systems was applied to social and organi-zational domains, one of the major principles that emerged was that in complex dynamic systems there should be a central organizing vision, but decentralized decision making. Taking clear lessons from nature, it became obvious that for success and survival, organizations and communities must have a shared vision or a commonly sought goal. But in situations that require responsiveness and agility, in other words, life in general, subgroups and even individuals should operate on the basis of decentralized control.

Decentralized decision making need not mean disconnected or unaligned decision making, nor need it mean that a small special team will control the whole organization. In fact, the opposite should be the case. When the team's mission and purpose are clear and when team members have a good understanding of the situation, decision making can be relatively simple and well aligned. There are, however, two other elements that enable opti-mal team operation and goal alignment. They are information flow and organizational values. We initiated our consideration of these elements at the team level; we now need to revisit them with a focus on leadership.

Information Flow

We have already noted that good information flow and communication are crucial to organizations. For special action teams, a free flow of relevant information is vital for success. Information must flow to and from all team members. They must readily share information, ideas, concerns, setbacks, and insights with one another; and they must do so expediently. But information must also flow abundantly to and from the team. The larger organization and the supporting elements must provide the team with all the information it requires, and without hesitation. Leadership must ensure that special teams have all the information they need.

On the other hand, given the roles and circumstances of special project teams, they have a responsibility to stay connected with the larger organization. For some teams such as emergency response units, constant communication is necessary. For others, such as new-product development teams, the ability to check in with senior authorities frequently and outside of normal reporting times may be all that is required. For most special teams, however, difficulty in accessing information and/or poor or infrequent communication between the team and the parent organization sets the stage for failure. To ensure that small teams are making the best decentralized decisions and that parent organizations are reaping optimal benefits from small team actions and learning, information must flow freely and easily in all directions.

Organizational Values

Mission clarity and the commander's (CEO's) intent demark the goal and specify what will count as task success. Abundant information flow specifies the current situation and keeps everyone aware and aligned. The function of organizational values is to specify how individuals will conduct themselves in pursuit of goals. Values denote the character of the team, the ideals that organizational members seek to exemplify in dealing with each other and with the larger community.

As noted earlier, for teams to perform satisfactorily, they must first constitute themselves. They must negotiate the treacherous storming phase of the team life cycle and move into the norming phase where they learn how to work together. To excel at the even higher performing level, team members must exemplify strong team values in their daily actions. The conditions of peaceful coexistence and clear role definitions of the norming phase must be surpassed and supplanted by dedication, intrinsic motivation, and a strong sense of obligation to the greater community and to each other.

Just as at the team level, values at the organizational level should set standards for the personal and interpersonal behaviors of all members. They imprint character, and they set expectations. They help to forge individual members into an integrated whole. Importantly, shared values imbue both teams and organizations with a sense of identity and, if they are praiseworthy in nature, with an esprit de corps.

There is, however, another crucial role that values play: they inform decision making. When choices must be made, and especially when they must be made under pressure and in a decentralized manner, the values that a organization lives by make seemingly difficult decisions a lot easier. When individuals truly understand and conscientiously observe high-minded principles, their behavior will be both honorable and consistent.

Rangers live by the Ranger Creed. Even in the great chaos of battle, they have demonstrated a dedication to the principles of the Creed and to each other. The Ranger Creed is an integrating aspect of Ranger culture. It does more than govern behavior; it provides the philosophy for a lifestyle. Ranger values connect individual Rangers, not just to their units but, in effect, to an extended family.

Great teams and great companies also live by high-minded principles. Personally, I have encountered clear and meaningful values in a number of great companies, and some companies are almost legendary because of the values that characterize their behavior.

■ **CASE STUDY**

DISNEY VALUES

Among many business managers, Walt Disney World is famous for its behind-the-scenes program. The wonderful magic of the park is replaced in the manager's mind by the normally hidden magic of a large and complex enterprise that is run especially well. Even park guests can take an abbreviated tour that gives a strong sense of the clarity and discipline under which Disney's "cast members" operate. One of the very first things in the introductory briefing given to guests is the set of Disney values: Safety, Hospitality, Efficiency, and Show. In fact, much of the remainder of the tour is an explanation and elaboration of how those values pervade the park and the conduct of the cast.

While those values are always operational, I had an unusual glimpse at how they were applied during a potential crisis. During one segment of our tour, we took a special ride through the workings of Space Mountain, Disney's high-thrills roller coaster in the dark that is the center of attraction for Tomorrow Land. At one point, the normally black environment was lit briefly. I thought this was for the benefit of the tour group, and I appreciated the look at the complicated infrastructure that is usually felt rather than seen. When we emerged from our secret look at the ride, I found out differently.

Our guide, who himself consistently exemplified the four values, explained what had happened. For some reason, one roller coaster car was gaining distance on the car in front of it. As yet there was no danger, but a control parameter had been crossed. The operating crewmembers immediately turned on the lights and effected a correction that adjusted the distance to its proper range. Within what seemed like only two or three seconds the correction had been made, the lights went off, and Space Mountain riders were returned to scary thrills in the black of "outer space." The value of Show was returned to its normal place in the value set. What the secret tour group learned was that Show had its high place, but if anything untoward became even a remote possibility, Safety became the dominant value. There was apparently no need to check with higher levels of authority, to get permission, to check policy. People knew their jobs and their responsibilities and executed them in an empowered fashion. At Disney, values are explicit and to the point, and there is even a clear order of precedence should values come into conflict with one another. The message here is that decision making is easy if your mission is clear and your values really inform and shape your behavior. ■

■ **CASE STUDY**

CORPORATE CHARACTER

Rangers Alex Gorsky and Fred Walker are employed by two different subsidiaries of Johnson & Johnson. Both view J&J's Credo as crucial guidance for their actions and decisions. Alex, as president of Janssen Pharmaceutica, says values in general provide a "moral compass" in his company, and the Credo in particular facilitates decision making. Fred, an executive director in marketing at McNeil Consumer and Specialty Pharmaceuticals, feels that the Credo "provides the basis for the operations of the entire corporation." He believes that just as the Ranger Creed sets standards for Rangers that are higher than those of the rest of the Army, the Johnson & Johnson Credo sets the bar higher for J&J employees.

My experiences with teams within McNeil are consistent with these perspectives. More than once, I have seen the Credo and J&J's extraordinary standards employed to inform decision making and team conduct. One may justifiably say that in terms of exemplary corporate character, Johnson & Johnson provides a textbook illustration. Twice J&J has put a great deal of money where its mouth is in exemplifying corporate responsibility to the community.

In 1982 and again in 1986, unknown individuals tampered with Tylenol, one of J&J's most popular and profitable products, by placing cyanide in capsules of the pain reliever. In the first incident, seven people died from the poisoning. J&J voluntarily recalled the product at the cost of $100 million against earnings and a drop of $1 billion in corporate market value. In the second instance, after one person died, J&J quickly pulled the product from every outlet, not just those in the region with the fatality. Further, the company decided that it would no longer manufacture over-the-counter products in capsule form, as their safety could not be guaranteed even in the tamper-proof containers that were made standard after the first incident. The second hit on the company was also financially devastating, but Johnson & Johnson's ethical behavior and corporate responsibility were so well appreciated, that within five months it had recouped most of its market share, and its growth continued beyond that time.[8] ∎

Besides Disney and Johnson & Johnson, there are many other great companies walking their talk. Malden Mills, the manufacturer of the cold-weather fabric Polartec, is well known for its family values that have helped the company and its employees sustain themselves through hard economic times. The values of the North Carolina software design firm, SAS, permeate every aspect of the company, from the way it handles money to the wonderful social and support programs it offers its employees. Year after year, it shows double-digit growth, and its employee turnover rate, even in the revolving-door high tech marketplace, is a mere 3 percent. Ben & Jerry's and The Body Shop are so driven by their standards and sense of corporate responsibility that they consider themselves "values-led businesses." Both companies see themselves as not just businesses, but forces for social changes. The Body Shop established its reputation by refusing to carry products that were developed through animal testing and by instituting recycling programs such as discounts on the return of perfume bottles for refilling. Ben & Jerry's works to incorporate social consciousness into as many of its policies and everyday activities as possible—even its ice cream manufacturing operations.[9]

■ CASE STUDY

ONE PERSON CAN MAKE A DIFFERENCE

In a dynamic system, and that could be a small team or a large conglomerate, everyone plays an important role. There are no insignificant people; there are no insignificant actions. Chaos theory, the study of complex systems, tells of the *Butterfly Effect*. This theory proposes metaphorically that a force as small as the flapping of a butterfly's wings in Brazil can set off a tornado in Texas next month. Strong imagery, and perhaps a little too simply stated, but scientists have the data to show that in complex systems in which the parts are strongly interconnected, a small act or change in one part of the system can have an impact on the entire system. And there are plenty of business examples, good or bad, that attest to the truth of the Butterfly Effect and its relationship to personal and organizational values. Consider the following two cases:

Our company facilitated some strategic thinking with one of the newspapers within the Gannett chain. While working with the newspaper, I heard more than once a story that was fast becoming part of the paper's mythology.

One day, very early in the morning before most people were even due to arrive at work, a person from the production staff noticed a couple of boxes of circulars on the floor. The circulars should have been shipped to a client about 100 miles away. The worker was completing his night shift and had no individual responsibility for the circulars or their delivery, but he knew that the newspaper was responsible and the client needed them almost immediately. Without waiting for others including management to arrive, the worker loaded the boxes into a vehicle and personally delivered them to the client on time. This act saved the newspaper's reputation and revenue because the person exemplified good values and shared ownership for *all* of the newspaper's responsibilities. When you are part of a high-performing team, you own everything the team is responsible for or does. And one person can make a difference.

Contrast that example with that of Nicholas Leeson, a twenty-eight-year-old stock trader in the Singapore branch of Barings Bank. Barings was a 232-year-old British establishment, so well regarded that Queen Elizabeth kept a good deal of her personal money in the bank. Leeson made a sequence of very risky investments that started to go sour quickly. Motivated by avarice and the fear of being caught, he compounded the situation and the bank's vulnerability by devising a devious cover-up. In a period of about four months, Leeson's imprudent investments, greed, and chicanery created first a small, then an ever-widening fissure in Barings' financial structure. By the time the true nature of his behavior was discovered, the damage was so great that the bank could not be saved from insolvency. For good or bad, one person can make a significant difference.[10] ∎

As we have seen, many companies are thriving because they have the twenty-first century philosophy of "doing good and doing well." They are good citizens of the larger community, and they seek to take good care of their workers. The accompanying result is that they are doing well in terms of reputation and substantial profits. But we can also see that worthy values must be more than high-sounding phrases on a sign in the reception area. They must inform and guide the actions of all on the team or in the company. When they do, good things seem to happen naturally; when they do not, they can spell disaster for teams and even whole organizations.

Learn Like Crazy

IMPROVING

Improving actions fall into these categories:

Developing involves investing adequate time and effort to develop individual subordinates as leaders. It includes mentoring.

Building involves spending time and resources to improve teams, groups, and units and to foster an ethical climate.

Learning involves seeking self-improvement and organizational growth. It includes envisioning, adapting, and leading change.[1]

—U.S. Army Field Manual 22–100

Don't Fight the Last War

Traditionally, the first responsibility of a military commander is to accomplish the mission, the second is to take care of the troops. In recent years, through U.S. Army doctrine, training, and operations, a third major responsibility has emerged: *Learn.*

We have already noted that Army leadership framework can be headlined in three small words: Be, Know, Do. Doing is further broken down into Influencing, Operating, and Improving. The last item, the call for constant improvement, challenges the military leader to learn, grow, and lead change. It demands that leaders develop their subordinates, improve the abilities of their units, and grow personally. This reaffirms what we have noted at both the individual and team levels: learning and development are crucial for long-term survival and success. Here we will reinforce and apply that principle at the leadership level.

For special operations leaders, the mandate for continual improvement and learning is clearly stated in the Army's leadership framework. Its basis, however, is in ever-evolving missions, enemies, and technologies. Likewise, for civilian leaders, the mandate is manifested in the constantly changing circumstances in which they operate and the challenges they must face.

There is a well-known expression that "an army always prepares to fight the last war." To a large extent, history bears out the truth of this adage. It is easy to understand why. Especially in cases in which the waging of the last war was successful, it is easy for military thinkers to build on that success—that is, to do more of what worked before. That kind of thinking, unfortunately, can be taken to the point of being ridiculous. One egregious example was the long-standing refusal of British senior officers to accept the concept of an armored tank. Proposed prior to World War I, the concept was rejected. Even as trench warfare produced the daily slaughter of thousands in no-man's-lands, the tank was rejected because it threatened the traditional role of artillery and cavalry! Amazingly, World War II was well under way before the British High Command fully endorsed the concept.

But the military is far from alone in such thinking. Most businesses and other civilian institutions tend to fight the last war. Most are very slow to change and innovate. Many seem almost to resist learning, as they repeat mistakes and extend troublesome patterns of behavior. Indeed, some have to teeter on the brink of failure before realization hits, and only then does leadership attempt restructuring or revitalization. In fact, the task of changing and innovating is often given to new leadership, as former leaders are saddled with the blame for downturns and moved out.

The Learning Imperative

Change is certain, and dependence on today's competencies lays the foundation for tomorrow's defeat. Leaders, therefore, need to accept change, anticipate needs, and develop competencies for the future. Learning is imperative. It must be ongoing, purposeful, deep, integrated, and fast. Individuals at all levels must, in other words, always be learning like crazy.

ONGOING, PURPOSEFUL LEARNING

As noted, organizations can be woefully slow to change. Sometimes, this is the result of poor leadership. But often the problem is not that leadership is blind or reluctant to change, rather it is that learning must be purposefully pursued, and too often people are too busy to take the time to learn. They are also too busy or too shortsighted to notice that the world is changing around them.

Sometimes external changes come slowly until they reach a critical point, then the shifts are dramatic and far reaching. The development of computer technology, for example, began in the 1940s and proceeded incrementally for half a century until the 1990s, when the world seemed to suddenly become wired and connected. At other times, a significant disruption comes unexpectedly, and the world (or industry) changes overnight. The development of atomic weapons brought a quick end to World War II and a beginning to the dangerous Cold War. The meltdown at Chernobyl and the accident at Three Mile Island quickly disrupted the momentum of the nuclear energy industry. The Tylenol tampering case was immediately disruptive. The shifts from mainframe computing to desktop computers and from independent doctors to managed care came at moderate speed.

LIMITED BY SUCCESS

Too often, individuals, organizations, and even whole industries are slow to change because they have been lulled into complacency. And what was the drug that put them to sleep? Often it is success. As paradoxical as it seems, success is one of the worst enemies of learning and innovation. If something, whether a process or a product, seems to be working or selling well, there is relatively little passion to question it, let alone change it. If current competencies seem adequate, people often feel little need to put any substantial effort into improving themselves or their organizations.

There is, of course, a sense of psychological security in the status quo, especially if it is viewed as at least moderately comfortable. It is not, however, just an "if it ain't broke, don't fix it" attitude that is at play here. Cognitively, we humans are generally bound by current reality; our imaginations are constrained by what our minds know to be the case *now*. Even when change is called for, we tend to hold onto the familiar. Consider, for example, that the first automobiles were truly horseless carriages; the horse was taken away, but the basic design remained that of a horse-drawn carriage. And even though the concept of railroading called for new thinking, early rail-road cars were really modifications of the then current mode of public over-land transportation, the stagecoach. Except for flanged wheels to fit onto the tracks, the design and usage were basically the same—including seating people on top of the cars! Things started to change when people began being thrown from those cars.[2]

SURVIVAL OF THE LEARNINGEST

History has clearly shown that the world does not stand still. The title of an important book by George Land, the "father of transformation theory," tells the story succinctly: *Grow or Die!*[3] For individuals, species, armies, corpo-rations, or nations the continuing challenge is to learn, adapt, and develop. This challenge applies in the natural world and in the business world. When one considers that more than 90 percent of all known species that ever existed are now extinct, it is clear that the failure to adjust to changing cir-cumstances can have deadly consequences. But, remarkably, the average lifespan of contemporary businesses is less than that of individuals! Rather than working for a company that a grandparent or parent worked for, a per-son would be lucky to work for a company that will stay in business during that person's working years.

And being the biggest and strongest in your domain does not guarantee success or even survival: the dinosaurs that ruled the earth did not survive a meteor's collision with Earth approximately 65 million years ago. Likewise, you may be the best typewriter manufacturer in the world, but if the world no longer needs typewriters, you may as well be making abacuses, slide rules, or eight-track stereos. (When, by the way, was the last time you went shopping for a typewriter?)

No, rather than current size, strength, or market share, what matters for long-term success is matching competencies to conditions. Survival consists in value that continually generates even greater value. But the locus of such excellence is not to be found in today's products or services, but rather in leadership, thinking skills, and aspirations. For individuals, teams, or cor-porations, the greatest challenge is to continually build and refine compe-tencies—not for the present, but for the uncertainties of the future. Like special operations forces, teams and organizations have to be agile, adaptive, responsive, and resilient—and they have to be prepared and geared up for their mission. It is too late to build competencies once a crisis hits or an opportunity presents itself. Those competencies have to be in place long before they are needed.

And this challenge is not met through occasional or incidental learning. It can only be met through ongoing, purposeful learning, that is, the level of learning required for success can only be achieved when learning is a crucial component of every day's work. Learning cannot be hit-or-miss or infrequent. Instead, it must be directed, and it must be continual. Building individual and organizational expertise must be a co-objective of every work task. Every individual must see learning as one of the most important things she must do each day.

AFTER ACTION REVIEW

The United States Army is the best-trained, most effective army in the world today. To reach that pinnacle, its combat units must regularly undergo highly realistic and very demanding training at such sites as the Joint Readiness Training Center in Louisiana and the National Training Center in California. At those sites, training mistakes can be very embarrassing, and successes exhilarating. In either case, lessons there and at other realistic training facilities are hammered home by means of the After Action Review or AAR.[4]

For more than twenty years, the U.S. Army has used this powerful technique to facilitate continual learning. The After Action Review is simple in form, yet potent in terms of impact. It takes the form of a nonevaluative, egalitarian dialogue conducted among participants immediately after actions or operations. Its focus is on improvement for the future. Lt. Col. Mark Meadows, a Ranger officer who currently serves as an observer/controller at the Joint Readiness Training Center, regards the AAR as the best mechanism for learning and growth that the Army has developed. He considers it "absolutely invaluable as a feedback mechanism," and he makes the further claim that the Army will always have the AAR as part of its training cycle. Col. Kurt Fuller, who has spent several years in the Ranger Regiment and currently commands a brigade of the 82nd Airborne Division, agrees. He feels the AAR is "the most important and most useful tool that the Army has ever developed in terms of capturing lessons learned from what has happened . . . and improving your capability to execute missions that may come in the future." He notes that

Rangers conduct the AAR both formally and informally at every level—from making improvements at the individual level to lessons learned at Joint Headquarters that deal with large units from different branches and different armed services.

The AAR is first conducted verbally and as promptly after an activity as possible. Later, with time given for deeper reflection, it is converted to writing. But written After Action Reviews do not become dust collectors on shelves; they may be incorporated into unit Standard Operating Procedures (see below) or accessed during the planning of new operations. Colonel Fuller notes that when the Rangers prepared for the seizure of an airport in Operation Just Cause in Panama, they pulled out the AARs from the similar mission they had executed previously during Operation Urgent Fury in Grenada. They wanted to be sure that any lessons from the first operation would be incorporated into the upcoming one.

The Army conducts AARs at the completion of any important activity or training experience, at which time participants are gathered into functional small groups to discuss the experience and turn it into learning. During the conduct of the AAR, differences in rank are downplayed; in fact, especially among Rangers, commanders expect to receive criticism from their subordinates. Everyone is encouraged to speak frankly about what he observed or experienced. The tone is nonevaluative in that the discussion is more about what happened, rather than who might be to blame. Besides looking at actions and results, assessments, especially at higher levels, are made regarding the overall process and planning that went into the mission.

Three questions provide the template for the dialogue: *What happened? Why do we think it happened? What did we learn?* Notice that even these questions are nonevaluative, as responses could be about successes, failures, surprises, hypotheses, and so on.

The first question calls for empirical data about the experience. Responses from all individuals are encouraged as the leader or facilitator seeks to aid the team in putting together a picture of what occurred that is as comprehensive as possible. The second question is designed to evoke perspectives and hypotheses; the focus is on determining contributing factors, perceptions, sequences, interrelationships, and influences. The final question prompts the group to turn the experience into a practical lesson. The output should result in explicit guidelines on how to conduct similar activities in the future.

There are two reasons why Rangers rely so heavily on the AAR. As Colonel Fuller notes, "Rangers are professionals who understand that no matter how well you do something, you can always do it better the next time." The second reason may be even more essential: learning helps combat soldiers to accomplish missions, win wars, and stay alive.

But in addition to its value as an important military learning tool, the AAR offers itself as a simple, yet potent technique for civilian special teams and leadership groups. Any major activity, and probably many lesser ones, should be quickly reviewed for lessons learned, and those lessons (what to do, what to avoid) should be made part of the team or organization's knowledge base for the future.

The following are guidelines for conducting an AAR with a special action team:

1. Conduct the After Action Review when the event or operation is still fresh in everybody's mind. If appropriate, conduct it immediately after the action.

2. Follow the structure and sequence provided by the three questions above.

3. If possible, have an unbiased and experienced facilitator guide the team through the process. The facilitator should set the stage, establish a psychologically secure common ground, prompt honest participation, and moderate the dialogue.

4. When applicable, incorporate records and visual materials such as sketches, flowcharts, and timelines in order to provide the fullest picture.

5. In examining the operation, proceed by phases. Look for threads or chains of events that may have been set in motion early.

6. Get people to talk about themselves and what they experienced. An AAR session must be honest and open for it to be effective. Encourage people to take responsibility (without praise or blame) for what they did or did not do. Ask: what could you do better?

7. Encourage focused attention and good listening. People must take in and understand what others experienced and how they perceive the course of events. Often people must adjust their perspectives in order to have insights.

8. Remember that the focus of the AAR is the future; it is on learning and growing. Require a nonevaluative, empirical tone. In the case of success, get the team beyond self-congratulation. In the case of failure, do not allow blaming.

9. Insights and lessons should be quickly recorded and incorporated into organizational procedures for the next operation.

The AAR's three questions are simple, open-ended, and evocative. If conducted well, the After Action Review can become a major vehicle for ongoing team and organizational learning.

DEEP AND INTEGRATED LEARNING

To take on the greatest challenges, special action teams may need to do some just-in-time learning. But given a short time frame, most of what they will be able to accomplish will be a function of the knowledge and skills that their members bring to the task. The greater those personal repertoires, the greater the likelihood of team success. But the development of personal ability is through the learning process, which should be a continuing process for any professional.

Ongoing, purposeful learning is the vehicle to professional development, and its culmination is in expertise[5]—that is, great ability and skill in a particular field. Expertise is deep understanding and keen awareness that allow an individual to perform at the highest levels and to take on the most difficult problems—and to make doing so look easy. To succeed you must be as good as you can be and for both the individual and the organization, expertise is the cornerstone of success. Its development, therefore, should be a strategic objective for both individuals and organizations. Establishing and facilitating that objective is the hallmark of great leadership.

The research across many fields makes one point very clear: expertise is a function of experience, a lot of experience. There is no shortcut to expertise. Researchers estimate that seven to ten years of experience is required to become an expert in a field. But expertise does not equate to longevity. We have all come across individuals who have been in a particular position or with a particular organization for many years, yet who have long ago stopped learning and growing. Putting in time is not what produces expert skill. For expertise to develop, experience must be made *meaningful.* That is, experts are those individuals who have accumulated a great depth and breadth of experience—and have learned a great deal from it. Their years of work have also been years of purposeful learning.

DEVELOPING THINKERS

The achievement of expertise represents ascension through levels of learning and development. In any one field, a person starts as a novice, then moves progressively to competence, proficiency, and, in the best case, onto expertise. Much of that development, especially at the lower levels, will come from experience that is translated into domain skills. Because much of what we learn we learn incidentally, simply being exposed to many, various situations in our line of work will rub off on us. In that mode, we pick up terminology and a decent amount of know-how. We develop a deeper level of knowledge, however, through formal instruction and reflection, either through apprenticeship or formal education combined with a serious personal effort to construct meaning. In this manner, we are likely to acquire the guiding principles and fundamental knowledge of the field.

But as noted earlier, domain skills, while terrifically important, are only one layer of knowledge and ability. People must also be good thinkers. They must develop the process skills of problem solving, decision making, and planning. They must be capable, critical, analytical thinkers, as well as fluid, creative thinkers. And so, the development of process skills is not something that should be left to chance. I asked Lt. Col. Dave Anders, who has served as a platoon leader in the Ranger Regiment, commander of the III Corps LRS company, and commander of the LRS Leaders Course within the Ranger Training Brigade, about this challenge of developing the thinking skills of Rangers. He believes that, "First, they have to know what right looks like." A strong and proven problem-solving/decision-making methodology has to be formally taught and reinforced until it is ingrained in the individual. When one is confronted with the stresses of Ranger School or combat or those to be found in civilian high-stakes situations, it is not the time to figure out how to think. Those well-developed thinking skills and strategies have to be brought to bear quickly and effortlessly.

Thus, beyond the purposeful development of domain skills, leaders and educators must ensure that strong general strategies of problem solving, decision making, and planning are taught formally, transferred into practice, and reinforced experientially until the prospective high-stakes team leader/member can immediately apply them even under stressful conditions. Rangers and other Army commanders employ the Military Decision Making Process, elements of which have been shared above. Additionally, there are a number of other proven cognitive strategies and models available to the individual or to organizational leadership. It may be appropriate, however, for a special action team to formally adopt a particular model and ensure that all team members are proficient in its use.

The cultivation of thinking skills through formal instruction and practical reinforcement actually represents an intermediate phase of cognitive development. As with domain knowledge, when process methodologies become highly internalized, as they do at the level of the expert, they are "forgotten." That is, they are so well learned and are used so effortlessly, that the expert no longer consciously activates them or is aware of them. They simply become the normal and natural way to think.

PROGRESSIVE PROBLEM SOLVING[6]

Another characteristic of experts is their *progressive problem solving*. Experts reach the heights in their fields by repeatedly taking on problems at ever higher levels, continually reaching a little beyond their last success. Working at the edges of their competence, they take on and solve problems of greater scale and those that require greater depth or breadth of understanding. They learn to adjust to increasing degrees of complexity, handle more constraints, or meet higher standards. They extend the breadth and depth of their abilities by learning from their successes and their failures and converting their experiences either way into knowledge and skill. They reflect on and internalize their lessons until their thinking and actions become automatic and relatively effortless.

There is probably nothing better for the production of learning and the development of expertise than solving real and challenging problems. This is an approach taken by smart military commanders. When asked how he approaches the development of thinking in Rangers and other special ops troops, combat veteran Mark Meadows says, "Let them solve problems." He challenges his subordinate leaders to solve problems and make decisions that are appropriate to their jobs and their level of development. He then reinforces that experiential learning with discussions and debriefings (see below). He provides counsel and encouragement and guides them through self-correction. He then moves them on to the next level of difficulty. And as they, like experts in general, proceed through each progressive level of challenge and development, they experience an important by-product of learning: confidence. Much as is the case in Ranger School, passing each successive test is self-empowering. As one's confidence grows, so does the willingness to take on the next level of challenge. The cycle of learning, confidence building, and application of new skills to new problems becomes a self-reinforcing loop.

THE VALUE OF FAILURE

> The only mistakes are the ones that go uncorrected.
>
> —Gen. George S. Patton Jr.

It is important to underscore that learning from failure as well as success is an important aspect of competency building and the development of expertise. Failure and mistakes are part of the learning process. We all slip and have lapses, and sometimes circumstances conspire against us. To paraphrase General Patton, we could suggest that the only failures are the ones we don't learn from. We need to recognize that failures and honest mistakes provide important opportunities for learning—perhaps more so than successes, because errors often come with a higher emotional charge that prompts learning. While the temptation may be to hide mistakes or forget about failures as soon as possible, doing so sets the stage for making stupid mistakes and repeating failures. It also closes the door on potentially important learning.

Serving as a Senior Observer/Controller at the Joint Readiness Training Center, Ranger Lt. Col. Mark Meadows sees his role as a coach, teacher, and mentor. But most of Mark's career has been as a troop commander. He served with the Rangers in Operation Desert Storm and, prior to that, jumped into Panama with the Regiment's 1st Battalion during Operation Just Cause. Having been born in Panama, Mark jokes that he's only been there twice—once to be born, once to help straighten things out. A highly accomplished combat commander, Mark knows the importance of executing operations as well as possible. Yet he remarks that, "Mistakes are great." He does not, of course, encourage them, and he recognizes that some are unrecoverable. But he also believes that people can't help but make occasional mistakes, and when they do, they are presented with a great opportunity for learning. His leadership approach to helping his subordinates learn from mistakes offers good guidelines for others. His first step is to point out the mistake if the person making it does not yet see it. Then he discusses with that person why it is a mistake and what its ramifications could be. But rather than dictate a correction, he helps his subordinate to think through the situation in order to learn the lesson and develop his own rectification. He finds that after guiding subordinates through this informal learning process, mistakes are rarely repeated.

Of course, we should attempt to avoid mistakes. We need, through personal discipline and the careful observance of SOPs, to guard as best we can against slip-ups, lapses, and mental errors. We especially need to guard against what Bob Dewar of the Kellogg Graduate School of Business at Northwestern University calls "dumb mistakes."[7] In this category, he lists: repeating your own mistake, repeating someone else's mistake, risking more than you can afford to lose, acting impulsively without thought, and doing something illegal or unethical. Avoiding dumb mistakes is another important motivation and one that reinforces the value of learning, including learning from others' mistakes as well as our own.

But when mistakes or failures do occur, we must turn them into lessons. We have to fight the misconceptions and embarrassment that people have toward these things. Mistakes and failures are a form of negative feedback; they help to redirect our efforts and keep us on course toward our goals. We need to recognize that they are often only temporary setbacks and, as a matter of fact, may play a key role in our long-term success.

Both the scientific method and the creative process have historically benefited from miscues. Scientists and inventors, in fact, often have a very positive view of failure. Semi Joseph Begun, a pioneer in magnetic recording technology, said, "Failures are precious if you learn from them." Soichiro Honda said, "Success is 99 percent failure." R. Buckminster Fuller went further, noting: "I only learn when I have failures." Some of the best advice that I have received regarding how to use failure came from Trudy Elion.[8]

■ **CASE STUDY**

LEARNING FROM FAILURE

Dr. Gertrude "Trudy" Elion was a great scientist. A Nobel Laureate and an inductee of the National Inventors Hall of Fame, she was featured by Tom Brokaw in his book *The Greatest Generation.* She received the Nobel Prize for her work that yielded the first drugs to treat leukemia. She used the learning from those efforts to develop drugs that dealt with the body's natural rejection mechanisms, thus facilitating organ transplants. She then went on to develop medicines for treating herpes and gout.

I was fortunate to meet Trudy when we both spoke at induction ceremonies at the National Inventors Hall of Fame. She outlined her creative process as doing foundational work on one problem, then having succeeded at that problem, using even moderate success to move on to higher-level challenges. She equated this version of progressive problem solving to moving around the face of a clock: success at twelve o'clock leads to work at one o'clock, which leads to work at two o'clock, and so on.

But while history records her work as a trail of successes, she was quick to point out that the work involved many failures. It was how Trudy Elion handled those failures that made her great. In fact, for her, there were no failures, because she viewed unsuccessful attempts as crucial lessons. She said such instances "told me something"; they were "positive indications." Probing why something did not work led to revelations about what would work. For her, failures became springboards to success. She noted: "Every failure is a step forward—a path you don't have to try again and an opportunity to explore new things. Have faith that persistence will cause a problem to reveal an answer." ■

Trudy Elion, like many other great thinkers, exemplifies expertise that comes from constructing significant meaning out of experience, including mistakes. She reminds us that outstanding achievement at ever higher levels does not usually take a path of unerring progress; it will likely be a path strewn with many failures. But with dedication, persistence, and learning from those mistakes, each achievement can open the door to more opportunity and greater achievement.

RECIPROCITY

Individuals who seek to take on the greatest challenges must aspire to expertise, and leaders must facilitate the development of such individuals. For as those individuals develop, so do their organizations. But there are two interrelated leadership challenges here: organizations must find ways to keep individuals growing professionally, and individual expertise must be converted into organizational competencies.

The easy answers to the first challenge are more money and more perks, but those are probably not where the real answers lie. Surely, people need to feel that they and their families are being taken care of in terms of financial security and that they will share in the fruits of their labors. But research indicates that these things may not be the chief motivating factors of creative experts. We have already indicated what some of those greater motivations may be. Hard-charging individuals should be given ample opportunity to pursue greater challenges, especially those for which they are intrinsically motivated. Individuals who want to learn and grow should not be thwarted or impeded in those efforts; rather they should be encouraged, and their professional growth facilitated. In pursuing their investigations, they should be given operational autonomy and allowed latitude for personal creativity. And they should enjoy managerial support in the form of mentoring, encouragement, championing of their efforts and, of course, fair treatment.

It is also fair that they take responsibility for providing the organization with a return on its investment. Such individuals should be encouraged to share their growing knowledge and skill by informing, advising, and supporting the work of others. They should be examples and standard bearers within the organization, active members of a community of practice and willing contributors to the organization's higher goals. And it is important to note that in taking on these responsibilities and roles, they are not just serving the organization and their field, they are also enjoying another aspect of personal fulfillment. Thus, a positive growth cycle for both the individual and organization is reinforced.

The development of expertise addresses the need for deep learning on the part of individuals. As to the second challenge of integrating individual expertise into organizational competence, we return to the notion of ongoing, purposeful learning, but we make these efforts more specific. In order to derive mutual benefits, individual learning should be aligned with organizational need; individual expertise should feed into organizational competency building. These objectives require that leaders have a sense of direction. Foresight and good strategic thinking must inform the ongoing process of competency development. This can be accomplished through the strong incorporation of scenario methodology and by stretching the use of branches and sequels thinking into more strategic timelines. It is also appropriate, however, that strategic thinking and its accompanying competency building be constantly reviewed. This is the approach of military leaders and planners, and it is one that should be adopted by civilian organizations. To truly prepare for the challenges of the future, the direction of strategic growth must frequently be reconsidered and reevaluated lest an organization find that it has prepared to "fight in a jungle and now finds itself in a desert."

Setting the strategic agenda and promoting individual learning are important first steps that must then be complemented by strong organizational learning. Even with good upfront thinking, there still must be steps taken to integrate and codify learning into team and organizational competencies. Lessons must be incorporated into the memory of the greater organization through effective information management systems, policy development, instruction, and training.

STANDARD OPERATING PROCEDURES

The Ranger Regiment addresses this last challenge through Standard Operating Procedures, which it has for just about everything including how to lace boots. Rather than lose knowledge, Rangers purposefully store learning in the form of SOPs. These principles and procedures then become a kind of unit memory. By developing, maintaining, and continually upgrading that knowledge base, Rangers stay current, and they prepare for the future. Lt. Col. Mark Meadows says, "Rangers are probably the world's best [at setting standards and establishing systems]. If they can put brushing your teeth into an SOP, they'll do it." And they do not deviate from those standards. By instilling SOPs in individual Rangers, the unit shares knowledge gained over generations and prevents the repeat of lessons learned the hard way. Rogers' Standing Orders directed the behavior of Rogers' Rangers in their pre-Revolution operations. But they and their upgrades also guided Rangers in Korea, Vietnam, Grenada, Panama, the Gulf War, Somalia, Afghanistan, and Operation Iraqi Freedom. In the form of Regimental SOPs, they continue to guide Rangers to this day. (And, of course, some of them are offered here as potential guides for civilian special action teams.)

These guidelines have a constructive, if somewhat paradoxical, effect: overall, they tend to reduce the need for creative thinking while at the same time freeing the mind for really important creative thinking.

Meadows remarks that in combat, "Time is never on your side." He views SOPs as a playbook that has already been well developed and prepared. Since the SOPs represent competencies, lessons, and standards that have been well integrated into Regimental thinking, he feels Rangers, when confronted with a demanding challenge, can begin immediately to focus on the problem at hand. He contrasts this to other organizations that have to, maybe too late, start thinking about what competencies may be needed and how they should prepare to prepare. As an experienced warfighter, Mark is big on learning and the incorporation of that learning into everyday operations. His point is that if you have to go back to the drawing board every time you confront a problem, "you will stay at the same level for the rest of your life, (and) the rest of your organization's life; and it may be a short life."

Because SOPs provide ready and time-tested answers to a great many questions, Rangers do not have to spend time reinventing the wheel. For that very reason, they can devote their efforts to new problems and challenges that do require inventive thinking. In the same manner, SOPs optimize military actions and behaviors. As they are internalized, they develop into the *automaticity* that characterizes experts; that is, they result in quicker awareness and pattern recognition and more instinctive and effortless responses to changing circumstances. Together, they contribute to *naturalistic decision making*, the ability to tap experience and expertise under stressful conditions in order to achieve objectives. They provide the foundation for and promote quick, knowledgeable action even in the midst of combat.[9]

SOPs are, in effect, a shared knowledge base. On civilian high-stakes teams they may be called SOPs, continuity files, best practices, or something similar. Special teams can make good use of SOPs or their variations provided three important points are observed. First, there is great benefit derived from shared knowledge. A shared knowledge base represents long-term organizational learning. When it is codified and stored, it not only neutralizes knowledge loss through changeover of personnel, it becomes the core of organizational capability. It provides the foundation for competency building and ongoing excellence. And, if it is made accessible through modern information management systems and/or promulgated through a strong professional development program, it actualizes and distributes intelligence throughout the organization.

The second point is that whether at the team or organizational level, the shared knowledge base must be upgraded and reviewed regularly.

Ranger Dave Anders says of SOPs: "There is no SOP that is written in stone. Any SOP is a living document. . . . As soon as someone comes upon a better way or an easier way or a smarter way, then those SOPs are adjusted." Learning must be ongoing. The fact that something worked well and has been recorded should not close down the learning process or halt the search for even better ways to do things. Learning and creativity are related activities. When a better solution or system is found, the knowledge base should be upgraded. Depending on the nature and importance of those new lessons, they should be transmitted to others immediately or made available for access on an as needed basis. It was noteworthy that during Operation Iraqi Freedom, there was a Central Command Headquarters "lessons learned team"[10] operating in real time parallel to the military operations on the ground and in the air. Rather than wait for the conclusion of hostility, lessons were being processed on an ongoing and immediate basis.

The third point is that learning must be converted to practice. Establishing and maintaining SOPs, continuity files or any other form of a knowledge base is a waste of effort if people do not know about them or do not use them. Every individual on a special team or in an organization should know where to go for the most up-to-date knowledge and procedures. In fact, leaders should make certain that important components of the knowledge base are pushed out to members to assure awareness, and they should further ascertain that members are using the lessons of the past. By ensuring the acquisition, easy access, and free flow of knowledge and information, a team or business unit becomes a true learning organization and derives maximum benefits from its learning.

DEVELOPING THE TALENT POOL

Rangers know that combat is the time to exemplify agility and skill; it is not the optimal time to develop them. Rather, training and rehearsal are the best times to build competencies and foster can-do attitudes. Likewise, the competencies that make for agility and versatility on civilian special teams should be forged well in advance of the intense circumstances they may face. Taking this cue, senior managers should have foresight regarding their organization's future needs for special action teams. Learning from the expertise studies, they should provide prospective team members with myriad opportunities to gain a great deal of diverse and meaningful experience at increasing levels of challenge. They should ensure that prospective team members work to enhance their domain and process skills and sharpen their interpersonal skills on a continuing basis. Such professional development would be an important prologue to participation on high-intensity teams. In addition to more general skill building, individuals and/or teams can also be scheduled for specialized training and rehearsals in order to acquire and develop the specific competencies they may need. And in those cases in which individuals may be designated to work together on some future team that may have to be activated quickly, for example, a crisis or emergency response team, it would be beneficial that they train and rehearse together in their team member roles before they are called into action. This portfolio of advance learning programs will help to ensure that organizations have a pool of talented, knowledgeable individuals who can quickly move into special teams as members and leaders.

We have noted thus far that learning must be ongoing and purposeful. The learning imperative requires that knowledge acquisition and competency building be major functions not only of special action teams, but also of any twenty-first-century organization. Good leadership and regular use of the AAR can help to address these requirements. Learning must also be deep in the form of individual development of expertise and integrated through the fusion of individual knowledge and abilities into team and organizational competencies. Forward-looking professional development programs and well-maintained, shared knowledge bases will help to accomplish these objectives. Now we need to address one more characteristic of contemporary learning: it must be fast.

FAST LEARNING

The reader may recall the case study, Calling Home for Firepower, in which paratroopers on Grenada used their commercial telephone cards to creatively connect with naval fire support. In that case, creative thinking saved the day, but broader learning and adjustments had to wait until the cessation of hostilities. Then the communications compatibility issue was addressed and systems reengineered. Often, however, new lessons and the modifications they call for cannot wait until work is completed. In many cases, a team will have to learn and adjust quickly in order to complete its mission. The following anecdote prompted quicker action:

■ CASE STUDY

KNOCKING NEXT DOOR FOR FIREPOWER

Sid Salomon was leading his Rangers on the breakout from Normandy. They were walking alongside a tank when an enemy sniper started to fire upon them. The tank crew was all buttoned up and unaware of the sniper's fire on the infantrymen. Sid repeatedly attempted to bang on the tank to get the crew's attention, but the thickness of the armor and the noise of movement prevented him from being heard. Finally, although it was dangerous for him, he stepped in front of the tank where he could be seen. He got the crew's attention and pointed to the sniper's location. The tankers quickly directed their guns in that direction and did away with the sniper. The unit proceeded forward.

Although daring, this was not the kind of event the Army wanted to repeat, and the proposed answer was a relatively simple one that could be effected quickly. The Army soon started modifying its tanks by placing a telephone on the tank hull, thus allowing infantry next to tank to talk directly to the tank crew even when the hatches were closed. ■

As is the case with Rangers, for special action teams learning must be fast and to the point. It is not generally the case that a high-stakes team will know or learn everything it needs up front and then implement its planned actions. The reality is that very often it is the concurrent learning that takes place *as* a team is doing its work that spells success. It was noted earlier that data collection and information processing were the responsibility of all team members. The focus there was on the content of a team's work. With our current attention on competency building, we need also to focus on the process of a team's work. Accordingly, one powerful strategy to consider is *action learning.*

Action learning involves two concurrent goals that reflect the two halves of the term. Actions are conducted to achieve a current objective and at the same time purposeful learning is sought in order to build competencies for the future. Action learning is a very purposeful, carefully designed process conducted by and for the people who do the work. It is used to test strategies and tactics and their impacts in realistic or under real-world conditions, rather than in hypothetical laboratory situations.

Ranger units apply a version of action learning while undergoing demanding and highly realistic training against clever opposing forces at the Army's major training centers in Louisiana and California. There "enemy forces" often have the upper hand because they are familiar with the terrain and may be more heavily armed than the Rangers. On other training exercises, however, Ranger planners may themselves go to extraordinary lengths to befuddle their units by building in events, conditions, or obstacles that the units are not expecting.

For special teams, action learning may take a couple of forms. A team may implement a planned course of action in a somewhat experimental mode in order to achieve an objective and gain knowledge at the same time. Although experimental, this does not represent a trial-and-error approach, since work still has to be accomplished. The team would use the best approach that could be designed, and then study its effectiveness as it is implemented. Team members would, in effect, be studying themselves and their impacts as they go about their work. They would pay strong attention to what is going well or what is problematic. With such an approach, learning would be focused on the processes and methods being used, but there may be other focal points as well.

Another way to conduct action learning is to direct efforts primarily to achieving a specific goal. During the progress of the work, however, the team would engage in frequent debriefings, assessments, and learning sessions. These sessions would be conducted both formatively (during the action process) and summatively (after completion of the work). The After Action Review would serve well to provide structure in either situation.

For high-stakes teams, and sometimes for whole organizations, the pace of learning cannot be leisurely, and circumstances do not always allow for lengthy and tranquil study interludes in between action phases. Rather, teams must act, adjust, experiment, and learn simultaneously. By fusing the learning process to work activities, the concept of action learning helps to make knowledge acquisition and competency building ongoing, instrumental aspects of all efforts. Complemented by intense training and ongoing professional development, action learning provides teams and organizations with an important vehicle for accelerating learning.

Developing

This chapter began with the excerpt on Improving from the U.S. Army Leadership Framework. Improving involves Building, Learning, and Developing. We have attended to the objectives of Building and Learning by focusing on individual learning and on the building of team and organizational competencies—all with a view to preparing for a dynamic future. Let us now turn to the objective of Developing, which calls on the leader to invest "adequate time and effort to develop individual subordinates as leaders," [11] and which includes the process of mentoring.

Civilian leaders must often develop a succession plan for someone to take over from them as they retire or prepare to move to another position in the future. Combat leaders face the possibility that "succession" may take place only moments after hostilities begin. Beyond the need for continuity of command in the face of casualties, however, Rangers look to develop broad and deep leadership throughout their ranks. There is recognition that being a Ranger means being willing and able to take on leadership roles as necessary, and Ranger School is, to a great extent, a leadership school. There is, however, a further responsibility to be addressed: good leaders develop other good leaders.

SUPPORTING GROWTH

Superiors should help to structure the professional development of their subordinates to provide them with significant opportunities to acquire and enhance leadership skills. There are a number of approaches that superiors can take in order to accomplish this. The first of these is formal education. In this regard, leaders should encourage/require their subordinates to take advantage of educational and professional development opportunities that address the skill clusters described earlier. In addition to courses and workshops aimed at building domain and process skills, however, leaders should encourage subordinates to engage in learning opportunities focused on the development of interpersonal and leadership skills per se. Beyond structured educational experiences, leaders can also prompt and support less formal connections that promote continual development of skill sets. Casual conversations, mini-lessons during team meetings, and other informal activities can contribute to an atmosphere of learning.

EMPOWERMENT

A second major approach to developing effective followers and younger leaders is through guided and supported experience. Through delegation, job rotation, and special assignments, leaders can provide their high potential subordinates with opportunities to take on responsibility and handle authority. The challenge level for these experiences should be raised commensurate with the individual's ability to move through increasing levels of responsibility at a pace that stretches them without overwhelming them.

Empowerment is the key concept here because two objectives are served at once: subordinates are given the opportunity to develop their leadership ability, and the organization builds capability through decentralized decision making. Accordingly, when subordinates are ready for delegated authority and responsibility, they should be given tasks that are challenging and authentic, and senior leaders should adopt a supportive, but otherwise hands-off, approach. Making a big deal about delegating trivial work and/or standing over the shoulder of subordinates are two ways of killing initiative and motivation, while at the same time stunting professional growth. On the other hand, when delegation and empowerment are handled in an authentic and challenging manner, the motivation and growth of subordinates are spurred, and organizational capability is enhanced.

Competent subordinates will be motivated to excel if they are given meaningful challenges and an understanding of the part they play in the overall mission. They will grow if they feel both supported and trusted. Seniors need to be available to answer questions, provide guidance, arrange resources, and champion efforts, but they should not impose their support on someone who would do fine without them. They should adopt an approach the Army calls "powering down without powering out." They should delegate well, trust and support subordinates, but otherwise stay out of their way. Yes, a superior may need to step in if something is going disastrously wrong or if people are being endangered. But generally, they should view a delegated task as an action learning opportunity for the subordinate and treat it accordingly. Successes should be celebrated; honest mistakes should be tolerated. Both should be the subject of feedback and After Action Reviews.

MENTORING

Beyond promoting study and providing empowered practical experience, leaders can provide subordinates with another very valuable service that can yield substantial long-term benefits: mentoring. *Mentoring* is a one-to-one learning relationship between a seasoned professional and a younger counterpart. Ideally, the two individuals choose each other, but some organizations have adopted programs in which mentors are assigned to work with designated subordinates.

The mentor-protégé relationship is usually conducted somewhat informally. The individuals involved may meet frequently or infrequently; they may speak to each other or correspond in writing. Sometimes, they may meet in what Ranger Mark Meadows calls "fireside councils," casual, yet substantial, discussions of leadership. In any case, the essence of their interaction is the teaching-learning dynamic. The senior person shares experience and offers advice with the intention of accelerating the growth of the protégé. The younger person has an opportunity for deeper learning, personal coaching, and wise counseling. While mentoring cannot replace personal experience, it can help a younger person to learn quicker, handle increasing levels of challenge, and avoid pitfalls.

Mentoring relationships are not solely content oriented; they often facilitate growth in thinking and interpersonal skills as well. Just as a knowledgeable coach can be instrumental in the development of an athlete, a mentor can contribute substantially to the professional and personal growth of a young leader. The value of guidance offered by a mentor can even exceed that of formal learning, as mentoring can enhance the protégé's practical experiences by helping to make them more meaningful.

But the mentor-protégé relationship is not a one-way street. Mentors often feel personal gratification from sharing their life experiences and being in service to another. It is also often the case that at some point roles reverse and the younger person helps the senior to learn new things.

Whether through mentoring, education, encouragement, or empowerment, leaders need to develop the abilities and nurture the character of their subordinates. Maintaining a broad focus, seniors should instruct and guide subordinates in the areas of domain, process, and interpersonal skills, as well as in leadership ability and character development. In doing so, leaders contribute to organizational growth and competency building, as well as to the professional and personal growth of their subordinates. The Army goal relative to this area is to have "leaders of leaders."[12] The result will be what Margaret Wheatley calls "leaderful organizations"—organizations with many people at every level who are willing and able to shoulder leadership responsibility as required.

SUMMARY: THE LEARNING IMPERATIVE

Learning, then, represents an imperative, a mandate of the highest order. This learning imperative applies first to leaders, who must be outstanding examples of continual learning for their teams and organizations. But the imperative must also flow from leaders. Beyond their personal growth, leaders must take responsibility to ensure that team and organizational learning has all the characteristics described above. They must promulgate the need for learning, establish and facilitate learning processes, and require that learning be as much a part of the organization's work as any other task.

Ensuring continual learning is a crucial challenge for every leader, but learning as a process and as a goal must be the responsibility of every individual on the team or in the organization. Team success and organizational survival depend upon that being the case. Learning begins with individuals, who must then share and integrate it so that team and organizational learning can take place. Learning must be ongoing and purposeful; it must be a crucial component of the team or organization's daily work. Given the breadth and speed of change in today's world, learning also must take place at an accelerated pace in order to ensure that competencies are in place before they are needed—and before it is too late.

I made reference above to Margaret Wheatley, the author of *Leadership and the New Science*. I have had the good fortune to learn directly from her. Meg has worked internationally with a great many organizations, including U.S. Army Special Operations. An anecdote of a conversation she had with a special ops leader has especially resonated and stayed with me. In their conversation of why learning was so important to the military, the soldier stated simply: "We'd rather learn than die."[13]

There can be no greater rationale for learning among Rangers and other military units. But the instinct to survive should apply to civilian organizations to no lesser degree. While business or institutional success would seem to be a primary motivation for learning, organizational survival is an even greater one. Survival is at the heart of the learning imperative.

14

Drive On!

U.S. Army Rangers "do the impossible" for a living. Their tradition, principles, and example teach us what we must do if we aspire to take on the toughest and most important challenges.

Form teams from the best individuals. Select people who are knowledgeable and highly competent. Look for individuals who are skillful problem solvers and thoughtful decision makers. Choose those who have dedicated themselves to the ideals and principles of their profession and who are strongly motivated to take on the toughest tasks. Select those who seek to be the best in their field and who recognize that being elite only comes through extra effort and living up to higher standards. Look for individuals who value teamwork and who are willing to invest the effort that it requires. Choose people whose character has been tested and who can be trusted with great responsibility. Assign leaders who respect their followers, who are willing to seek the counsel of subordinates, and who see strength in diversity.

Take on worthy challenges. Match special action teams to missions that are strategically important, that is, to goals that will significantly contribute to the organization's future. Recognize the potential of these teams and use them in situations they are qualified for and that will stretch their abilities rather than waste their efforts.

Ensure unfaltering support from the organization. Provide high-challenge teams with the resources they need. Establish the importance of their mandates within the organization and make certain that others provide them with any assistance that may be required. Ensure that any information that they may require will promptly be made available to them. Allow teams tactical freedom; give them a sense of direction and then stay out of their way. Trust and empower them to make decisions on the spot and on the basis of their best judgment. Be ready to protect and champion their efforts.

Lead by example. Be visionary. Set high standards and expectations. Share the risks, hardships, and work of the team. Put the needs of team members before your own, and value accomplishment more than recognition. Understand that leadership is a function of followership; bring out the best in team members and be worthy of your leadership role. Be courageous. Be steadfast in your commitment to the vision and confident in your manner. Be the best example of the team's values.

Forge high-performing teams. Meld the skills and abilities of team members so that strengths are multiplied and weaknesses are cancelled out. In terms of roles and procedures, get your act together quickly, and then put effort into surpassing expectations. Use buddy systems and action subteams to ensure comprehensive coverage and redundancy. Match assignments to individual capabilities. Ensure free and rapid communication. Create positive synergy by establishing and maintaining interdependent relationships. Respect subordinates, superiors and colleagues; be honest and straightforward with them, and be loyal to them at all times. Care for and support one another. Do more than your share. Learn continuously.

Train and prepare beyond the challenge. Make thoughtful and well-informed decisions. Plan in detail to develop the best operational designs. Rehearse when possible and think ahead always. Maintain a bias for action and a sense of urgency. Be agile—develop and polish competencies well in advance of when they may be needed. Be versatile—expect change and disruption and plan transitions to alternate and follow-up plans. Be responsive—prepare for both crises and opportunities and handle each with calm mind and focused effort.

Accomplish the mission. Ignore people who say that an important goal can't be achieved. Keep the purpose of the mission in mind at times, and do what is necessary to accomplish that purpose. Recognize that a task stops being impossible when you figure out how to do it, develop the required competencies, and have the strength of will to get it done.

Rangers Lead the Way!

Appendix A

The Ranger Creed

R   **Recognizing** that I volunteered as a Ranger, fully knowing the hazards of my chosen profession, I will always endeavor to uphold the prestige, honor, and high esprit de corps of the Rangers.

A   **Acknowledging** the fact that a Ranger is a more elite soldier who arrives at the cutting edge of a battle by land, sea, or air, I accept the fact that as a Ranger, my country expects me to move farther, faster, and fight harder than any other soldier.

N   **Never** shall I fail my comrades. I will always keep myself mentally alert, physically strong, and morally straight and I will shoulder more than my share of the task, whatever it may be, one hundred percent and then some.

G   **Gallantly** will I show the world that I am a specially selected and well-trained soldier. My courtesy to superior officers, neatness of dress, and care of equipment shall set the example for others to follow.

E   **Energetically** will I meet the enemies of my country. I shall defeat them on the field of battle for I am better trained and will fight with all my might. Surrender is not a Ranger word. I will never leave a fallen comrade to fall into the hands of the enemy and under no circumstances will I ever embarrass my country.

R   **Readily** will I display the intestinal fortitude required to fight on to the Ranger objective and complete the mission, though I be the lone survivor.

Appendix B

Standing Orders Rogers' Rangers

1. Don't forget nothin'.
2. Have your musket clean as a whistle, hatchet scoured, sixty rounds powder and ball, and be ready to march at a minute's warning.
3. When you're on the march, act the way you would if you was sneaking up on a deer. See the enemy first.
4. Tell the truth about what you see and what you do. There is an army depending on us for correct information. You can lie all you please when you tell other folks about the Rangers, but don't never lie to a Ranger or officer.
5. Don't never take a chance you don't have to.
6. When we're on the march we march single file, far enough apart so one shot can't go through two men.
7. If we strike swamps, or soft ground, we spread out abreast so it's hard to track us.
8. When we march, we keep moving till dark, so as to give the enemy the least possible chance at us.
9. When we camp, half the party stays awake while the other half sleeps.
10. If we take prisoner, we keep 'em separate till we have had time to examine them, so they can't cook up a story between 'em.
11. Don't ever march home the same way. Take a different route so you won't be ambushed.
12. No matter whether we travel in big parties or little ones, each party has to keep a scout 20 yards ahead, 20 yards on each flank, and 20 yards in the rear so the main body can't be surprised and wiped out.

13. Every night you'll be told where to meet if surrounded by a superior force.

14. Don't sit down to eat without posting sentries.

15. Don't sleep beyond dawn. Dawn's when the French and Indians attack.

16. Don't cross a river by a regular ford.

17. If somebody's trailing you, make a circle, come back onto your own tracks, and ambush the folks that aim to ambush you.

18. Don't stand up when the enemy's coming against you. Kneel down, lie down, hide behind a tree.

19. Let the enemy come till he's almost close enough to touch, then let him have it and jump out and finish him up with your hatchet.

Notes

The primary purpose of this section is to provide a reference of valuable resources that were researched for this book and to point the reader to sources for further study. This section also includes some additional details and explanatory notes. Notes are arranged by chapter.

Chapter 1: **Rangers Lead the Way**

Several sources provided background information that was synthesized in this chapter. Perhaps the most helpful was the voluminous *To Fight with Intrepidity: The Complete History of the U.S. Army Rangers, 1622 to Present* (Pocket Books, 1998). This book by Ranger John D. Lock, is remarkably comprehensive and detailed. John Lock also (surreptitiously) wrote a journal of his days in Ranger School, *The Coveted Black and Gold: A Daily Journey Through the US Army Ranger School Experience* (2001), which is available through Xlibris Corporation). It is remarkable that such a book could be composed under such conditions.

Other helpful books include:

Elite Warriors: 300 Years of America's Best Fighting Troops by Lance Q. Zedric and Michael F. Dilley (Pathfinder Publishing of California, 1996). This book, which also describes other special operations forces, provides an especially good description of early Ranger operations.

U.S. Rangers: From Boot Camp to the Battle Zones by Ian Padden (Bantam, 1985) gives special focus to Ranger operations during World War II and on Grenada.

Ranger: Behind Enemy Lines in Vietnam by Ron Field (Publishing News Limited, 2000) includes many color and black-and-white photographs, as well as several historical illustrations. Its primary focus is on Ranger Long Range Reconnaissance Patrols (LRRPs) in Vietnam.

Rudder's Rangers: The True Story of the 2nd Ranger Battalion D-Day Combat Action was written by Lt. Col. Ronald L. Lane, an Army Airborne Ranger. This book is packed with details and descriptions of the 2nd Battalion's assaults on Pointe-du-Hoc and Pointe de la Percée on June 6, 1944.

Ranger, (U.S. Army Infantry School, Fort Benning, Georgia, 1966) is a small pamphlet that describes Ranger Training for Vietnam-era Rangers. It also includes a brief history of the Rangers.

The Spearheaders (Popular Library, 1960) was written by one of Darby's Rangers, James Altieri. It provides rich detail of the training of the 1st Ranger Battalion under the British Commandos and of that battalion's operations from Africa to Italy.

U.S. Special Forces: Airborne Rangers written by Alan M. Landau et al. (Lowe & B. Hould Publishers, 1999). This book, which includes sections on the Delta Force and Navy SEALS, contains good background information and many photographs.

1. The quotation that opens this chapter is from Lock's *To Fight with Intrepidity* (cited above), p. xv.
2. *Northwest Passage* was written by Kenneth Roberts (Haas Press, 1983).
3. The source of Greene's commendation to Marion is found in *To Fight with Intrepidity*, pp. 182–83.
4. Mosby's combat philosophy is quoted in *To Fight with Intrepidity*, p. 198.
5. Colonel Vaughn's praise of the Rangers is cited in Altieri's *The Spearheaders*, p. 47.
6. The marching cadence also comes from *The Spearheaders*, p. 206.
7. Patton's praise for Darby and his description of Darby's heroics at Gela are recorded in Patton's autobiography, *War as I Knew It* (Houghton Mifflin, 1947) pp. 58–59.
8. The Axis Sally threat is from *The Spearheaders*, p. 191.
9. "Toughest, most desperate and dangerous" is a quote from John Lock in *To Fight with Intrepidity*, p. 268.
10. Omar Bradley's description of Rudder's D-Day mission comes from *To Fight with Intrepidity*, p. 268.
11. The description of the D-Day operations comes primarily from *Rudder's Rangers* (cited above). Additional details came from a personal interview with Sid Salomon, who quickly became the Ranger commander at Pointe de la Percée. For more details on the 2nd Battalion's operations following D-Day, see Salomon's

book *2nd U.S. Ranger Infantry Battalion: Germeter-Vossenach-Hurtgen-Bergstein-Hill 400, Germany* (Birchwood Books, 1991).

12. The famous anecdote of how the Rangers got their unofficial motto is found in many sources, including *To Fight with Intrepidity*, p. 286.

13. For a history of the 1st Special Service Force, see *The Devil's Brigade: The Hell-for-Leather Saga of the Wildest, Toughest Fighting Men of World War II* by Robert H. Adleman and Col. George Walton (Bantam, 1966).

14. See Charles Ogburn Jr.'s *The Marauders* (Crest Books, 1956) for a description of the operations of Merrill's Marauders in Burma.

15. For a dramatic telling of the 6th Battalion's rescue of the Bataan prisoners of war, see Hampton Sides's *Ghost Soldiers: The Forgotten Epic Story of World War II's Most Dramatic Mission* (Doubleday, 2001).

16. "One of the most well conceived . . ." is found in *Elite Warriors* (cited above), p. 152. General MacArthur's description is in *To Fight with Intrepidity*, p. 303.

17. Colonel Puckett's quotation comes from *To Fight with Intrepidity*, p. 316.

18. The Abrahms Charter can be found in *U.S. Army Field Manual 7–85, Ranger Unit Operations* (Headquarters, Department of the Army, 1987), p. F-10.

19. *Black Hawk Down: A Story of Modern War* by Mark Bowden (Atlantic Monthly Press, 1999) provides a vivid and detailed description of the Battle of Mogadishu.

20. Information on the Rangers' airborne assault on Kandahar can be found in *Time*, October 29, 2001.

21. Ranger actions in Operation Iraqi Freedom were reported on Savannahnow.com, the website of *Savannah Morning News*, April 29, 2003.

22. Information on the rescue of Pfc. Lynch can be found in *USA TODAY*, April 2, 2003.

Chapter 2: **Move Farther, Faster, Fight Harder**

1. The Ranger Creed, which is quoted in parts throughout the book can be found in the *Ranger Handbook* (Ranger Training Brigade, U.S. Army Infantry School, Fort Benning, GA, 2000), p. i. See Appendix A for the entire Creed.

2. For detailed information on Lockheed's Skunk Works, see *Skunk Works: A Personal Memoir of My Years at Lockheed* by Ben R. Rich and Leo Janus (Little, Brown & Co., 1994).

3. For information on the birth of the Macintosh, see *Apple Confidential: The Real Story of Apple Computer, Inc.* by Owen W. Linzmayer (No Starch Press, 1999).

4. The information on the two Taurus projects comes from *Car: A Drama of the American Workplace* by Mary Walton (W. W. Norton, 1997).

5. Rogers' Standing Orders can be found in the *Ranger Handbook*, (Ranger Training Brigade, U.S. Army Infantry School, Fort Benning, Georgia, 2000), p. ii. For interesting historical notes and the original set of twenty-eight orders, see Appendices B and C in Lock's *To Fight with Intrepidity*, pp. 571–78.

6. The Principles of War and related operational tenets are described throughout the book and are treated in depth in chapter 7. The primary source for these principles is *U.S. Army Field Manual 3–0, Operations* (Headquarters, Department of the Army, 2001).

Chapter 3: **Don't Forget Nothin'**

1. This running cadence and others can be found in *Run to Cadence: U.S. Army Rangers, Run to Cadence: U.S. Army Airborne Rangers* and *Run to Cadence: U.S. Army Airborne Rangers, Vol. 2*, produced by Documentary Recordings in 1984, 1986 and 1996.

2. The anecdote regarding the Navy reservist/geologist can be found in *Time*, March 11, 2002.

3. The story of the mine rescue, "The Man Behind the Miracle," was posted on CNN's website on July 28, 2002, and can be found at http://pittsburgh.about.com/ gi/dynamic/offsite.htm?site=http://www.cnn.com/2002/US/07/28/mine. turning.point/index.html.

4. Some good references on both offensive decision making and avoiding cognitive biases include Jonathan Baron's *Thinking and Deciding* (Cambridge University Press, 1988); J. Edward Russo and Paul J. H. Schoemaker's *Winning Decisions: Getting It Right the First Time* (Currency Doubleday, 2001); and Max Bazerman's *Judgment in Managerial Decision Making, 3rd Edition* (John Wiley & Sons,1994). Books that put the spotlight on what could go wrong with thinking include *Decision Traps: The Ten Barriers to Brilliant Decision-Making and How to Overcome Them* by J. Edward Russo and Paul J. H. Schoemaker (Fireside, 1990); *How We Know What Isn't So: The Fallibility of Human Reason in Everyday Life* by Thomas Gilovich (Free Press, 1991); *Inevitable Illusions: How Mistakes of Reason Rule Our Minds* by Massimo Piattelli-Palmarini, (John Wiley & Sons, 1994); *How to Think about Weird Things: Critical Thinking for a New Age, 2nd Edition, by* Theodore Schick Jr. and Lewis Vaughn (Mayfield Publishing, 1999); and *Judgment Under Uncertainty: Heuristics and Biases* edited by Daniel Kahneman, Paul Slovic, and Amos Tversky (Cambridge University Press, 1982).

5. Foundational references on emotional intelligence include *Emotional Intelligence* by Daniel Goleman (Bantam Books,1997), and *Multiple Intelligences: The Theory in Practice* by Howard E. Gardner (Basic Books, 1993). Goleman with Annie

McKee and Richard E. Boyatzis followed up with a related volume, *Primal Leadership: Realizing the Power of Emotional Intelligence* (Harvard Business School Press, 2002).

6. A scholarly book on new perspectives of cognition is *The Tree of Knowledge: The Biological Roots of Human Understanding* by Humberto R. Maturana and Francisco J. Varela (Shambhala Publications, 1998).

Chapter 4: **Be the Best**

1. One source for this formula for motivation is "Synthesis of Research on Strategies for Motivating Students to Learn," by Jere Brophy, *Educational Leadership,* October 1987.

2. One of the best treatments regarding types of motivation and their effects on productivity can be found in Teresa Amabile's *The Social Psychology of Creativity* (Springer Verlag, 1983). See also her *Creativity in Context: Update to the Social Psychology of Creativity* (Westview Press, 1996).

3. The source for the Ranger Imprint is *U.S. Army Manual 21–50, Ranger Training and Ranger Operations* (Headquarters, Department of the Army, 1962), p. 4.

4. The feel of Ranger School comes from my personal experience. And while no verbal description will begin to convey the demands and hardships of Ranger School to a non-Ranger, some good descriptions can be found in Alan and Frieda Landau's *Airborne Rangers* and John Lock's personal journal, *The Coveted Black and Gold* (both cited above).

Chapter 5: **Select the Best**

1. Information on Ned Herrmann's Whole Brain Model can be found in his books, *The Creative Brain* (Brain Books, 1989) and *The Whole Brain Business Book: Unlocking The Power of Whole Brain Thinking in Organizations and Individuals* (McGraw-Hill, 1996). See also Dorothy Leonard's and Susaan (sic) Straus's article "Putting Your Company's Whole Brain to Work" in *Harvard Business Review,* July–August, 1997, pp. 111–21.

2. For more on intrinsic motivation, see the Amabile works cited above.

Chapter 6: **Forge the Team**

1. Details about the principle of Objective can be found in *U.S. Army Field Manual 3–0, Operations,* p. 4-12.

2. The research on agenda setting and tactical freedom for teams can be found in Teresa M. Amabile and Stanley S. Gryskiewicz, *Creativity in the R&D Laboratory* (Center for Creative Leadership, 1987).

3. The Ranger Creed can be found in Appendix A. As noted earlier, the source of the Creed is the *Ranger Handbook*, p. i.

4. Tuckman's model as well as other models of team cycles can be found in *Pfeiffer and Company Library of Theories and Models, Vol. 25, Group* (Pfeiffer, 1995).

5. The quotation from Senator Smith is from *U.S. Army Field Manual 22–100, Army Leadership: Be, Know, Do* p. 2-19.

6. Details about the principle of Unity of Command can be found in *U.S. Army Field Manual 3–0, Operations*, p. 4-14.

Chapter 7: **Be Agile, Versatile, and Responsive**

Descriptions and details regarding the Principles of War outlined in this chapter can be found in *U.S. Army Field Manual 3–0, Operations*, p. 4-12–4-15. Details on the tenets of initiative, agility and versatility can be found in *U.S. Army Field Manual 3–0*, pp. 4-15–4-18.

1. Theodore Roosevelt's quotation is from *U.S. Army Field Manual 22–100, Army Leadership: Be, Know, Do* p. 7-6.

2. Nordstrom's quality of service, management philosophy, and innovative approaches are described in Tom Peters's *Thriving on Chaos: Handbook for a Management Revolution* (Knopf, 1988).

3. The U.S. Army's perspectives on initiative, decentralized decision making, and mission-type orders can be found in *U.S. Army Field Manual 3–0, Operations*, pp. 4-15–4-16.

4. The research on keeping a tight focus on organizational strength is found in Jim Collins's *Good to Great* (HarperBusiness, 2001). Collins refers to the approach as the Hedgehog Concept.

5. For an interesting article on maneuver applied to business, see "Maneuver Warfare: Can Modern Military Strategy Lead You to Victory?" by Eric K. Clemons and Jason A. Santamaria in *Harvard Business Review*, April 2002, pp. 57–65.

6. The account of this "Battle in the Cola Wars" can be found in *Odyssey* by John Sculley with John A. Byrne (Harper & Row, 1987), pp. 30–31.

7. I am indebted to Col. Kurt Fuller, who provided details of the ingenuity displayed at Port Salines in a personal interview on April 25, 2003. Colonel Fuller made the combat assault on that airfield with the 2nd Ranger Battalion.

8. The account of the Apollo 13 accident came from a personal conversation with Edgar Mitchell on April 21, 1995. There is also a description of the incident in his book with Dwight Williams, *The Way of the Explorer* (Putnam, 1996), pp. 35–39.

9. The source for the Grenada case study is *U.S. Army Field Manual 3–0, Operations*, p. 5-13.

10. The source for the information on the Battle of Germantown was a commemorative article by Michael Schaffer in *The Philadelphia Inquirer*, September 29, 2002.

11. The definitions of agility and versatility can be found in *U.S. Army Field Manual 3–0, Operations*, pp. 4-16–4-17.

Chapter 8: **Create Positive Synergy**

1. For a comprehensive treatment of feedback, including James Watt's centrifugal governor, see George P. Richardson's *Feedback Thought in Social Science and Systems Theory*, (Pegasus Communications, 1999).

2. An interesting history of cybernetics and its relevance to the mind and systems thinking can be found in Fritjof Capra's *The Web of Life: A New Scientific Understanding of Living Systems* (Anchor Books, 1996).

3. For more on Chris Argyris's perspective, see "Good Communication that Blocks Learning," *Harvard Business Review*, November 15, 2000.

Chapter 9: **Be, Know, Do**

The chief military reference for this chapter is *U.S. Army Field Manual 22–100, Army Leadership: Be, Know, Do* (Headquarters, Department of the Army, 1999).

1. General Meyer's quotation comes *U.S. Army Field Manual 22–100, Army Leadership: Be, Know, Do*, p. 1-2.

2. The story of Sid Salomon's actions on D-Day comes from *Rudder's Rangers* and a personal interview with Mr. Salomon.

3. A full description of U.S. Army values can be found in *U.S. Army Field Manual 22–100, Army Leadership: Be, Know, Do*, pp. 2-2–2-10.

4. I am indebted to Steve Jacobs for the concept of Personal Weirdness Factor.

5. The quotation "Developing the right values . . ." is found in *U.S. Army Field Manual 22–100, Army Leadership: Be, Know, Do*, p. 2–26.

6. Field Marshall von Moltke's version of Murphy's Law comes from *The Coveted Black and Gold* (cited above), p. 159.

7. General Marshall's quotation comes from *The Coveted Black and Gold*, p. 61.

8. The U.S. Army's definition of audacity is in *U.S. Army Field Manual 3–0, Operations*, p. 7-6.

9. Napoleon's quotation can be found in *The Coveted Black and Gold*, p. 140.

10. *The Coveted Black and Gold*, p. 175, was the source for General Lee's quotation.

11. The U.S. Army's perspective on taking care of the troops is stated in *U.S. Army Field Manual 22–100, Army Leadership: Be, Know, Do*, pp. 3-1–3-5.

12. For a biographical sketch of Dick Meadows, see "A Special Warrior's Last Patrol" by Maj. John Plaster at http://teamhouse.tni.net/lastpatrol.html.

13. The Taoist excerpt comes from *Tao Te Ching*, Lao Tsu, translation by Gia-Fu Feng and Jane English (Vintage, 1972).

14. See *Good to Great* (cited above).

Chapter 10: **Visualize, Describe, Direct**

1. The introductory quotation is from *U.S. Army Field Manual 3–0*, pp. 5-1–5-2.

2. For the military descriptions of the Visualize, Describe, Direct process, see *U.S. Army Field Manual 3–0, Operations*, pp. 5-1–5-18.

3. Von Moltke's quotation can also be found in *U.S. Army Field Manual 3–0, Operations* p. 6-3.

4. I am grateful to Col. Kurt Fuller for information on the raid at H3. Colonel Fuller led that raid as the company commander of B Company, 1st Ranger Battalion.

5. For information on the Military Decision Making Process at different levels, see chapter 2 of *U.S. Army Field Manual 7–20, The Infantry Battalion* (Headquarters, Department of the Army, 1992); chapter 2 of *U.S. Army Field Manual 7–10, The Infantry Rifle Company* (Headquarters, Department of the Army, 1990); or chapter 2 of the *Ranger Handbook* (cited above).

6. The excerpt is from *U.S. Army Field Manual 3–0, Operations*, p. 6-1.

7. The excerpt on planning can be found on p. 6-2 of *U.S. Army Field Manual 3–0, Operations*.

8. The description of Intelligence comes from *U.S. Army Field Manual 101–5–1, Operational Terms and Graphics* (Headquarters, Department of the Army, United States Marine Corps, 1997), pp. 1-83–1-84.

9. The information on cola research can be found in Cynthia Crossen's *Tainted Truth: The Manipulation of Fact in America* (Simon & Schuster, 1994).

10. The excerpt on Information Superiority can be found in *U.S. Army Field Manual 3–0, Operations* p. 11-2. Chapter 11 of this field manual serves as a good general resource for the military concept of information superiority.

11. The concepts of critical information requirements and Commander's Critical Information Requirements can be found in *U.S. Army Field Manual 101–5, Staff Organization and Operations* (Headquarters, Department of the Army, 1997) and *U.S. Army Field Manual 3–0, Operations*, pp. 11-13–11-14.

12. The excerpt on Intelligence Preparation of the Battlefield comes from *U.S. Army Field Manual 7–20, The Infantry Battalion*, p. 2-25.

13. The statement regarding the individual soldier's involvement in intelligence preparation can be found in *U.S. Army Field Manual 34–1, Intelligence and Electronic Warfare Operations* (Headquarters, Department of the Army, 1994).

14. Thomas Kuhn's famous work is *The Structure of Scientific Thinking, 2nd Edition,* (University of Chicago Press, 1970).

15. The "Too-Hot Fire" comes from Gary Klein, *Sources of Power: How People Make Decisions* (MIT Press, 1998), p. 32.

16. The information on the tracks in the mud and graffiti episodes comes from Col. Kurt Fuller who was serving with the units involved at the time these incidents took place.

17. For an interesting article on weak signals and the secondary source of the National Intelligence Council excerpt, see "Weak Signals: Detecting the Next Big Thing" by S. Dyer Harris and Steven Zeisler in *The Futurist*, November–December 2002, pp. 21–28. I originally learned of the Enron information from Mr. Zeisler's presentation at the 2002 World Future Society conference. His source article was "The Fall of Enron: Media Missed Clues to Enron's Troubles," by David Shaw, January 26, 2002, available at www.mediaforesight.org/LAT_enron.htm.

18. The first quotation on the leader's recon comes from the 1992 edition of the *Ranger Handbook,* p. 2-10. The second quotation can be found in the 2000 edition of that handbook on p. 5-1.

19. Rogers' Standing Orders can be found in the *Ranger Handbook,* p. ii. The quotation from General Patton comes from *U.S. Army Field Manual 3–0, Operations* p. 11-10.

20. My memory is not definite that the call sign for the observation plane on this particular night was Dark Delta, but Dark Delta was a call sign for such flights. For a similar anecdote, see *Once a Warrior King: Memories of An Officer in Vietnam* by David Donovan (Ballantine, 1985). This memoir was written by a fellow member of Advisory Team 84 and covers approximately the same time period as my service on that team.

Chapter 11: **Be Prepared for Anything**

1. The source of Rogers' Standing Orders is the *Ranger Handbook,* p. ii.

2. Two important resources for this introductory information on risk, including the sources of organizational risk are *Managing Risk: Critical Issues for Survival and Success into the 21st Century*, Alan Waring and A. Ian Glendon (International

Thomson Business Press, 1998) and *Root Cause Analysis: A Tool for Total Quality*, Paul F. Wilson, et al. (American Society for Quality, 1993).

3. General Patton's quotation comes from *U.S. Army Field Manual 3–0, Operations*, p. 6-3.

4. The excerpts on rehearsals come from *U.S. Army Field Manual 7–20, The Infantry Battalion*, p. 2-24.

5. The General Motors assumptions can be found in Russo and Schoemaker's *Winning Decisions: Getting It Right the First Time* (Currency, 2001), p. 42. Royal Dutch/Shell's approach is described in Peter Senge's *The Fifth Discipline* (Currency/Doubleday, 1994), pp. 179–81.

6. Good resources on scenario development include *The Fifth Discipline Fieldbook: Strategies and Tools for Building a Learning Organization* by Peter Senge et al. (Currency/Doubleday, 1994); *The Art of the Long View* by Peter Schwartz (Currency/Doubleday, 1999); and "Scenarios: Uncharted Waters Ahead" by Peter Wack in *Harvard Business Review*, September–October 1985.

7. Two good sources on prevention planning and barrier analysis are Wilson et al., *Root Cause Analysis* (cited above), and Charles H. Kepner and Benjamin B. Tregoe's *The New Rational Manger* (Princeton Research Press, 1981).

8. The excerpt is from *U.S. Army Field Manual 3–0, Operations*, pp. 6-1–6-2.

9. Source information on branches and sequels can be found in *U.S. Army Field Manual 3–0, Operations*, p. 6-5.

10. The excerpt is from *U.S. Army Field Manual 3–0, Operations*, p. 6-3.

11. One source for the People Express case study is Peter Senge's *The Fifth Discipline* (cited above), p. 131.

Chapter 12: **Accomplish the Mission**

1. For the heraldic grant of arms to the 75th Ranger Regiment, see *Airborne Rangers* (cited above), p. 89.

2. For information on the Swiss watch case study, see Joel Barker's *Paradigms: The Business of Discovering the Future* (HarperBusiness, 1993) pp. 15–18.

3. Information on the discovery that led to Scotchgard can be found on the 3M website, www.3m.com. Information on the invention of Post-it Notes can also be found at that site.

4. For information on the Commander's Intent, see *U.S. Army Field Manual 3–0, Operations* p. 5-14 and *U.S. Army Field Manual 101–5–1*, p. 1-34.

5. The excerpt is from *U.S. Army Field Manual 3–0, Operations*, p. 6-5. General Patton's quote comes from *U.S. Army Field Manual 22–100, Army Leadership: Be, Know, Do*, p. 6-23.

6. The source for "Initiative at Normandy" is *U.S. Army Field Manual 22–100, Army Leadership: Be, Know, Do,* pp. 1-16–1-17.

7. The reference for the Taurus anecdote is *Car: A Drama of the American Workplace* by Mary Walton (cited above).

8. Sources used for the Tylenol case study include: the Johnson & Johnson web site (www.jnj.com); *Robert Wood Johnson: The Gentleman Rebel* by Lawrence Foster (Lillian Press, 1999); and the corporate social responsibility page at mallenbaker.net.

9. The information on Malden Mills came from a *60 Minutes* report that aired on July 6, 2003 on CBS. The remarkable treatment given to SAS employees was described in a *60 Minutes* report that originally aired on CBS on October 13, 2002. Information on the role of values at Ben & Jerry's and The Body Shop can be found in *Ben & Jerry's Double Dip: Lead with Your Values and Make Money, Too* by Ben Cohen and Jerry Greenfield (Fireside, 1998).

10. For information on Nicholas Leeson's impact on Barings, see *Time*, March 13, 1995.

Chapter 13: **Learn Like Crazy**

1. The excerpt that introduces this chapter is found in *U.S. Army Field Manual 22–100, Army Leadership: Be, Know, Do,* p. 2-28.

2. The concept of structured imagination accounts for these examples. It is discussed in chapter 6 of *Creative Cognition: Theory, Research, and Applications,* by Ronald A. Finke, Thomas B. Ward and Steven M. Smith (MIT Press, 1992).

3. Transformation theory is described in George Land's *Grow or Die: The Unifying Principle of Transformation* (John Wiley & Sons, 1986).

4. For an article that provides background on the AAR and its potential for adoption by civilian organizations, see "After Action Review: Linking Reflection and Planning in a Learning Practice" by Marilyn J. Darling and Charles S. Parry in *Reflections: The SoL Journal,* Winter 2001, pp. 64–72.

5. For research and theory on the development of expertise, see *Toward a General Theory of Expertise: Prospects and Limits,* edited by K. Anders Ericsson and Jacqui Smith (Cambridge University Press, 1991); and *Surpassing Ourselves: An Inquiry into the Nature and Implications of Expertise* by Carl Bereiter and Marlene Scardamalia (Open Court, 1993).

6. For information on progressive problem solving, see Ericsson and Smith, *Surpassing Ourselves* (cited above).

7. The source of Dewar's thoughts on dumb mistakes is *Reinventing Strategy: Using Strategic Learning to Create & Sustain Breakthrough Performance* by Willie Pietersen (John Wiley & Sons, 2002), pp. 178–79.

8. Information on Trudy Elion can be found in *The Greatest Generation* by Tom Brokaw (Random House, 1998).

9. The concept of automaticity is addressed in *Surpassing Ourselves*, pp. 114 and 145. Helpful sources on naturalistic decision making include: *Decision Making in Action: Models and Methods*, edited by Gary Klein, et al. (Ablex Publishing Corporation, 1993); *Linking Expertise and Naturalistic Decision Making*, edited by Eduardo Salas and Gary Klein (Lawrence Erlbaum Associates, 2001); and Gary Klein's *Sources of Power: How People Make Decisions* (MIT Press, 1998).

10. The information on the lessons learned teams was presented by U.S. Secretary of Defense Donald Rumsfeld in a news conference on April 15, 2003.

11. The quotation on Developing comes from *U.S. Army Field Manual 22–100, Army Leadership: Be, Know, Do*, p. 2-28.

12. The phrase "leaders of leaders" is found in *U.S. Army Field Manual 22–100, Army Leadership: Be, Know, Do*, p. 1-13.

13. Margaret Wheatley's primary work is *Leadership and the New Science: Discovering Order in a Chaotic World, 2nd Edition* (Berrett-Koehler, 1999). In addition to her written works, I have enjoyed the benefit of studying directly with her in her seminars at Sundance, Utah, and the Albert Einstein Medical Center's Cape Cod Institute. The anecdote of the special operations soldier's response came from a Cape Cod seminar in August 1996.

Index

Abrams, Gen. Creighton, 25
Abu Abbas, 31
Achille Lauro hijacking, 31
action learning, 267–68
action plan, 188
action points, 227
adjunct team members, 70
advisors, role of, 88–90
Afghanistan, 5, 30, 46, 53, 93, 263
After Action Review (AAR), 253–56, 266, 268
agility, 99, 103, 127, 190, 242
Aidid, Mohamed Farrah, 28, 29
Air Force PJs (Parajumpers), 29, 56
al-Qaeda, 30, 46, 93, 203
American Creativity Association (ACA), 162
Anders, Lt. Col. Dave, 92, 103, 216
    on accomplishing missions, 231
    contingency planning and, 227, 228–29
    on Standard Operation Procedures (SOPs), 265
    on thinking skills, 257
Apollo 13 rescue, 118–19, 127
approval plan, 189
Argyris, Chris, 140
Art of Command, 185
Arthur Anderson accounting firm, 151, 202
assumptions, 220–24
astronaut crews, 33, 118–19, 194

automaticity, 264
avoidance behavior, 139
Axis Sally, 15

barrier analysis, 225
Bataan Death March, 20
Begun, Joseph, 260
behavior, norms of, 80, 81
being, leadership and, 148–53
Bemis Heights, Battle of, 11
Ben & Jerry's, 247
Biêt-Dông-Quân (BDQ), 24
"Black Death," 15
Body Shop, The, 247
Bradley, Gen. Omar, 17
branches, 226–30, 263
British Commandos, 13, 14
budget allocations, 43
bureaucracy, 34, 103, 112
Burgoyne, General, 11
Bush, George H. W., 28
business intelligence, 192

C-rations, 4
Cambodia, 199
Camden, Battle of (Revolutionary War), 12
Camp Carson (Colorado), 23
catastrophic failure/success, 228–29
chains of command, 87–88
Challenger space shuttle, 194
chaos, 116, 118–19, 172, 232
chaos theory, 247
character, 55–59, 61, 73, 148–49
Chrysler Corporation, 150–51
Church, Capt. Benjamin, 10, 24
Churchill, Winston, 149
Civil War, 12, 115
Clinton, Bill, 29, 150
Coca-Cola, 107–8, 193–94

Cold War, 33, 251
Collins, Jim, 178
command, unity of, 38, 87–91, 109–10, 112
commander's (CEO's) intent, 78, 232, 236–41
commitment, 60
communication, 51, 109, 122, 123, 128, 130
    ambiguous, 140
    influence and, 164–66
    information flow, 132–34
communities of practice, 44
competitive intelligence, 190
complacency, 101, 251
computers, 132, 217
confidence, 55
confidentiality agreements, 111, 112
consensus, 81
contingency planning, 227–28, 231
Cornwallis, General, 11
Cota, Brig. Gen. Norman D., 18
courage, 3, 6, 56–57
courses of action (COAs), 186–87
Cowpens, Battle of (Revolutionary War), 11
creativity, 111, 117–19, 121
    leadership and, 156, 157
    Personal Weirdness Factor (PWF) and, 155
    reciprocity and, 262
critical information requirements (CIR), 195–96
Croix de Guerre (French medal), 19
Crossen, Cynthia, 193

Darby, Maj. William Orlando, 13–16
debriefings, 258
decision making, 78, 81, 170, 182–87. *See also*
    planning
    decentralized, 102–5, 232, 241–42
    decision trees, 227–28
    extended, 224–30
    learning and, 257
    naturalistic, 264

   rehearsal and, 215–17
   storming and, 83
defensive thinking, 211
Delta Force, 25, 29, 54, 92, 176
description, leaders and, 180–81
Desert One, 26
Devil's Brigade, 19
Dewar, Bob, 260
dialogue sessions, 165
differences, understanding and valuing, 52–53
direction, leaders and, 181–82
discipline, 57, 185
disruption, of adversaries, 116
Distinguished Service Cross, 15, 22
diversity, 69
domain skills, 42–47, 68–70, 257
Downing, Wayne, 176

economy of force, 38, 109
Edison, Thomas A., 169
Eglin Air Force Base (Florida), 4, 23, 62
egos, dealing with, 90–91, 140
82nd Airborne Division, 49, 88, 99, 174, 253
   in Grenada, 27, 118, 122
   in Korea, 21
   in Vietnam, 23
   in World War II, 237
Eisenhower, Dwight D., 14, 15, 182, 184, 230
Elion, Gertrude, 260–61
elitism, 125–26
emotional intelligence, 50
empathy, 174
empowerment, 124, 147, 270
Enron Corporation, 151–52, 201–2
estimate of situation, 186, 190–91, 218
excellence, 58
expertise building, 44, 256, 262
external security, 110–11
extrinsic motivation, 59, 166

failure, learning from, 259–61
Federal Bureau of Investigation (FBI), 33, 104, 171, 205, 218, 240
feedback, 84, 134–42
firefighting teams, 33
First Special Service Force (FSSF), 19
Fleming, Alexander, 197
focus group reports, 89
Ford Taurus, 33, 238–39
Fort Benning (Georgia), 4, 23, 62
Fort Bragg (North Carolina), 88, 122, 176
French and Indian War, 10
Fry, Art, 235
Fuller, Capt. Kurt, 184, 220, 227, 253–54
Fuller, R. Buckminster, 260

Gandhi, Mahatma, 149, 169
General Motors, 221–22
General Systems, 242
generalists, 96
Germantown, Battle of (Revolutionary War), 122–23
ghost conflicts, 87
"ghost soldiers," rescue of, 20–21
Gibbons, Capt. Sam, 237
Giuliani, Rudy, 115
Good to Eat (Collins), 178
Gordon, Gary, 30
Gorsky, Alex, 57, 124–25, 148, 169, 179, 245–46
gossip, 132
Green Berets, 88, 176, 199, 209
Greene, Gen. Nathanel, 12, 123
Grenada, 5, 26–27, 117, 121–22, 127, 220, 254. *See also*
    Operation Urgent Fury (Grenada)
  creative thinking in, 266
Grow or Die! (Land), 252
growth, 43–44, 269

Haise, Fred, 118
Hamilton, Alexander, 123
hardships, shared, 84–85

heroes, 148
Herrmann, Ned, 71
hindsight bias, 202
Honda, Soichiro, 260
honor, 58–59
"Hoo-ah Schools," 56
Hostage Rescue Team (FBI), 33
Howe, Gen. William, 123
Huhn, Sgt. Jack, 17
humor, connection and, 79
Hyena Pack, 85–87

Iacocca, Lee, 150–51, 152, 164
identity, of teams, 78, 80
inclusion, of team members, 79–80
information flow, 132–34, 242–43
information superiority, 194–95, 208
inspection teams, 225
intellectual property, 110
intelligence gathering, 108, 133, 134, 192–210. *See also*
    reconnaissance
  flexibility and, 226
  multiple minds and, 203–5
  weak signals, 197–203
internal security, 111–12
Internet, 192
interpersonal norms, 81–82
interpersonal skills, 50–53, 61, 72–73, 104, 154
intrinsic motivation, 59, 74, 166, 243, 262
Invention/Discovery (I/D) teams, 120–21, 127, 155, 195,
    228, 233
Iranian hostage crisis, 26, 176
Iraq, 31, 93, 119, 183–84. See also Operation Desert Storm;
    Operation Iraqi Freedom; Persian Gulf War

Janssen Pharmaceutica, 57, 124, 179, 245–46
jigsaw approach, 95–96
job rotations, 43
John F. Kennedy Special Warfare Center (SWC), 88, 89, 198

Johnson & Johnson, 245–46
Joint Antiterrorism Task Force, 33
Joint Readiness Training Center (Louisiana),
    253, 259
Jones, Bill, 23
Juntune, Joyce, 161–63

kickoff activities, 79–80
King, Martin Luther, Jr., 169
King Philip's War, 10
Klein, Gary, 200
knowing, leadership and, 153–63
Korean Conflict, 21–23, 125, 263
Kosovo, 201, 216, 220
Krueger, Lt. Gen. Walter, 20
Kuhn, Thomas, 197, 198
Kuwait, 183, 229

labor, division of, 109
Land, George, 252
Landgraff, Dick, 239
Lay, Kenneth, 151, 152
leadership, 3, 6, 38, 45, 60, 128
    attitude of, 168–73
    bias for action and, 169–70
    calm voice of, 171, 172–73
    catastrophe and, 115
    by example, 274
    information flow and, 243
    interpersonal skills and, 73
    knowing the team, 159–60
    leader as first among equals, 177–78
    learning and, 256
    principles of, 36
    Ranger training and, 63
    team formation and, 79, 81
    three dimensions of, 147–48
    trust and, 93
learning, 38, 69, 95, 96, 249–50, 272

fast, 266–68
integrated, 256–66
ongoing, 251–56
Lee, Gen. Robert E., 171
Leeson, Nicholas, 248
Legion of Honor (French medal), 149
light teams, 34–36
Lincoln, Abraham, 149
Littrell, Sfc. Gary, 24
Lock, Maj. John D., 9
Lockheed Martin, 32–33, 126
Lomell, Sgt. Leonard, 17
Long, Bob, 47
long-distance operations, 11
Long Range Reconnaissance Patrol (LRRP), 23–24
Long Range Surveillance Unit (LRSU), 3
Lovell, James, 118
Lynch, Pfc. Jessica, 31, 93, 103, 214

MacArthur, Gen. Douglas, 21
Macintosh (Apple) computer, 33, 126
majority rule, 81
Malden Mills, 246
maneuver, 38, 106–8, 226
Marion, Brig. Gen. Francis, 11–12
Marshall, Gen. George C., 14, 23, 169
mass, 38, 105–6
McNeil Pharmaceuticals, 45, 206–7, 246
Meadows, Lt. Col. Mark, 69, 159, 168, 176, 217–18
   on After Action Review (AAR), 253
   on mentoring, 271
   on problem solving, 258
   on Standard Operation Procedures (SOPs), 263, 264
   on value of mistakes, 259–60
Meadows, Maj. Richard "Dick," 176
medical trauma units, 33, 69, 94
membership changes, 96–98
mentoring, 270–71
Merrill, Brig. Gen. Frank D., 19

Merrill's Marauders, 19–20, 21, 24
metacognitive strategies, 187
METT-T Anaylsis, 191
Meyer, Gen. Edward C., 147
micromanagement, 103, 104, 177
Military Decision Making Process (MDMP),
    186, 258
mine collapse (Pennsylvania, 2002), 46–47
mission, 75, 77, 95
    accomplishment of, 231, 274
    change in, 227
    checklist for success, 142–43
    clarity of, 130, 232–36, 241
    clear statement of, 78
    leader's knowledge of, 161–63
    rapid deployment and, 100
mission-type orders, 77
Mitchell, Edgar, 118–19
Mogadishu (Somalia), 28–30, 92
Moltke, Field Marshall Helmuth von, 164, 182
morale, 160
Morgan, Capt. Daniel, 11
Mosby, John Singleton, 12–13
motivation, 38, 59–63, 124
    influence and, 166–68
    micromanagement and, 17
    positive feedback as, 137
Mucci, Lt. Col. Henry "Hank," 20

Napoleon Bonaparte, 170
Navy SEALs, 29, 31, 56, 93
negative feedback, 136, 137
niche talent, 45
Night Stalkers, 29, 30
noncommissioned officers (NCOs), 23, 126, 131
Nordstrom department store, 104–5
Noriega, Manuel, 27
norming phase, 83, 243
Northwest Passage, 10, 11

objectives, 38, 100–101
offensives, 38, 101–5, 170, 211
101st Airborne Division, 237
Operation Anaconda (Afghanistan), 30
Operation Anvil (WWII), 19
Operation Avalance (WWII), 15–16
Operation Desert Storm, 28, 183–84, 216, 220, 240, 259.
    See also Persian Gulf War
Operation Enduring Freedom (Afghanistan), 30, 93
Operation Husky (WWII), 15
Operation Iraqi Freedom, 31, 103, 123, 199, 214
  Iraqi soldiers' defeat in, 240
  Standard Operation Procedures (SOPs) in, 263, 265
Operation Just Cause (Panama), 27–28, 214, 254, 259, 263.
    See also Panama
Operation Overlord (WWII), 16–18
Operation Torch (WWII), 15
Operation Urgent Fury (Grenada), 26–27, 117, 254.
    See also Grenada
operational checklists, 225
organizational values, 243–48
overconfidence, 231
ownership, shared, 91–92

Panagakos, Nick, 104, 171, 193, 205, 240
Panama, 5, 27–28, 214, 216, 220, 254. *See also* Operation
    Just Cause (Panama)
paratroopers, 21, 166, 237
Patton, Gen. George, 15, 208, 214, 236, 259
peak performance, 7
People Express Airlines, 229–30
Pepsi-Cola, 107–8, 193–94
perfectionists, 58
performance reviews, 88
performing phase, 83
Persian Gulf War, 5, 28, 183–84. *See also* Operation Desert Storm
  "catastrophic success" of, 229, 230
  Standard Operation Procedures (SOPs) in, 263
persistence, 56

personal responsibility, 60

Personal Weirdness Factor (PWF), 155, 156

planning, 182, 232, 257. *See also* decision making
  development of decision process, 214–24
  situation analysis and, 190–91
  turning decisions into action, 188–89
  understanding situations, 190–214

playbook, decision making and, 227

Pollock, David, 22

positive feedback, 137–38

precaution/opportunity protocols, 224–25

Presidential Unit Citation, 19, 21

prevention planning, 225, 227

Price, Capt. Robert, 20

Principles of War (U.S. Army), 37–38

problem formulation, 85–86

problem solving, 257, 258–59

process leaders, 88, 90, 91

process norms, 81, 82

process plans, 186–87, 187

process skills, 47–50, 70–72, 154

procrastination, 226

Proctor and Gamble, 107

promotions, 43

Puckett, Lt. Ralph, 22

Purple Heart, 149

Ranger Assessment Phase (RAP), 62

Ranger Buddy system, 14, 21, 96, 109, 274

Ranger Creed, 29, 31, 32, 81, 244, 275
  corporate values and, 246
  on responsibility, 91
  Standing Orders and, 36–37
  on trust, 92

Ranger Hall of Fame, 22

Ranger Instructors, 84, 113, 134

Ranger School, 3–4, 11, 49, 55, 57, 208
  ambush training, 113–14
  "cooperate and graduate" tenet, 79

mountain phase, 84
  problem solving in, 259
  purpose of, 60–63
Ranger Tab, 3–4, 23, 49, 73, 169
Ranger Training Center, 22–23
Rangers
  as brotherhood, 4
  decision making in, 242
  in Grenada, 117–18
  intelligence training, 200–201
  in Korea, 21–23
  Long Range Surveillance (LRS), 216
  motivation and, 166
  relationship with Army, 125–26
  risk and, 211, 212
  tradition of, 9–13, 36
  in Vietnam War, 23–24
  in World War II, 13–21
reciprocity, 261–63
reconnaissance, 109, 119–21, 205–10. *See also*
    intelligence gathering
Red Falcons, 48
referent power, 149
rehearsal, 215–17, 218
research and development (R&D), 33, 42–43, 188,
    195, 234
resources, concentration and disposition of, 105, 106
respect, 51–52, 72, 81, 176–77
responsibility, 17, 91–92, 109
Revolutionary War, 122–23
risk, 212–14
Rogers, Capt. Robert, 10–11, 24, 181
Rogers' Rangers, 10–11, 263, 277–78. *See also* Standing
    Orders (Rogers' Rangers)
role models, 148
Roosevelt, Eleanor, 149
Roosevelt, Theodore, 103
Royal Dutch/Shell, 222
Rudder, Lt. Col. James Earl, 16–19

Salomon, Capt. Sid, 18, 149–50, 151, 152,
    169, 171
  communication with tank crew, 267
  on planning, 232
SAS firm, 246–47
Saving Private Ryan (film), 150
Scarcelli, Betsy, 73, 102, 241
scenarios, 219–24
Schneider, Maj. Max, 18
Sculley, John, 108
security, 38, 110–15
Seiko watches, 234, 235
self-confidence, 170, 171
self-knowledge, 154–59
senior management, 101, 104
  concentration of resources and, 105
  domain skills and, 71
  economy of force and, 109
  feedback and, 138, 139–40, 141
  information flow and, 133
  internal security and, 112
  planning and, 189
  support for high-stakes teams, 124–25
  unity of command and, 110
September 11, 2001, terrorist attacks, 61, 119,
    213, 240. *See also* terrorism
  Afghanistan campaign and, 5, 46
  intelligence gathering and, 134, 202–3
  strong leadership and, 115
sequels, 226–30, 263
serendipitous mistakes, 235–36
75th Ranger Regiment, 25
Shepherd, Alan, 118
Sherman, Gen. William Tecumseh, 115
Sherman, Patsy, 235
Shughart, Randy, 30
Silver, Spence, 235
Silver Star, 149, 150
Simmons, Col. Arthur "Bull," 24, 176

simplicity, 38, 122–24
situation analysis, 190–91
skill and trait clusters, 42–53
Skunk Works (Lockheed Martin), 32–33, 126
Smith, Margaret Chase, 84
Smith, Stan, 235
socialization, 80
Somalia, 28–30, 53, 92, 263
Sources of Power (Klein), 200
Special Forces, 56, 88
special operations, 44, 61, 214, 250
Special Operations Command, 27
specialists, 95–96, 132–33
sports teams, 129
Standard Operation Procedures (SOPs), 22, 114,
    254, 260, 263–65
Standing Orders (Roger's Rangers)
  on ambush avoidance, 115
  "Don't Forget Nothin'", 41
  full list of, 277–78
  origin of, 36–37
  on reconnaissance, 208
  Standard Operation Procedures (SOPs) and,
    263
  on taking chances, 211
  on telling truth, 134
  on versatility, 99
Stanton, Elizabeth Cady, 149
start-up companies, 99
storming phase, 83, 85, 86, 243
stovepiping, 103, 104
Stuart, Gen. Jeb, 12
styles, 71–72, 159
surprise, 38, 116–22
surveys, 89
Swamp Fox, 12
SWAT teams, 33
Swigert, John, 118
synergy, 129, 131, 133

tactical freedom, 77–78
Tainted Truth (Crossen), 193
talent pool, development of, 265–66
Taliban, 30, 46, 93
Tao Te Ching, 177
Tarleton, Lieutenant Colonel, 12
task versus purpose, 76–77
team cycles, 82–83, 97, 98, 130
teams
  best and worst, 128–32
  differences and, 52, 79
  distinguished from groups, 78–79
  formation of, 273
  individuals and, 41–42, 67–68
  initial challenges, 75–87
  leader's knowledge of, 159–60
  leader's moral example, 153
  mind power and, 94–96
  repertoire of skills, 69
  three dimensions of, 36
  varieties of, 232
technical consultants, 89
temporary assignments, 43
terrorism, 30, 31, 33, 46, 212. *See also*
    September 11, 2001, terrorist attacks
Texas Instruments, 234, 235
thinkers, development of, 257–58
3M Company, 112, 235
transfers, 43
transparent leadership, 177
Truscott, Brig. Gen. Lucian, 14
trust, 92–94, 128, 177
Tuckman, Bruce, 82
turf issues, 90

unanimity, 81
uncertainty, 182, 184–85, 196, 212–14,
    252
urgency, sense of, 101–2, 119

U.S. Army
  After Action Review (AAR) and, 253–55
  elite units in, 125–26
  formula for battle commanders, 179, 181, 185
  "Hoo-ah Schools" of, 56
  Leadership Framework, 54, 147–48, 152–54,
    164, 249, 269
  rapid deployment force, 99
U.S. Army Field Manual
  on action, 163
  on art of command, 179
  on attainable objectives, 75
  on character, 55
  on combat rehearsal, 215
  on information superiority, 194–95
  on intelligence preparation, 196
  on leadership quality, 153
  on learning, 249
  on planning, 188, 190, 226, 227, 236
  on pride and confidence, 60
  on unity of command, 87

Vann, John Paul, 198–99
Vaughn, Colonel, 13
Vietnam War, 5, 23–24, 88, 89, 172–73
  ambush prevention in, 114–15
  feedback in, 135–36, 141
  intelligence gathering in, 198–99, 208–9
  Rangers' relationship to Army and, 125, 126
  Standard Operation Procedures (SOPs) in, 263
  teamwork in, 130–31
visualization, 180, 206

Walker, Fred, 45, 74, 76, 180, 206–8, 245–46
Walls, Billy, 22
Walt Disney World, 244–45
war, principles of, 75–78, 182
  attainable objectives, 100–101
  economy of force, 109

maneuver, 106–8
mass, 105–6
offensive, 101–5
security, 110–15
simplicity, 122–24
surprise, 116–22
unity of command, 87–91, 109–10
wargaming, 186, 217–19, 221, 224
warning sytems, 225
Washington, George, 11, 122–23
Watt, James, 136
weak signals, 197–203
Weiner, Norman, 136
Westmoreland, Gen. William, 5
Wheatley, Margaret, 271, 272
Whole Brain Model, 71
wild cards, 90
World War II, 13–21, 125, 136, 149–50, 219
    commander's intent at D-Day, 236–37
    use of tanks in, 250
World Wide Web, 132

yes-people, 140

About the Author

A former U.S. Army Airborne Ranger, Anthony Le Storti is the president of IDEATECTS, Inc., a management and consultant firm dealing with cognitive skills development, leadership, and the dynamics of human systems. He has consulted for numerous Fortune 500 companies and lectured widely on creativity and management.